Jarosław Dobrzyński
Colour illustrations
Lieuwe de Vries

Lockheed F-104 STARFIGHTER

Published in Poland in 2015
by STRATUS s.c.
Po. Box 123,
27-600 Sandomierz 1, Poland
e-mail: office@mmpbooks.biz
for
Mushroom Model Publications,
3 Gloucester Close,
Petersfield,
Hampshire GU32 3AX
e-mail: rogerw@mmpbooks.biz

© 2015 Mushroom Model
Publications.
http://www.mmpbooks.biz

All rights reserved. Apart from any fair dealing for the purpose of private study, research, criticism or review, as permitted under the Copyright, Design and Patents Act, 1988, no part of this publication may be reproduced, stored in a retrieval system, or transmitted in any form or by any means, electronic, electrical, chemical, mechanical, optical, photocopying, recording or otherwise, without prior written permission. All enquiries should be addressed to the publisher.

**ISBN:
978-83-63678-39-5**

Editor in chief
Roger Wallsgrove

Editorial Team
Bartłomiej Belcarz
Robert Pęczkowski
Artur Juszczak
Dariusz Karnas

Colour drawings
Lieuwe de Vries

Scale plans
Daiusz Karnas

DTP & Layout
Stratus s.c.

Printed by
Drukarnia Diecezjalna,
ul. Żeromskiego 4,
27-600 Sandomierz

www.wds.pl
marketing@wds.pl

PRINTED IN POLAND

Table of contents

The birth of the Starfighter	3
The Starfighter for NATO	17
The ultimate	51
The ultimate Starfighter – F-104S	51
Operators	60
The F-104 in combat	96
Special versions	102
F-104G and F-104S technical description	107
Specifications	112
Flying the F-104	114
F-104 Production	115
In Detail	122
General View	122
Fuselage	126
Wing	134
Electronic Systems	138
Cockpit	142
Radar	150
Cannon	151
Stores	154
Engine	158
Fuselage details	163
Undercarriage	167
Bibliography:	176

Acknowledgements

The author would like to thank: Przemysław Skulski, Hans Rolink, Nils Mosberg, Bartłomiej Belcarz, George Papadimitriou, Henk Schuitemaker, Jerzy Dziedziniewicz, Nikos Livados, Ludovic Mac Leod, Grzegorz Karnas, Dariusz Karnas, D. Guisinger.

Title page: Lockheed F-104S Starfighter taxis at Pratica di Mare AB. (Ludovic Mac Leod)

Get in the picture!
Do you have photographs of historical aircraft, airfields in action, or original and unusual stories to tell? MMP would like to hear from you! We welcome previously unpublished material that will help to make MMP books the best of their kind. We will return original photos to you and provide full credit for your images. Contact us before sending us any valuable material:
rogerw@mmpbooks.biz

The birth of the Starfighter

The late 1940s and early '50s was an era of breaking barriers and setting new flight speed records. In 1944 the first jet powered aircraft – German Messerschmitt Me 262 and Arado 234, British Gloster Meteor – entered combat. In 1947 Chuck Yeager broke the sound barrier in the Bell X-1 rocket–powered aircraft and in 1953 Scott Crossfield exceeded Mach 2 (twice the speed of sound) in the Douglas D-558-2 Skyrocket. The Korean War (1950 – 1953) was dominated by jet-powered aircraft, primarily the F-86 Sabre and MiG-15 fighters.

In 1951 Clarence "Kelly" Johnson, Lockheed's vice president of engineering and research, and creator of many notably Lockheed aircraft like the P-38 Lightning and P-80 Shooting Star, travelled to Korea with Lt. General Benjamin Chidlaw, chief of the USAF Materiel Command, and Lee Atwood, vice president of North American Aviation, the manufacturer of the USAF's main fighter at that time, the F-86 Sabre. He hoped to find out what the USAF's fighter pilots expected from a new type of fighter. The two most important things wanted by the pilots were speed and altitude. In response to these demands, Johnson decided to create a simple day superiority fighter, in which all was subordinated to performance – speed, climb and altitude.

The first prototype XF-104 53-7786 FG-786 on Rogers Dry Lake at the Air Force Flight Test Center, Edwards AFB, California. The XF-104 is easy to distinguish by the lack of inlet shock cones and a shorter fuselage. (USAF)

After having considered several layouts the team led by Johnson decided on a fighter with a long, cylindrical fuselage, housing the radar, pilot's cockpit, avionics equipment, gun and ammunition, fuel tanks and a big jet engine, very short trapezoid wings with a very thin profile, sharp leading and trailing edges and significant dihedral. This layout, especially the straight and extremely thin wing, was inspired by the Lockheed X-7 experimental rocket/ramjet drone, used for trials of ramjet engines and missile guidance systems. The latter was expected to fly at speeds from Mach 1.7 to Mach 3 at altitudes from sea level to 80,000 feet. It was launched from beneath a B-29 mother ship with a 467 kN (105,000 lbf) rocket booster assembly fitted with large vertical and horizontal stabilizers, which would accelerate the X-7 to supersonic

The first prototype XF-104, FG-786, in flight, 1954. (USAF)

The first prototype XF-104, FG-786, in flight over Edwards AFB, 1954. (USAF)

speed. After the rocket motor burnout the booster assembly would separate and the ramjet would take over. Sixty-one X-7A drones were built. In 1960 an X-7A broke all contemporary speed and altitude records for air-breathing vehicles, reaching Mach 4.31 and 106,000 feet.

In January 1953 the Lockheed team received the letter of approval for the L-246 design, and in March 1953 was awarded the contract by the Air Force to build two XF-104 prototypes and the work began. The time needed by Lockheed to build the XF-104 was exceptionally short. The first XF-104 prototype, number 53-7786, FG-786, was presented to the Air Force for Phase I and II of flight testing in February 1954. Continuing their tradition of "Star" names for jet fighters Lockheed named the aircraft the "Starfighter".

High-speed taxi and lift-off tests were conducted on 27 February 1954 and on March 4 the XF-104 made its maiden flight with Lockheed test pilot Tony LeVier at the controls. During the first and second flights the landing gear failed to retract and fuel pressure problems occurred as well. The XF-104 was powered by a Buick-built Curtiss-Wright J65-W-6 engine rated at 34.7 kN (7,800 lbf) in place of the planned General Electric J79, not yet ready, hence its performance was worse than expected. The second XF-104, FG-787, was fitted with the J65 W-7 engine with afterburner, which gave a maximum thrust of 45.8 kN (10,300 lbf). The first prototype was retrofitted with such an engine.

As the armament testbed FG-787 was fitted with the M61 cannon and AN/ASG-14T-1 fire control system. FG-787 achieved a top speed of Mach 1.79 at 60,000 feet (18,000 m) on March 25 1955, piloted by Lockheed test pilot J. Ray Goudey. This was the highest speed achieved by the XF-104. On 18 April 1955, FG-787 was lost in a crash caused by explosive cockpit depressurization during firing trials. Lockheed test pilot Herman Salmon ejected successfully. The flight test program of the XF-104 was completed in August 1956.

Basing on the experience gained in XF-104 testing, the YF-104A pre-production variant was developed. It was lengthened to 16.66 m (54.5 ft), powered by a General Electric J79 GE3 engine and featured modified landing gear and air intakes with shock cones. The contract called for 17 YF-104As and six F-104A standard production aircraft. Subsequently the US Air Force ordered 147 F-104As for Tactical Air Command and Aerospace Defense Command and 26 two-seat F-104B

Four aircraft of the "century series" in flight. Clockwise from left to right: Lockheed XF-104 Starfighter, McDonnell F-101 Voodoo, Convair F-102 Delta Dart, North American F-100 Super Sabre. (USAF)

Pre-production YF-104A 55-2961 on the lakebed. (USAF)

trainers for pilot conversion. Apart from the YF-104s, 17 production F-104A aircraft were used in the flight testing program.

On 7 May 1958 Major Howard Johnson of 83rd FIS set a world altitude record of 27,813 m (91,246 ft) in YF-104A 55-2969 at Edwards AFB. Nine days later, on 16 May 1958 at Edwards AFB Capt Walter W. Irwin of 83rd FIS set a world speed record of 2,252 km/h (1,404 mph) in the same YF-104A 55-2969. That was the first time one aircraft held both the world altitude and speed records.

Early production versions

F-104A

The first production model was the F-104A (Lockheed model 183-93-02). A total of 153 units were built by Lockheed in seven production blocks – F-104A-1-LO to F-104A-30-LO. It was far fewer than originally planned – only 170 YF-104A and F-104A were ultimately built out of 722 planned. The F-104A was powered by the General Electric J79-GE-3A engine, delivering 42.7 kN (9,600 lbf) of dry thrust and 65.8 kN (14,800 lbf) with afterburner. It was armed with a M61A1 Vulcan cannon, and two AIM-9B Sidewinder infrared homing air-to-air missiles with the AN/ASG-14-T1 fire control system. During service the Lockheed C-1 downward-firing ejection seat was replaced by an upward-firing Lockheed C-2 seat, a ventral fin was added to the aft fuselage and a Boundary Layer Control (BLC) system was added to the flaps. The GE-3A engines were later replaced by improved GE-3B engines, starting in April 1958. Due to unsolved problems with the M61 cannon, most F-104As were built only with provision for the internal gun, which was replaced by ballast and the gun port was faired over.

The first F-104As entered service with the 83rd Fighter Interceptor Squadron at

Lockheed test pilot Tony LeVier sitting in the cockpit of the XF-104, FG-786. (Lockheed)

Hamilton AFB, California in January 1958. Later in that year three other ADC units received the type. The Starfighter was originally intended to replace the F-100 Super Sabre in the Tactical Air Force beginning in 1956, but by the time the F-104A was ready for delivery the USAF requirements had changed. Due to the Starfighter's short endurance, problems with the cannon and small weapons load, TAC lost interest in the Starfighter. That could have been the end of the aircraft but ADC's need to bridge the gap between the obsolete F-102 Delta Dagger and introduction of the F-106 Delta Dart convinced the USAF commanders to introduce the F-104A as a stopgap measure. The F-104A was not well suited for the interceptor role, since it lacked adequate endurance and had no all-weather capability, but its high speed and climb rate made it attractive for the ADC. In its first year of service with the USAF the F-104A Starfighter became the first operational interceptor with the capability of flying with sustained Mach 2+ speed. Due to its appearance and performance the F-104 was named "the missile with a man in it".

In October 1958 twelve F-104As of the 83rd FIS were disassembled and sent aboard C-124 Globemasters to Taiwan in Operation Jonah Able to support the defense of the island against communist China during the Quemoy crisis.

On 13 and 14 December 1958, USAF pilots Lt William T. Smith and Lt Einar Enevoldson set several time-to-climb records, flying F-104A 56-0762 over NAS Point Mugu, California:

3,000 meters (9,800 ft) in 41.85 seconds
6,000 meters (20,000 ft) in 58.41 seconds
9,000 meters (30,000 ft) in 81.14 seconds
12,000 meters (39,000 ft) in 99.90 seconds
15,000 meters (49,000 ft) in 131.1 seconds
20,000 meters (66,000 ft) in 222.99 seconds
25,000 meters (82,000 ft) in 266.03 seconds

The F-104A's career in the USAF was relatively brief. In 1960 they were retired from first-line units. Some were handed over to US Air National Guard squadrons. In 1960 24 airplanes were modified as QF-104A target drones and three as NF-104 aerospace trainers. Three went to NASA. Forty-four aircraft were delivered within US military assistance programs to the Republic of China Air Force on Taiwan. Other foreign operators of the F-104A were Pakistan (14) and Jordan (22 aircraft).

An F-104A Starfighter of Arizona Air National Guard. Note the lack of cannon and the cannon port faired over. (USAF)

The F-104A 56-0761 was used for testing the "C" version modifications. It was the only F-104A fitted with a refueling probe. (USAF)

The prototype of the F-104B, 56-3719. (USAF)

An F-104C in flight. (USAF)

F-104D 57-1316 of the USAF, assigned to Naval Weapons Test Center, in flight. (US Navy)

F-104B

The prototype of the two-seat dual control combat trainer version of the F-104A was built quite by hand at Lockheed's plant at Palmdale, using an F-104A airframe (c/n283-5000, 56-3719) taken out of the production line at Burbank. The first F-104B-1-LO (Lockheed model 283-93-03) was transported by road to Edwards AFB and there made its maiden flight on 16 January 1957. As the service test aircraft it was unofficially designated YF-104B. It had no automatic pitch control system, nor the fire control system and larger area vertical tail of later F-104Bs. It was also used to test the downward-firing ejection seats fitted initially to USAF Starfighters and after the tests was modified to F-104B production standard. The first production F-104B was delivered to the USAF in September 1957 and the last in November 1958. The instructor's seat was mounted behind the pilot in the place formerly occupied by the M61 cannon, which was deleted. The armament was reduced to two wingtip-mounted AIM-9 missiles, but the AN/ASG-14-T1 fire control system was retained, as were provision for two underwing and two wingtip-mounted drop tanks. Other features differing the B model from the A model were repositioning of the nosewheel strut from the rear to the front of the landing gear well, which meant that the wheel retracted backward instead for forward as on the F-104A, increasing the vertical stabilizer area by 21% and adding a power boosted rudder. Twenty-six units were built. They served alongside the F-104As as type conversion and proficiency trainers. Five F-104Bs were delivered to the RoCAF on Taiwan, two to Pakistan and five to Jordan. In December 1959 one F-104B was handed over to NASA.

7

F-104C

The F-104 was intended to be a tactical fighter to replace the F-100 Super Sabre, and since the F-104A had not met this requirement Lockheed continued development of the aircraft. This resulted in the third production variant of the F-104, the F-104C fighter-bomber (Lockheed model 483-04-05) which first flew on 24 July 1958. The last F-104C was delivered in June 1959. Only 77 units were built, a further 363 were cancelled.

Externally the C model was almost identical to the A. The most important change was the new uprated J-79-GE-7A engine, delivering 44.48 kN (10,000 lbf) dry thrust and 70.3 kN (15,800 lbf) with afterburner. The more powerful engine enabled the F-104C to carry more payload – two 1,000 lb (454 kg) bombs or 170 gal tanks, a Mk 28 nuclear bomb, AIR-2 Genie nuclear unguided air-to-air rocket (never used) or four AIM-9 Sidewinder missiles. An in-flight refueling probe was added on the port side of the forward fuselage. Blown flaps (BLC) were installed from the outset. Within program "Grindstone" of 1961 ventral rails for AIM-9 Sidewinder missiles were added to improve the F-104C's air-to-air capability.

The first unit to receive the new Starfighter model, in September 1958, was the 476th Tactical Fighter Squadron of the 479th Tactical Fighter Wing at George AFB, California. Subsequently the 479th TFW's three other squadrons – the 434th, 435th and 436th – were also equipped. On 14 December 1959 Capt. Joe Jordan set a world altitude record of 31,513 m (103,389 ft) in the F-104C s/n 56-0885. It was the first aircraft to take off under its own power and exceed 100,000 feet (30,480 m). He also set a 30,000 m (98,000 ft) time-to-climb record of 904.92 seconds. In 1965 and 1966 squadrons of the 479th TFW were deployed to South East Asia, where they flew both air superiority and ground attack missions. After returning from the SEA theatre the remaining F-104Cs were transferred to the Puerto Rico ANG, where they continued in service until 1975.

F-104D

A two-seat combat-capable trainer variant of the F-104C was designated F-104D (Lockheed model 383-04-06). It was configured much the same as the F-104B, with the cannon installation replaced by the aft cockpit. The differences included a higher canopy with a clear panel between side-opening canopy sections. Twenty-one were built by Lockheed and delivered to TAC units, a further 83 were cancelled.

Lockheed's pre-flight line at Palmdale, California in 1958. (Lockheed)

Lockheed F-104D Starfighter, Sacramento Aerospace Museum, California. (US National Archives).

YF-104A (early stage), 1/72 scale.

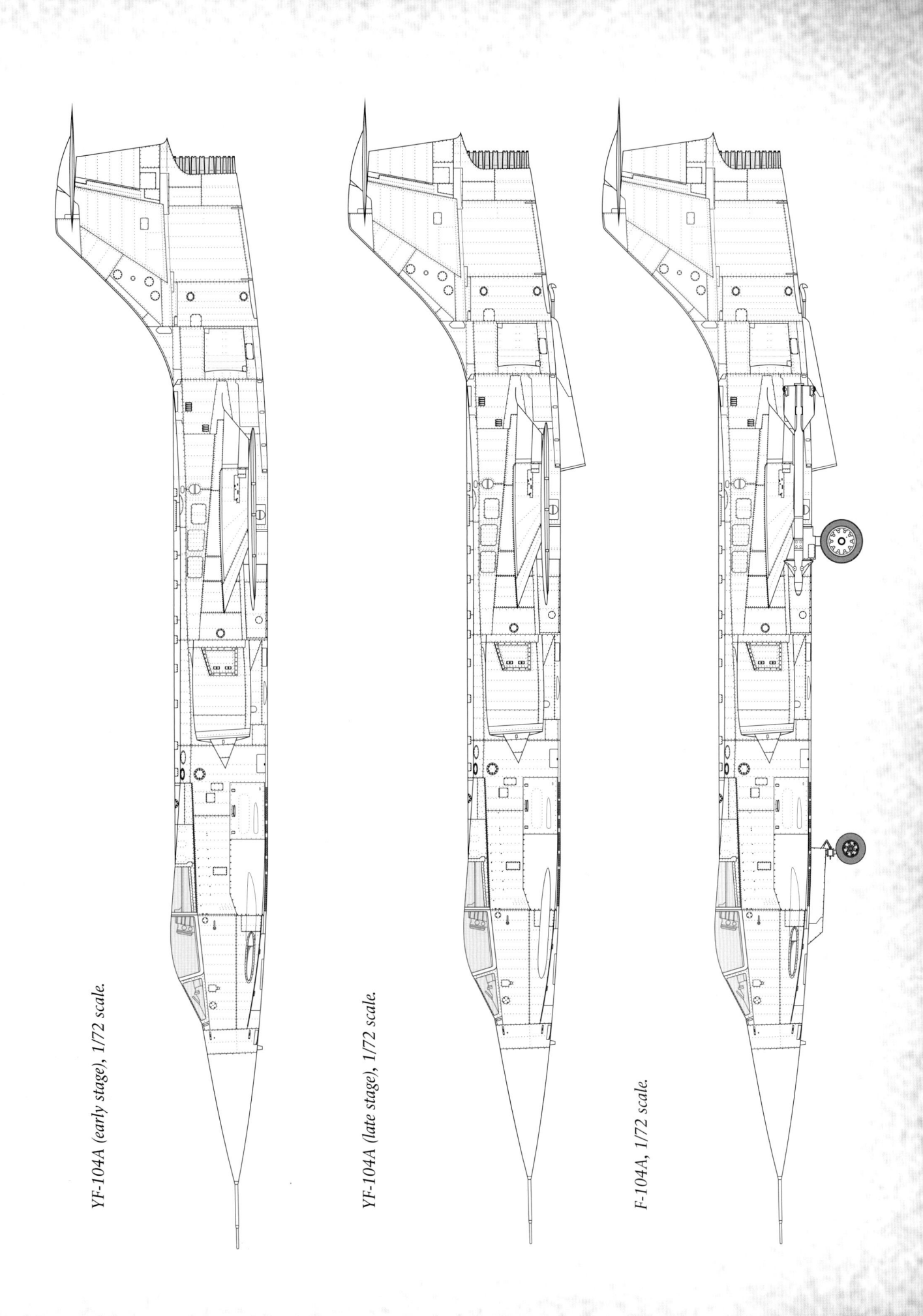

YF-104A (late stage), 1/72 scale.

F-104A, 1/72 scale.

F-104C, 1/72 scale.

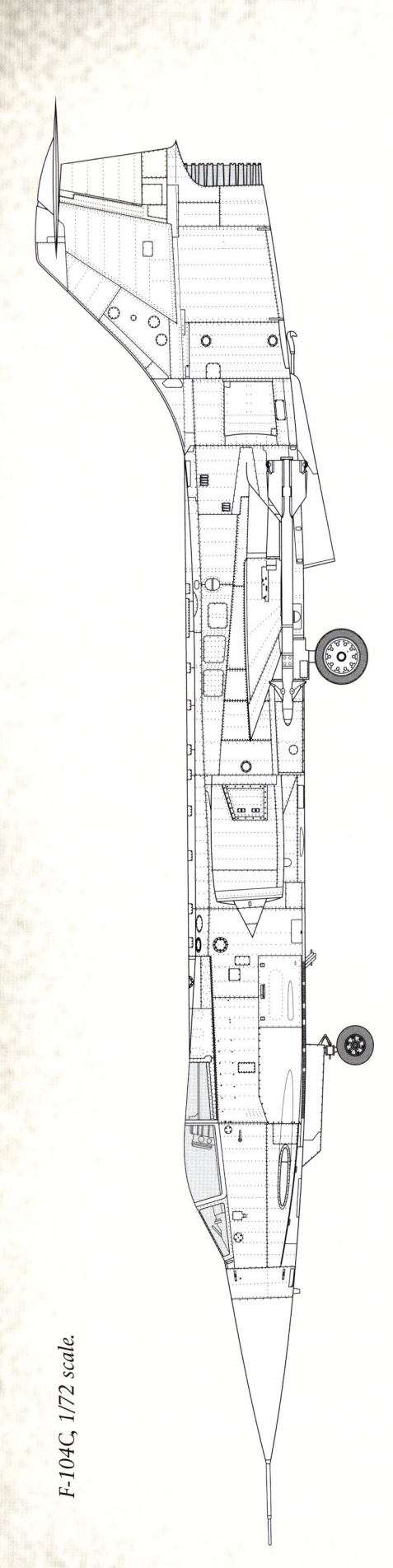

F-104C with refuelling probe, 1/72 scale.

F-104B, 1/72 scale.

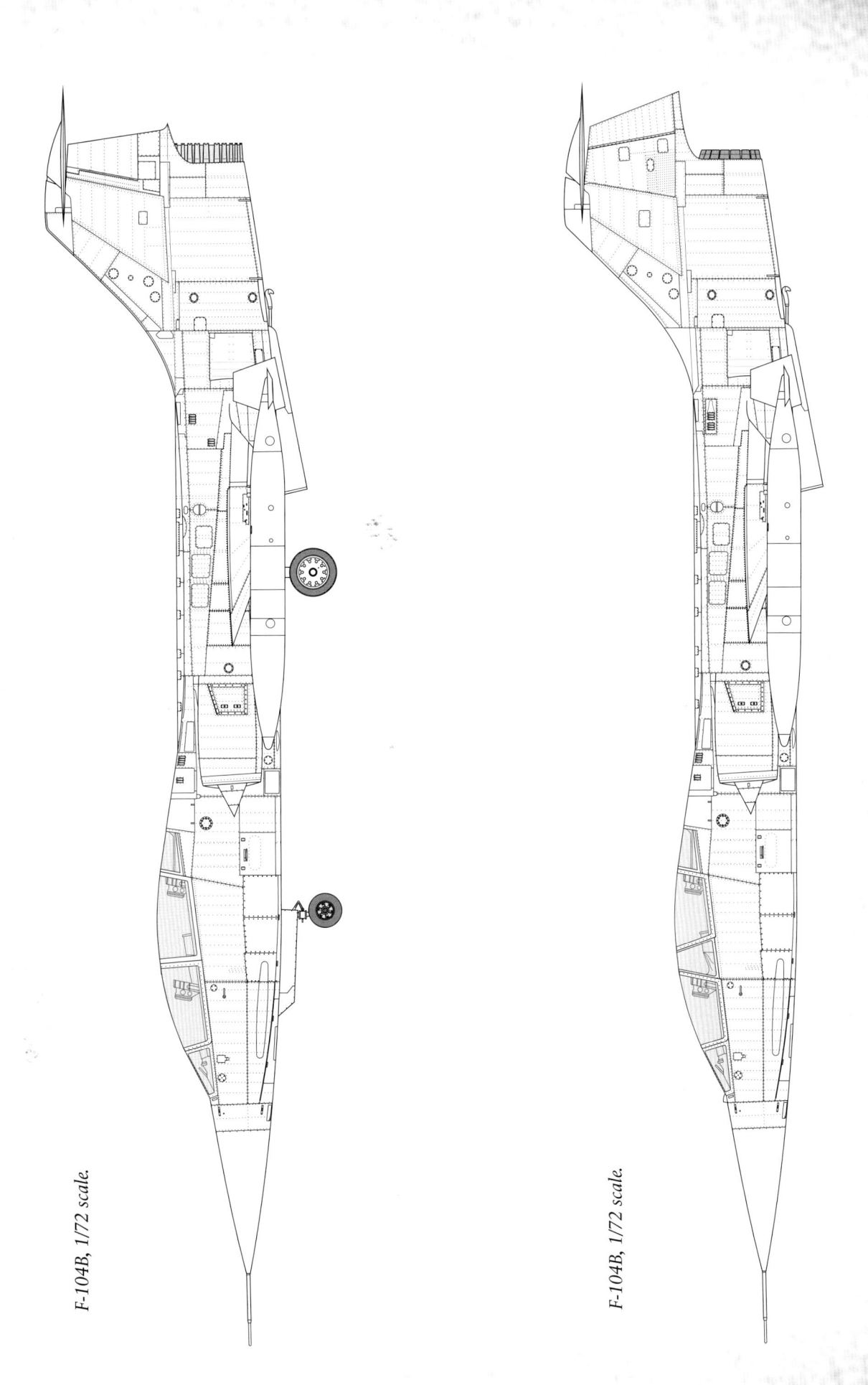

F-104B, 1/72 scale.

YF-104 prototype 53-7786, FG-786, USAF, Edwards AFB, 1954. Aircraft natural metal overall with unpainted wings. Serials and letters in black. National insignia in four positions. (See also page 13)

F-104A 56-0791 of the 83rd Fighter Interceptor Squadron USAF, Tao Yuan AB, Taiwan, September 1958. Aircraft in natural metal finish with white upper wings and light grey wing undersides. Radome is white with a black anti-glare panel running up to the forward windscreen.

F-104B prototype FG-719, serial number 56-3719. Aircrat in natural metal finish with unpainted wing. Experimental pitot tube painted white with stripes – most likely red.

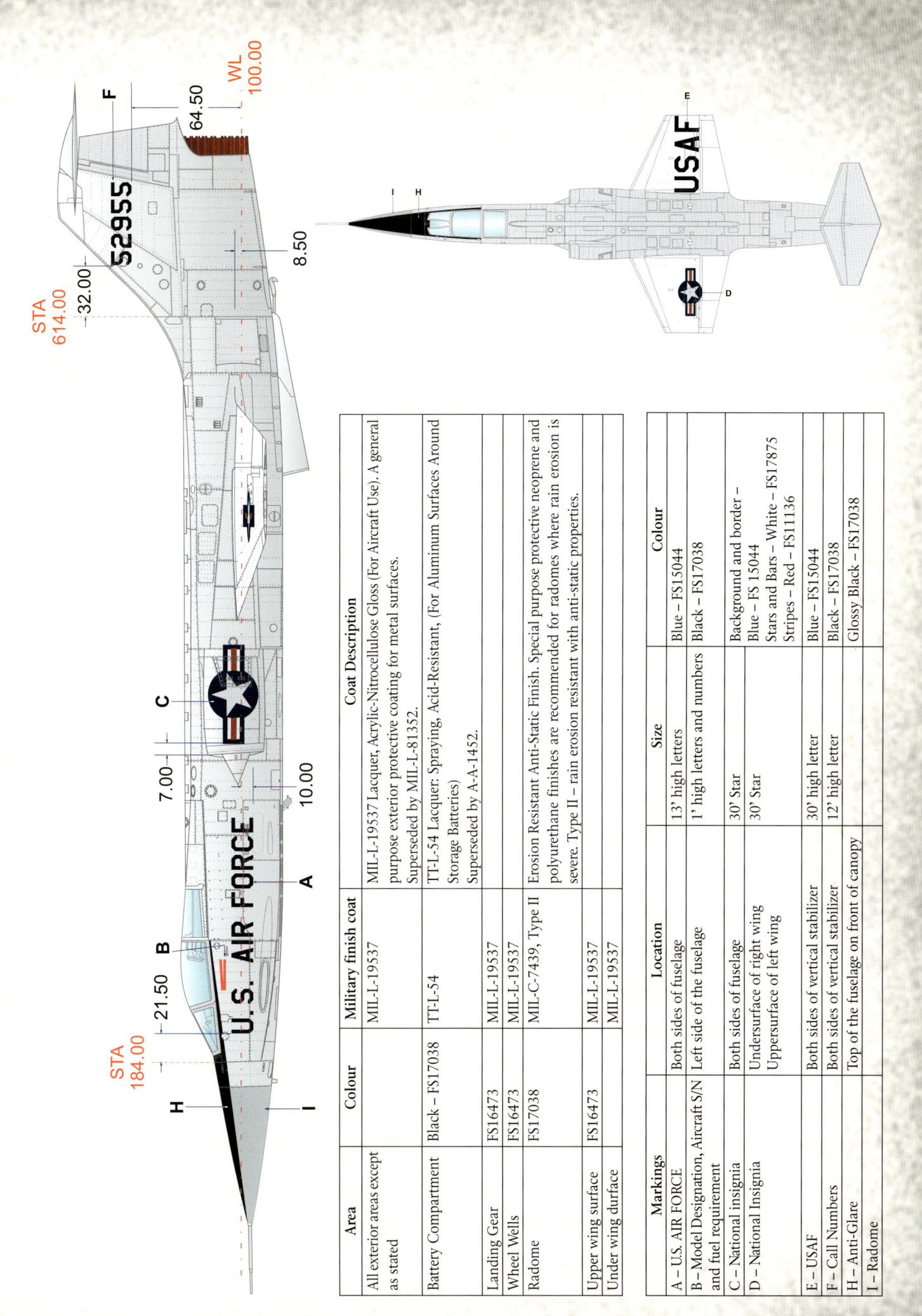

Area	Colour	Military finish coat	Coat Description
All exterior areas except as stated		MIL-L-19537	MIL-L-19537 Lacquer, Acrylic-Nitrocellulose Gloss (For Aircraft Use). A general purpose exterior protective coating for metal surfaces. Superseded by MIL-L-81352.
Battery Compartment	Black – FS17038	TT-L-54	TT-L-54 Lacquer: Spraying, Acid-Resistant, (For Aluminum Surfaces Around Storage Batteries) Superseded by A-A-1452.
Landing Gear	FS16473	MIL-L-19537	
Wheel Wells	FS16473	MIL-L-19537	
Radome	FS17038	MIL-C-7439, Type II	Erosion Resistant Anti-Static Finish. Special purpose protective neoprene and polyurethane finishes are recommended for radomes where rain erosion is severe. Type II – rain erosion resistant with anti-static properties.
Upper wing surface	FS16473	MIL-L-19537	
Under wing durface		MIL-L-19537	

Markings	Location	Size	Colour
A – U.S. AIR FORCE	Both sides of fuselage	13" high letters	Blue – FS15044
B – Model Designation, Aircraft S/N and fuel requirement	Left side of the fuselage	1" high letters and numbers	Black – FS17038
C – National insignia	Both sides of fuselage	30" Star	Background and border – Blue – FS 15044 Stars and Bars – White – FS17875 Stripes – Red – FS11136
D – National Insignia	Undersurface of right wing Uppersurface of left wing	30" Star	
E – USAF	Both sides of vertical stabilizer	30" high letter	Blue – FS15044
F – Call Numbers	Both sides of vertical stabilizer	12" high letter	Black – FS17038
H – Anti-Glare	Top of the fuselage on front of canopy		Glossy Black – FS17038
I – Radome			

13

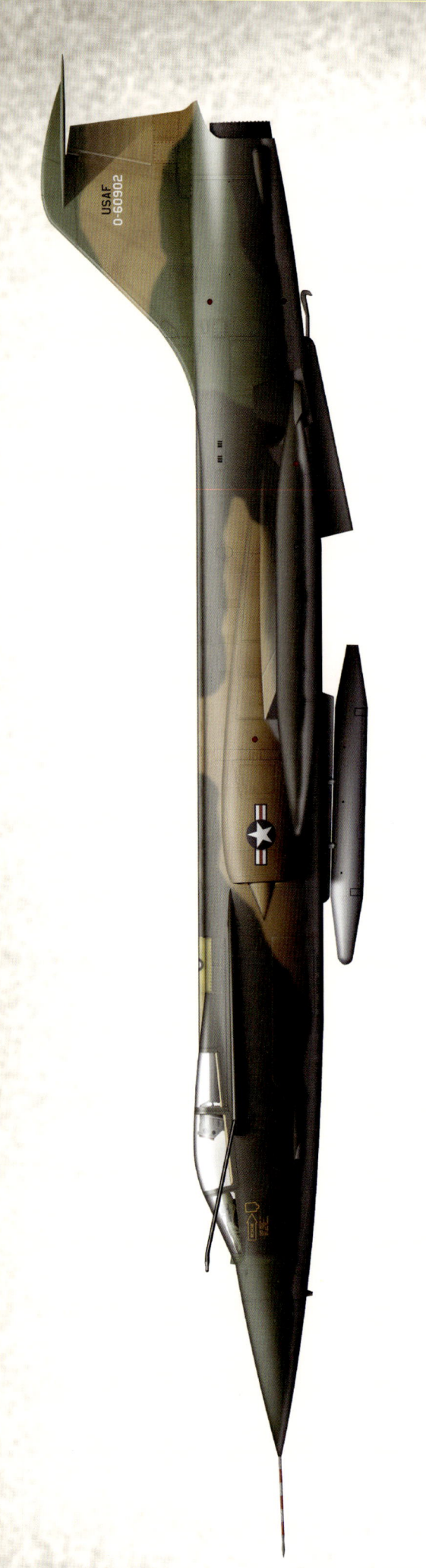

F-104C 56-0902 435th TFS USAF Udorn, Thailand 1966. Aircraft is painted in the standard South East Asia camouflage pattern. Dark Green – FS34079, Medium Green – FS34102 and Tan – FS30219 uppersurfaces with Grey – FS36622 undersurfaces.

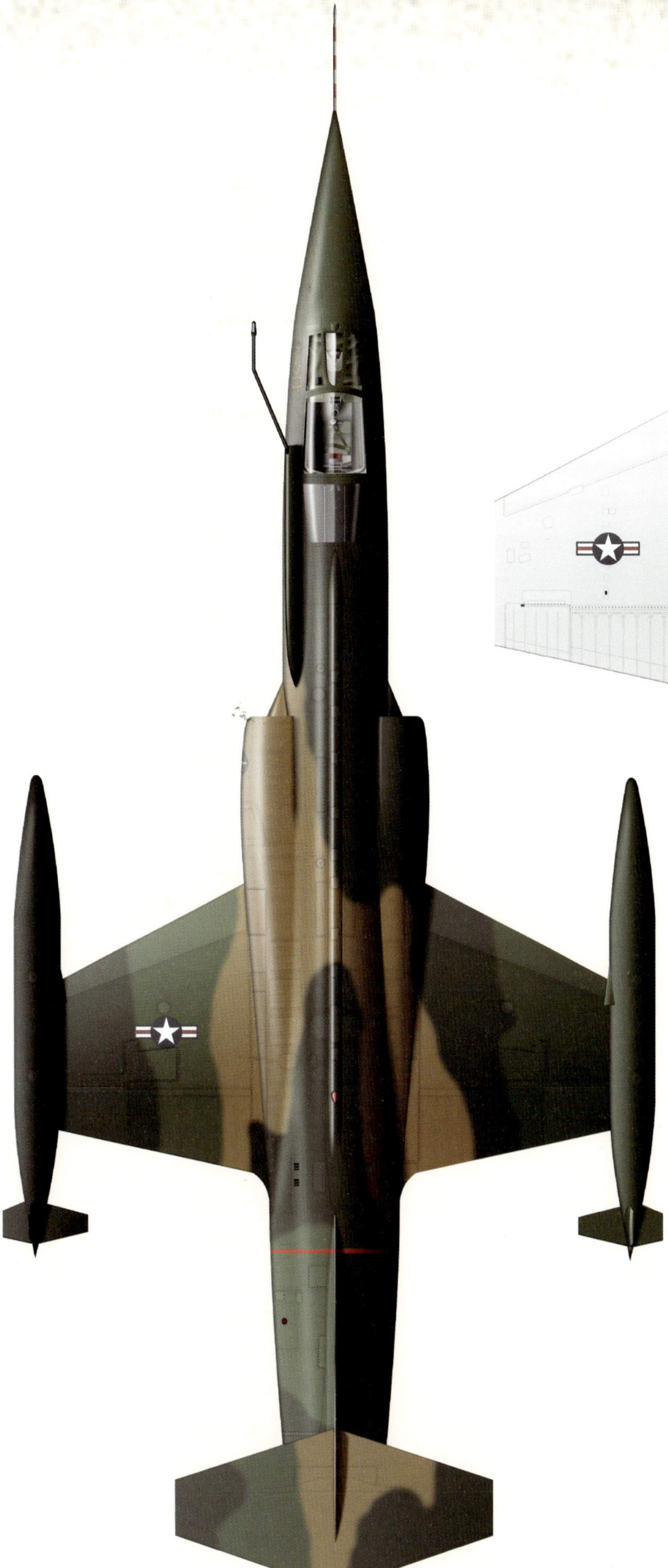

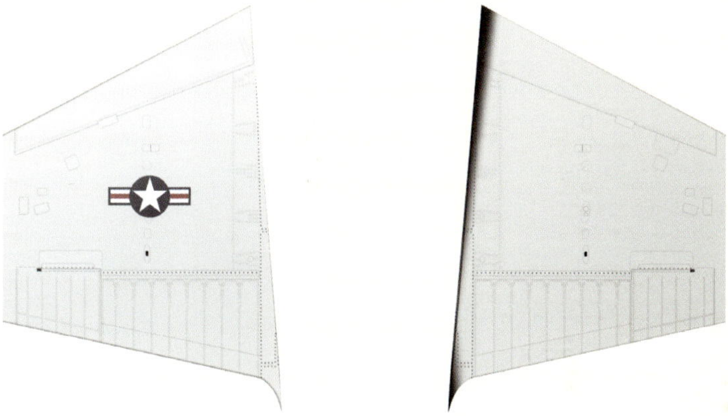

F-104D 57-1318, 194th TFS, Puerto Rico ANG 1970. Aircraft is painted in a standard South East Asia paint scheme.

F-104G FX 02 of 350th Squadron, Belgian Air Force, Beauvechain 1963. Aircraft in natural metal finish with white upper wings and light grey wing undersides. Radome is white with a black anti-glare panel running up to the forward windscreen.

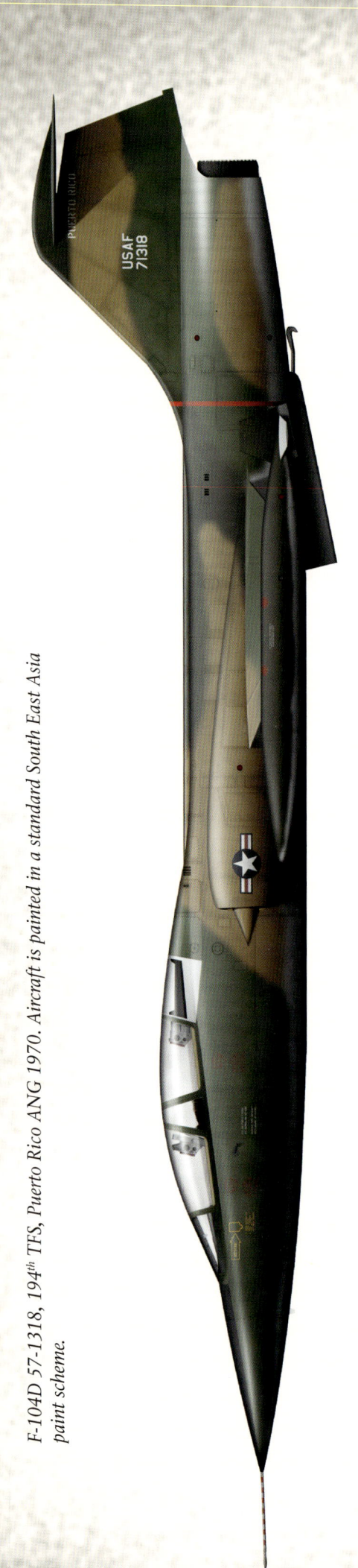

The Starfighter for NATO

Republic F-84F Thunderstreak, the immediate predecessor of the F-104G in European NATO countries, here in Belgian markings. (BAF)

In 1957 the West German *Luftwaffe*, established in 1955, facing a growing communist threat in the east started to look for a primary all-weather fighter interceptor, fighter-bomber and photographic reconnaissance aircraft. The new aircraft was to replace the Republic F-84F Thunderstreak in the strike role, the North American F-86 Sabre in the air defense role, and the Republic RF-84F Thunderflash in the photo-reconnaissance role. These types were obsolete at the moment of purchase and even before the last unit was formed the *Luftwaffe* had looked to replace them. Since Germany at the time had no aviation industry of its own the German government began evaluating French, British and American designs. At first the Starfighter was not the favorite. The Germans were interested in an unusual British design, the Saunders Roe SR.177 (a derivative of the SR.53 experimental aircraft, powered by a Gyron turbojet engine and a Spectre rocket motor for high altitude boost). The British had a much more capable aircraft, the English Electric Lightning Mach 2+ interceptor, which had roughly equal speed and climb rate as the Starfighter and much better maneuverability but the British government for unknown reasons decided to relegate the Lightning to the background and promote the SR.177 instead. The SR.177 program was cancelled in the infamous Duncan Sandys Defence White Paper in 1957.

In December 1957 two experienced *Luftwaffe* fighter pilots, *Oberstleutnant* Albert Werner and *Major* Walter Krupinski, a World War II fighter ace with 197 victories, travelled to California to evaluate the F-104 Starfighter, which was about to enter USAF service. The other US-made aircraft taken into consideration was the Grumman F11F-1 Tiger. In 1958 Walter Krupinski also tested the Mirage IIIC and the comparison revealed better overall performance of the Starfighter. Besides, the Mirage and the F11 Tiger were in their prototype stages, while the F-104A had already been introduced into USAF service. The F-104A and B that the German pilots had tested had no all-weather capability and limited weapons load, but Lockheed proposed a more sophisticated F-104G model (Lockheed designation 683-10-19), then called the "Super Starfighter" with necessary structural strengthening enabling it to carry a greater weapons load, rudder surface increased by 21% in comparison with previous single-seat Starfighter models, more powerful J79-GE-11A engine and a very modern avionics suite comprising Autonetics NASARR F15A-41B air-to-air and air-to-ground targeting radar and Litton LN-3 inertial navigation system. They also agreed to grant a production

German F-104G 26+88 during engine tests in 1983. Note the intake covers, protecting the engine against foreign object damage. (DoD)

17

license to the German aviation industry. It was expected that other European NATO countries like the Netherlands, Belgium, Italy and Norway would follow Germany and also buy the Starfighter.

The German defense minister Franz Josef Strauss signed the contracts with Lockheed on 18 March 1959. They stipulated the supply of 30 unarmed F-104F (Lockheed model 483-04-08) twin-seat trainers and an initial batch of 96 F-104Gs as well as license production of the F-104G.

As Lockheed had predicted, countries neighboring Germany also decided to purchase the F-104G. The first was the Netherlands, which after eliminating the Northrop NF-156 (F-5) Freedom Fighter, Convair F-106 Delta Dart, Republic F-105 Thunderchief and the Mirage III, placed an initial order for 100 F-104Gs on 20 April 1960. Twenty-five of them were to be obtained free from the US Military Assistance Program (MAP) budget. The Netherlands had initially hoped to receive 100 aircraft from the MAP and buy a further 100 by direct purchase but when the US government refused to increase the number of MAP-funded aircraft and made the offer depending on Italy being co-opted into the Starfighter consortium, the Dutch reduced the order to 95 aircraft. Two months later, on 20 June 1960 Belgium followed. In February 1961 the USAF placed an order for MAP F-104Gs (followed by additional order in June 1962). On 2 March 1961 Italy signed a contract for license production of the F-104G. This was the "Deal of the Century". Subsequent countries to acquire the F-104G were Norway and Turkey in 1963, Denmark and Greece in 1964 and Spain in 1965.

As the scale of license production was formidable a multi-national consortium had to be created. The consortium was led by German company Messerschmitt and comprised four Work Groups (Arbeitsgemeinschaft – ARGE) in four countries.

ARGE-Süd (Work Group South), in southern Germany consisted of Messerschmitt at Augsburg, Heinkel at Speyer, Dornier at Munich and Siebel at Donauwörth. It built 210 F-104Gs for the Luftwaffe and Marineflieger. Later, to replace losses, MBB (Messerschmitt-Bolkow-Blohm), built an additional 50 F-104Gs. Messerschmitt was the main contractor tasked with the final assembly and flight testing. It had no proper production facility with an airfield, so the new one had to be built at Manching, Bavaria.

The clearance for Starfighter production at the German plants came on 1 December 1960. The first F-104 G components arrived from the USA to Manching on 13 June 1961. Their reassembly began on 22 June and on 25 July, this aircraft took off as the first "Manching" Starfighter.

The first German series production aircraft took off on its maiden flight on 5 October 1961, and the Works Manager at that time, Willi Langhammer, delivered the first German F-104G to the German Air Force in December that year.

Messerschmitt was responsible for construction of the pilot seat, the fuselage, empennage and the installation of the powerplant, the final assembly, flight testing (carried out at Manching) and painting. Siebel initially manufactured the canopy, the electronics bay hatch cover, the escape hatch, the nose landing gear doors, the fuel rank cover and the hydraulic access door, and was responsible for the forward fuselage and nose radome assembly, air scoops and the rear fuselage. Dornier constructed the mid-fuselage panels, upper panel assemblies for the fuselage, the mid-

F-104G 20+37 of the Luftwaffe *preserved at* Luftwaffenmuseum der Bundeswehr Berlin – Gatow. *(Przemysław Skulski)*

RF-104G D-8101 of 306 Squadron RNLAF. Note the lack of cannon and the ventral bulge with cameras.

Four F-104Gs of the RNLAF in flight. (RNLAF)

fuselage side panels and the nose landing gear. Heinkel was initially responsible for the main landing gear and the drop tanks, and manufactured the main landing gear doors, airbrakes, wings, fins, rudders, horizontal stabilizers and other minor equipment. As production gained pace other manufacturers started making some of these components.

ARGE Nord (Work Group North) at Schiphol, Amsterdam, comprised Fokker at Schiphol and Aviolanda at Dordrecht in the Netherlands and the German manufacturers, Hamburger Flugzeugbau (HFB) at Hamburg, Weserflugzeugbau and Focke-Wulf at Bremen. This group built 153 F-104Gs and 101 RF-104Gs for West Germany and 96 F/RF-104Gs for the Netherlands. Fokker was responsible for installation of the powerplant and 'loose' equipment, the construction of the pilot seat, final assembly, painting and flight testing,. Fokker also manufactured the electronics bay hatch cover, escape hatch, after fuselage, wing, empennage, horizontal stabilizer, fin, rudder, and the drop tanks for all three European work groups.

Aviolanda built the F-104G's forward fuselage, nose radome, nose and main landing gear doors, canopies and fuel tank covers for all three work groups. HFB manufactured the windshields for all three work groups and the majority of fuselage panels for the Dutch work group. Weserflugzeugbau made mid-fuselage panels for the Dutch work group. Focke-Wulf built the hydraulic access doors, scoops and ducts for the same work group.

ARGE-West (Work Group West) at Gosselies, Belgium comprised Avion Fairey S.A. and SABCA (*Societe Anonyme de Constructions Aeronautiques*). It built 187 F-l04Gs (100 for the Belgian Air Force, and 87 for West Germany) using fuselage nose radomes, air scoops, ducts and aft fuselage sections made by Siebel, and air brakes, main landing gear doors, horizontal stabilizers, fins and rudders made by Heinkel and nose landing gears made by Dornier.

The Italian Group at Turin-Caselle, comprising Fiat, Aerter, Macchi, SIAI Marchetti, Piaggio, and SACA, built 329 F/RF-104G and F-104S Starfighters: 104 F-104Gs for Italy, 25 for the Netherlands and 15 for Germany, 20 RF-104Gs for Italy and 35 for Germany and 206 F-104S aircraft for Italy and 40 for Turkey.

The F-104Gs were manufactured in two variants – all-weather fighter (AWX) and fighter-bomber. The AWX version was originally armed with M61A1 Vulcan cannon and AIM-9B Sidewinder missiles and had no centerline weapons pylon, while some aircraft of the fighter-bomber version had the centerline pylon, but had no cannon, replaced by an additional fuel tank. It varied depending on the country – Italian interceptors had no cannon, while the fighter-bombers had one. Later the fighter-bombers were refitted with cannons within overhauls and modification programs. In German service some AWX fighters were also later converted to fighter-bombers.

To co-ordinate the entire multinational program the NATO Starfighter Management Office (NASMO) was established at Koblenz, West Germany. BMW at Munich, Fabrique Nationale at Brussels and Fiat in cooperation with Alfa Romeo undertook the license production of the GE J79-GE-11A engine.

Apart from the F-104G fighter/bomber variant, the photo reconnaissance variant RF-104G was also developed. A total of 198 were built. They differed from the F-104G by having no cannon and ammunition,

TF-104G D-5803 of CAV (Conversie Aanvals Vlucht – Strike Conversion Flight, known also as Conversie Afdeling Volkel), taxis at Volkel on 20 October 1982. (Hans Rolink)

19

these being replaced by photographic equipment, which could comprise either three KS-67A cameras in the nose, or a fixed flat-sided ventral camera pod. RF-104Gs of the Royal Netherlands and Italian air forces were later retrofitted with the ventral removable Dutch Orpheus camera pod. Many RF-104Gs were also later converted to F-104G standard.

Lockheed at Burbank manufactured 139 F-104Gs during 1960–62 and 40 RF-104Gs during 1962–1963 (of them only 24 were in true reconnaissance configuration, the rest were armed like the F-104G) and during 1963–64 Canadair manufactured 140 F-104Gs. All these aircraft were delivered to foreign users under MAP.

The F-104G production program continued until 1972. By then the five production consortia had manufactured 1,092 units of the F-104G and 214 of the RF-104G (including 16 armed aircraft with this designation).

For pilot conversion trainer versions were necessary. The first was the F-104F (model 483-04-08), procured for the *Luftwaffe*. Thirty aircraft were built during 1959–1960 by Lockheed. It was similar to the F-104D. It was powered by the J79-GE-11A turbojet, but it did not have the strengthened airframe and the all-weather NASARR fire-control system of the F-104G and was not combat-capable. The main trainer version built by Lockheed for all F-104G operators was the TF-104G (Lockheed model 583C-10-20), which was identical to the F-104G, except for only the missing cannon and smaller fuel capacity. A total of aircraft 220 were built by Lockheed. Of these, 23 were assembled by Messerschmitt, 12 by Fiat and nine by SABCA.

In TF-104G registered N104L, Jacqueline Cochran set three women's world's speed records. On 11 May 1964, she averaged 2,300 km/h over a 15/25 km course, on 1 June she flew at an average speed of 2,097 km/h over a 100-km closed-circuit course, and on 3 June she flew at an average speed of 1,814 mph over a 500-km closed-circuit course.

Above: *Italian F-104Gs of 4º Stormo being readied for take-off. (AMI)*

Royal Danish Air Force Canadair CF-104 Starfighter (CL-90) "R-851" (683A-1151/104851/RCAF 12851) preserved at Aalborg Forsvars-og Garnisonsmuseum. This aircraft was transferred to Denmark in June 1972, from the Canadian Air Force in Europe after a conversion to the F-104G standard. Here it served with Eskadrille 726 at Aalborg AB until October 1983. *"R-851" was painted in a wraparound dark green colour scheme during its service time and here it sports a fake early Danish F-104G paint scheme. Note the displayed General Electric J79-GE-11A engine. (Nils Mosberg)*

Royal Danish Air Force Canadair CF-104 Starfighter (CL-90) "R-888" preserved at Dansk Flymuseum at Stauning. This aircraft was transferred to Denmark in June 1972, from the Canadian Air Force in Europe after conversion to F-104G standard. (Przemysław Skulski)

F-104G F-FN of the Royal Norwegian Air Force. (RnoAF)

F-104G 61-3269 of the 69th Tactical Fighter Training Squadron, 58th Tactical Training Wing at Luke AFB, Arizona carrying two practice AIM-9J Sidewinder missiles, photographed in 1979. The 58th TFTW conducted the F-104 conversion of German pilots. (USAF)

21

F-104G 6695 of the Hellenic Air Force preserved at the War Museum in Athens. (Jarosław Dobrzyński)

F-104G FX12 of the Belgian Air Force preserved at the Royal Museum of the Armed Forces and of Military History in Brussels. (Bartłomiej Belcarz)

CF-104 12702 with Vinten reconnaissance pod. (CAF)

F-104G 23+37 of JG 71 "Richthofen", Luftwaffe, Wittmundhafen 1974. Aircraft in the Norm 62 paint scheme of "Gelboliv" – RAL6014 (FS24064), over "Basaltgrau" – RAL7012 (FS26152). Undersides were either "Silbergrau" or "Weissaluminium" – RAL9006 (FS17178) or RAL7001 (FS36320). Tank markings were in bright orange called "Leuchtorange". Radome is white with a green anti-glare panel.

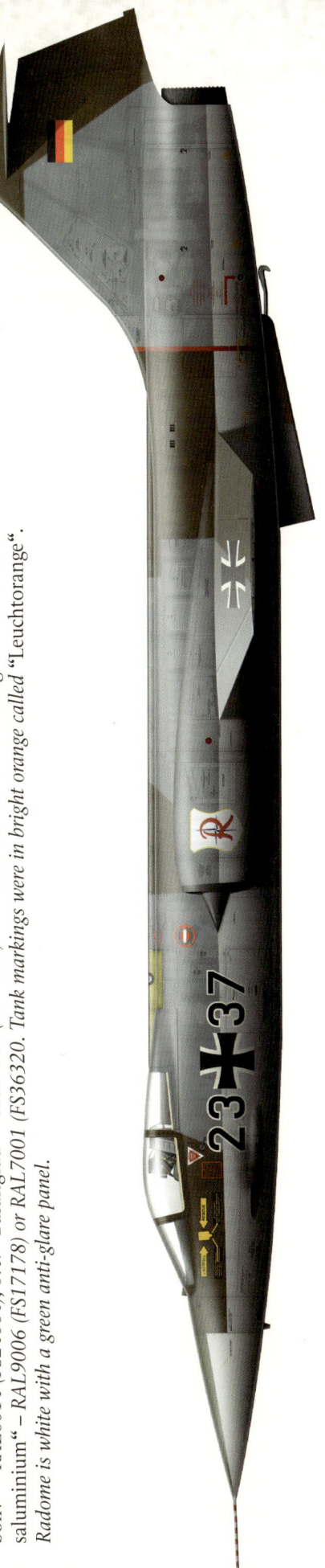

F-104G 26+72 of MFG 2, Marineflieger, Eggebek 1983. Aircraft painted in Marine Norm 76 paint scheme with dark grey – RAL7012 (FS26152) upper surfaces and light grey – RAL7001 (FS36320) or natural metal lower surfaces. Radome is white with no anti-glare markings.

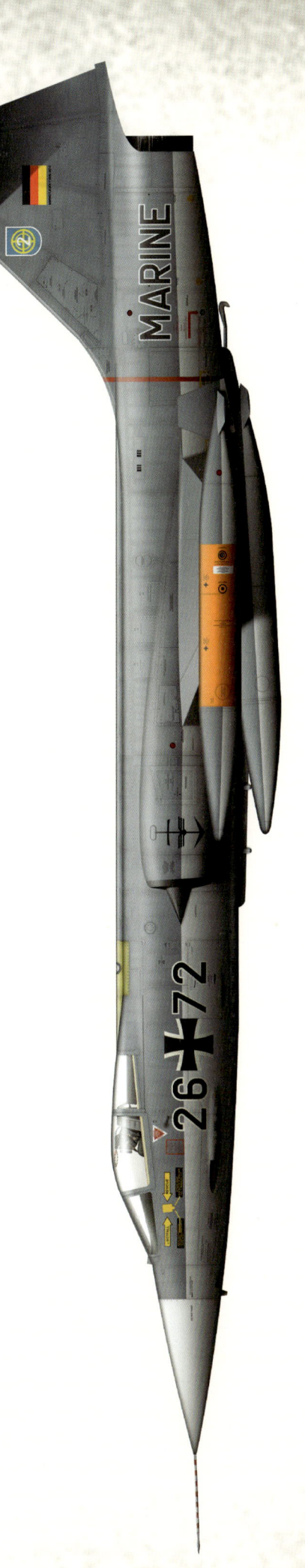

The Starfighter in Canada

In late 1950s the Canadian government had to make a number of financially and politically expensive decisions. The first concerned the replacement of eight squadrons of North American/Canadair F-86 Sabre day fighters, and four squadrons of Avro CF-100 Canuck all-weather/night fighters, serving in the European Air Division. Rapid technological development of jet aircraft made these types obsolete and a new, supersonic, aircraft was needed. Secondly, NATO had adopted a doctrine of "limited nuclear warfare" and was pressuring Canada to undertake a nuclear strike role for its European based aircraft. Simultaneously the indigenous Canadian combat aircraft the Avro CF-105 Arrow was undergoing flight trials, so a decision on its further development and production was required. Many defense experts and politicians had the opinion that the era of manned combat aircraft was gone and they would be replaced by rocket missiles.

In the evaluation of replacement aircraft for the European Air Division more than 10 different types were taken into consideration, including the Avro CF-105 Arrow, Lockheed F-104 Starfighter, Dassault Mirage IIIC, McDonnell F-4 Phantom, Douglas A-4 Skyhawk, Northrop F-5 Freedom Fighter, Fiat G-91, Republic F-105 Thunderchief, Grumman F11F-1F Super Tiger, Vought F-8 Crusader and Hawker Siddeley Buccaneer.

Initial requirements had been for a twin-engine, two crew aircraft, but these were dropped as the list got smaller. For quite a long time the F-4 Phantom was favored, but it was too expensive, and could not be supplied in time. In February 1959 the CF-105 Arrow program was cancelled and the choice had narrowed to two contenders, the Grumman F11F and the Lockheed F-104. Then the US Navy canceled the F11F program (only two were built).

On 2 July 1959 it was announced in the House of Commons that Canada had selected the Lockheed F-104 Starfighter as the replacement for the Sabre Mk.6 in service with the RCAF's European Air Division. As the Canadian government wanted equipment to be fitted in accordance with RCAF requirements, it elected to manufacture the aircraft under license in Canada rather than buying them from Lockheed. On 14 August it was announced that Canadair at Montreal-Cartierville, Quebec would license-build the CF-104s and that General Electric J79 engines would be license-built by Orenda Engines, Ltd. at Malton, Ontario. The CF-104 was powered by Canadian-built J79-OEL-7 rated at 44.48 kN (10,000 lbf) dry thrust and 70.3 kN (15,800 lbf) with afterburner. In addition, Canadair was to manufacture wings, tail assemblies, and rear fuselage sections for 66 Lockheed-built Starfighters destined for the West German *Luftwaffe*. The license production contract was signed on 17 September 1959. Lockheed sent F-104A-15-LO serial number 56-0770 to Canada to act as a pattern aircraft for CF-104 manufacture. It was later fitted with CF-104 fire control systems and flight control equipment (but not the strengthened airframe of the true F-104G) and turned over to the RCAF, where it was assigned the serial number of 12700. The RCAF eventually took delivery of 239 CF-104 Starfighters as follows:

Single Seat: One F-104A, (12700), manufactured by Lockheed Aircraft Corporation, of Burbank, California, accepted in March of 1961 as a production pattern.

200 CF-104s (12701–12900), manufactured under license by Canadair Limited, at Cartierville Quebec and delivered from March 1961 until December 1963. They were designated CL-90 by the Canadair factory. The initial RCAF designation was CF-111 but was later changed to CF-104.

Dual Seat: 22 CF-104Ds Mk I (12631–12652), accepted between January 1962 and September 1963, and 16 CF-104Ds Mk II (12653–12668), all accepted in November 1964. Both batches were manufactured by Lockheed at Palmdale, California.

The maiden flight of the CF-104 took place on 26 May 1961, at Palmdale. The aircraft, s/n 12701, had been built in Cartierville, airlifted to Palmdale and was flown by a Lockheed pilot, Ed Brown. The second CF-104 (12702) also made its first flight at Palmdale. The first flights in Canada took place at Canadair on 14 August 1961 with 12703, flown by Canadair pilot R.M. Kidd and later the same day, 12704, flown by Lockheed pilot Glen Reaves.

CF-104 12704 in flight. (CAF)

CF-104 12868 with Vinten reconnaissance pod. (CAF)

The CF-104 was basically similar to the F-104G, but in accordance with RCAF requirements was optimized for the nuclear strike and reconnaissance roles. The CF-104 was fitted with R-24A NASARR radar dedicated to the air-to-ground mode only in place of the NASARR F15A-41B radar of the F-104G, optimized for both air-to-air and air-to-ground modes. The cockpit layout was altered. Another difference from the F-104G was the ability of the CF-104 to carry the Vinten Vicon ventral reconnaissance pod with four cameras, bolted directly to the fuselage. Initially in the CF-104 an additional fuel tank was fitted in the place of the 20-mm M61A1 cannon and its associated ammunition. The main undercarriage members were fitted with longer-stroke liquid springs and carried larger tires. The CF-104 also differed from the F-104G in retaining the removable refueling probe that was fitted to the F-104Cs of the USAF (although the CF-104Gs never flew with them).

The 200th and last CF-104 (No. 12900) was completed on 4 September 1963 and delivered to the RCAF on 10 January 1964. Many early production aircraft were modified to the standard of the last production machines. CF-104s were initially assigned Canadian serials 12701 through 12900. On 2 May 1970, they were re-serialed as 104701 through 104900. The Lockheed-built F-104A pattern aircraft was re-serialed from 12700 to 104700. Following the delivery of the last CF-104, Canadair switched to the manufacture of F-104Gs for delivery to NATO allies under the provisions of MAP.

Three US Naval Air Reserve McDonnell F-4N Phantom IIs of Fighter Squadron VF-201 fly in formation with three Canadair CF-104 Starfighters from 417 Squadron of the Canadian Forces over the woods of Alberta in 1976. US Navy

Starfighter in Japan

In 1959 Japan was also looking for a new fighter aircraft, but its service chiefs favored the Grumman F11A Super Tiger. However, before the choice was announced Lockheed and Japanese politicians supporting the Starfighter made use of the F-104's 1958 and 1959 altitude and speed records in lobbying for the Starfighter's acceptance. A historical irony was the fact that the Starfighter's main supporter was Gen. Minoru Genda, the chief of air staff who in 1941 planned and carried out the attack on Pearl Harbor. During a visit at Lockheed, after a flight in a Starfighter Genda called it the world's best fighter and the license production contract was signed on 29 January 1960. Japan announced the intention to equip its newly created Japan Air Self Defense Force (JASDF) with 230 F-104J aircraft in the air superiority role. An industrial cartel headed by Mitsubishi Heavy Industries was given the responsibility for the license manufacture of the Starfighter in Japan. At first, the Japanese Starfighter would be assembled in Japan from Lockheed-supplied components, but ultimately the Starfighter would be built in Japan entirely from Japanese-manufactured components.

The Japanese Starfighter was given the designation F-104J. It was basically similar to the F-104G, but was specialized as an all-weather interceptor only, since post-war treaty restrictions at that time did not allow Japan to possess any aircraft with offensive capabilities.

The F-104J was powered by a J79-IHI-11A engine license built by Ishikawajima-Harima. It was fitted with the NASARR F-15J-31 fire control system optimized for the air-to-air mode, and was armed with a 20-mm M61A1 cannon, four AIM-9 Sidewinder air-to-air missiles and two external fuel tanks. No other stores were carried.

The first Lockheed-built F-104J (Model 683-07-14) flew on 30 June 1961. Three F-104Js were built by Lockheed. Deliveries of Mitsubishi-assembled F-104Js lasted from March 1962 through March 1965, totaling 29 units. The delivery of Mitsubishi-manufactured F-104Js lasted from March 1965 through 1967, totalling 178 aircraft

The F-104DJ (Model 583B-10-17) was the two-seat trainer version of the F-104J for Japan. It had electronics and other items compatible with those of the single-seat version. Twenty aircraft were built by Lockheed and reassembled in Japan between July of 1962 and January 1964. No F-104DJ two-seaters were constructed by Mitsubishi.

The F-104J entered with the *Koku Jietai* (Japanese Air Self Defence Force, JASDF) in March 1962. The first JASDF unit to convert to the F-104J was the 201st *Hikotai* (fighter squadron), which was a provisional training unit based at Komaki and later moved to Chitose. The two hundred and ten F-104Js and the twenty F-104DJ operational trainers were used by seven *Hikotais* (the 201st to 207th) of the *Koku Jietai*.

Beginning in December 1981, the Japanese Starfighters were replaced by Mitsubishi-built F-15J/F-15DJ Eagles. The last JASDF F-104J was retired by the 207th *Hikotai* in March of 1986.

After the retirement from front line operations, some F-104s were used by ADTW (Air Development and Testing Wing) for miscellaneous duties such as chase planes.

The last duties for JASDF F-104Js were to be unmanned target drones. Two F-104Js were modified to UF-104J experimental drones and tested by ADTW. After that, 14 Starfighters were converted to UF-104JA target drones and all of them were shot down at the firing range located near Iwo-Jima.

F-104J Starfighters of the Japanese Air Self Defence Force being prepared for a training sortie during the Cope North '81 exercise. (DoD)

F-104J 36-8563 of the JASDF. JASDF

F-104J 46-8650 of the JASDF. (DoD)

Accidents

The Starfighter was a very demanding and difficult aircraft to fly. It required from the pilot very high flying skills, precision and obedience to the flight operating instruction, as it did not tolerate any mistakes. This difficulty was related mainly to the necessity of maintaining constant high speed, including take-off and landing, and the aircraft's tendency to stall at high angles of attack, which resulted from the very high wing loading. Pilots used to older, much simpler subsonic aircraft had to completely change their flying habits.

In West Germany the F-104 quickly gained a bad reputation because of the high number of accidents, often resulting in fatalities. Due to this fact it quickly became known as "*Fliegender Sarg*" (flying coffin) and "*Der Witwenmacher*" (widow maker). From 29 March 1961 to 26 April 1989 a total of 298 German Starfighters were lost in accidents, claiming the lives of 116 pilots (on the other hand, 171 pilots managed to eject safely and eight pilots did so twice). The worst period, known as the "Starfighter Crisis", were the years 1965 and 1966 when the accident rate was highest. Most of the crashes were caused by human error – either pilot or maintenance mistakes.

However, the attrition rate in German service was not much greater than that of the F-104 in service with several other air forces, including the USAF. Other countries, like Italy, Belgium and the Netherlands had similar loss rates. Canada lost 46% of its 200 single-seat CF-104s in flying accidents. In *Luftwaffe* service the loss rate of Starfighters was similar to that of the Republic F-84F Thunderstreak, the Starfighter's direct predecessor, which amounted to 36%.

Some of the Starfighter crashes could indeed be traced to technical problems with the F-104G itself. Problems with the engine and fuel system were the major causes of accidents, particularly in the early period of operations of the Starfighter. Three of the first four crashes of German Starfighters were caused by engine failures in flight or on take-off. The first fatal crash was particularly dangerous and by a miracle claimed only one victim. On 25 January 1962 the F-104F

27

BB+366 encountered afterburner blow-out during a formation take-off for a training flight. The trainee, *Oberleutnant* Horst Völter managed to eject but the instructor, *Hauptmann* Lutz Tyrkowski, was killed. The aircraft hit a factory building near the airfield, but only one person inside was slightly hurt. Particularly troublesome was the hydraulically operated variable afterburner nozzle, which had a tendency to open unexpectedly, which resulted in rapid loss of thrust. Contamination of the Starfighter's liquid oxygen system, causing loss of consciousness of the pilot, was listed as a contributing factor in some of the accidents. Problems with asymmetric flap deployment and the boundary layer control system also occurred. The landing gear turned out to be not strong enough, since it had been designed for the lighter A and C models. Using an aircraft originally designed as a light day fighter in the roles of fighter-bomber, interceptor and nuclear strike was also mentioned among the reasons.

Yet human error, either by pilots or ground crews, was the major cause of the majority of the accidents. Insufficient training was one of the main factors. German Starfighter pilots were only flying 13–15 hours a month, compared with the NATO average of about 20 hours. Human errors in the cockpit were a substantial cause of the Starfighter crisis. Numerous accidents were the results of mistakes on the part of the pilot in handling the technology and flying errors, like failure to abort take-off in time, a significant number of compressor stalls, mid-air collisions, hitting the ground during low-level flight, failure to maintain minimum speed during the landing approach, incorrect landing configurations, spatial disorientation when flying on instruments and so-called pitch-ups, when too high an angle-of-attack resulted in the aircraft's sudden stall.

Another factor was the fact that the initial training of *Luftwaffe* pilots took place in the USA. The reason given for training *Luftwaffe* pilots in Arizona rather than in Germany was that the clear air and good flying weather in the American Southwest was much more conducive to pilot training than was the often poor weather of Northern Europe. The sudden transition from the clear desert skies of Arizona to the cloudy and foggy skies of northern Europe may have been another factor in the rash of crashes. The high rate of crashes while in *Luftwaffe* service could be blamed more on the hazards of flying at high speeds at low level in the bad weather of Northern Europe than on any intrinsic flaw with the F-104G. Many Starfighter crashes were CFITs (Controlled Flight Into Terrain). A good example of this was one of the best known German Starfighter victims, *Oberleutnant zur See* Joachim von Hassel of MFG 2, the son of Kai-Uwe von Hassel, the former Minister of Defence and later the chairman of the Bundestag. On 10 March 1970 his aircraft hit the ground during a ground-controlled approach to Eggebek air base. German electro music group Welle: Erdball wrote a song dedicated to him, titled "Starfighter F-104G".

Proper qualifications of the technical personnel were also a major factor contributing to flight safety. The Starfighter was a much more sophisticated aircraft than earlier generation jets and required 38–45 hours of maintenance for every flight hour, whereas many of the *Luftwaffe* ground crew personnel were hastily trained conscripts. Some aircraft were also destroyed on the ground, without human losses, in accidents during maintenance.

There also were accidents which certainly could have been avoided, since they were caused by needless bravado and lack of imagination, either of pilots or high level commanders. The most striking example was the most disastrous Starfighter crash on 19 June 1962 in which four aircraft and four pilots were lost. For 20 June 1962 a big ceremony on the occasion of the first *Luftwaffe* unit, *JaboG* 31, becoming operational on the F-104 was to take place at Nörvenich air base. The idea of adding splendor to the ceremony by group aerobatics display performed by a formation of four F-104Fs emerged and was accepted by the *Inspekteur der Luftwaffe*, *General* Josef Kammhuber, even though it was known that the Starfighter was not well suited to that kind of task and young German pilots had insufficient experience. On 19 June a four-ship formation with an American instructor, USAF Captain Jon Speer in the lead, and *Oberleutnants* Bernd Kuebart, Heinz Frye and Wolfgang von Stürmer took off for the final rehearsal. During a series of climbing and descending turns the formation flew into a cloud. The leader lost spatial orientation and executed the turning maneuver too tightly and at too low altitude, leading the formation out of the cloud in too steep a dive, thus having no time to pull out. All four aircraft crashed in a brown coal quarry at Knapsack, a few kilometers east of the Nörvenich base.

Sometimes the pilots behaved irresponsibly. On 18 March 1971 the F-104G 23+63 of JG 71 crashed on approach to Wittmundhafen air base during a night visual landing exercise due to a pitch-up (stall caused by too high angle of attack). The pilot, *Oberleutnant* Wolfgang Lippe ejected too late and was killed. An inquiry revealed that there had been a secret sweepstake among the pilots as to who could fly the fastest visual pattern. In this case it ended in a pitch-up because the last turn before the landing was flown too tightly.

Sometimes dangerous situations ended happily. On 2 June 1965 F-104G DA+103 of JaBoG 31 flown by *Hauptmann* Siegfried Heltzel had a mid-air collision with a Do 28 near Koblenz. The Do-28 D-IBEW crashed, but *Hptm* Heltzel managed an emergency landing at Nörvenich at a speed of 435 km/h. It was the fastest landing speed ever reached and it made an entry in The Guinness Book of Records in 1988.

Crash site of a German F-104G. (Stratus)

At the height of the Starfighter political crisis in mid-1966, the *Luftwaffe* commander, *General* Wernher Panitzki, was forced to resign after he had criticized Germany's Starfighter procurement program as being politically-motivated. His successor was the World War II fighter ace Lieutenant General Johannes Steinhoff, who had flown Me 262 jets during the war. Steinhoff had not initially been a Starfighter fan, and he had complained about the Bonn Defence Ministry's failure to implement the recommendations of his 1964 report on F-104G survival measures. One of Steinhoff's first moves was to review the F-104G's ejection system to enhance the probability of a successful escape by a pilot at low level. The Lockheed C-2 ejection seat initially fitted to the F-104G had been fitted with a more powerful Talley Corp 10100 rocket booster by November 1966 to give it true zero-zero capability. However, it was found that the Talley rockets had a destabilizing effect after ejection, and had to be removed. After the German Starfighter had to be grounded once again for fixes to the C-2 seats in December of 1966, it was decided to switch over to Martin-Baker Mk GQ7A zero-zero ejection seats. A contract was signed on 8 March 1967 to re-equip the entire remaining German F-104G fleet with the Martin-Baker seats. This took about a year to complete. The first successful use of a GQ7 seat to escape from a German F-104G took place during a ground-level overshoot at Ramstein on 24 September 1968.

Systematically, all technical deficiencies were corrected at great cost. During 1963 – 1968, 645 technical modifications were made to the airframe. By the time the F-104 was retired 1,498 modifications had been introduced.

The J79-GE-11A engines were found to be quite troublesome and MTU developed an improved version with blades of the first turbine stage made of new alloy called Udimet 700 and new afterburner nozzle and fuel systems. This version, designated J79-MTU-J1K, had thrust increased to 46.5 kN dry and 70.9 kN with full afterburner engaged. The first F-104G equipped with this new engine flew on 31 October 1969 and later most of the German Starfighters remaining in service were re-engined.

Another part of the program to reduce the Starfighter accident rate was the revision of the training techniques and procedures. It soon began to pay off. The Starfighter accident rate dropped by about half in 1968. However, this was only temporary, and 15 – 20 Starfighters crashed every year between 1968 and 1972. Crashes continued at a rate of nine to 11 aircraft per year until the mid 1970s and early 1980s, when all German F-104Gs began to be replaced by F-4F/RF-4F Phantoms and Tornados.

The Lockheed bribery scandal

The "Deal of the Century" was not all clean business. In late 1975 and early 1976 a U.S. Senate investigating committee led by Senator Frank Church concluded that from the late 1950s to the 1970s Lockheed representatives had corrupted members of friendly governments to guarantee contracts for military aircraft. In 1976 it was publicly revealed that Lockheed had paid $22 million in bribes to foreign officials in the process of negotiating the sale of aircraft, including the F-104 Starfighter. Former Lockheed lobbyist Ernest Hauser testified to Senate investigators that in 1961 the German Minister of Defence Franz Josef Strauss and his party the CSU had taken at least a 10 million dollar bribe for West Germany's purchase of more than 900 Starfighters. Strauss denied these charges and sued Hauser for slander. The allegations were not corroborated and the issue was dropped. It re-emerged in November 1976 during the *Bundestag* elections. There was another inquiry which revealed that most of the documents related to the F-104 purchase had been destroyed in 1962.

In the Netherlands Prince Bernhard, the husband of Queen Juliana and inspector-general of the Dutch Armed Forces received a 1.1 million dollar bribe from Lockheed to influence the Dutch government to select the F-104 rather than the Mirage III. This fact was revealed in 1976 and caused a serious crisis in the Royal Family. On 26 August 1976 a censored, but devastating for Prince Bernhard, report was released to the Dutch public. It included the Prince's letter of 1974 to Lockheed Corporation, demanding "commissions" be paid to him for Dutch military aircraft purchases. No criminal charges were pressed on the Prince by the Dutch government out of respect for Queen Juliana, but he was forced to resign from all his numerous public and business positions. He always denied the charges, but after his death in 2004 interviews in which he admitted taking the money were published. He said: "*I have accepted that the word Lockheed will be carved on my tombstone.*" Queen Juliana's abdication in 1980 was partially caused by her husband's behavior.

The Dutch Prince Bernhard and Queen Juliana returning from Italy because of developments in the Lockheed scandal. In the back seat Juliana with her dog Sara. The Netherlands, 26 August 1976.

This page: F-104G, 1/72 scale.

F-104G with Kormoran missile, 1/72 scale.

F-104G with reconnaissance pod and four fuel tanks, 1/72 scale.

F-104G with Sidewinder missiles, 1/72 scale.

F-104G with AGM-12 and Sidewinder missiles, 1/72 scale.

This page: F-104G upper and underside views. 1/72 scale.

This page: F-104G front and rear views. 1/72 scale.

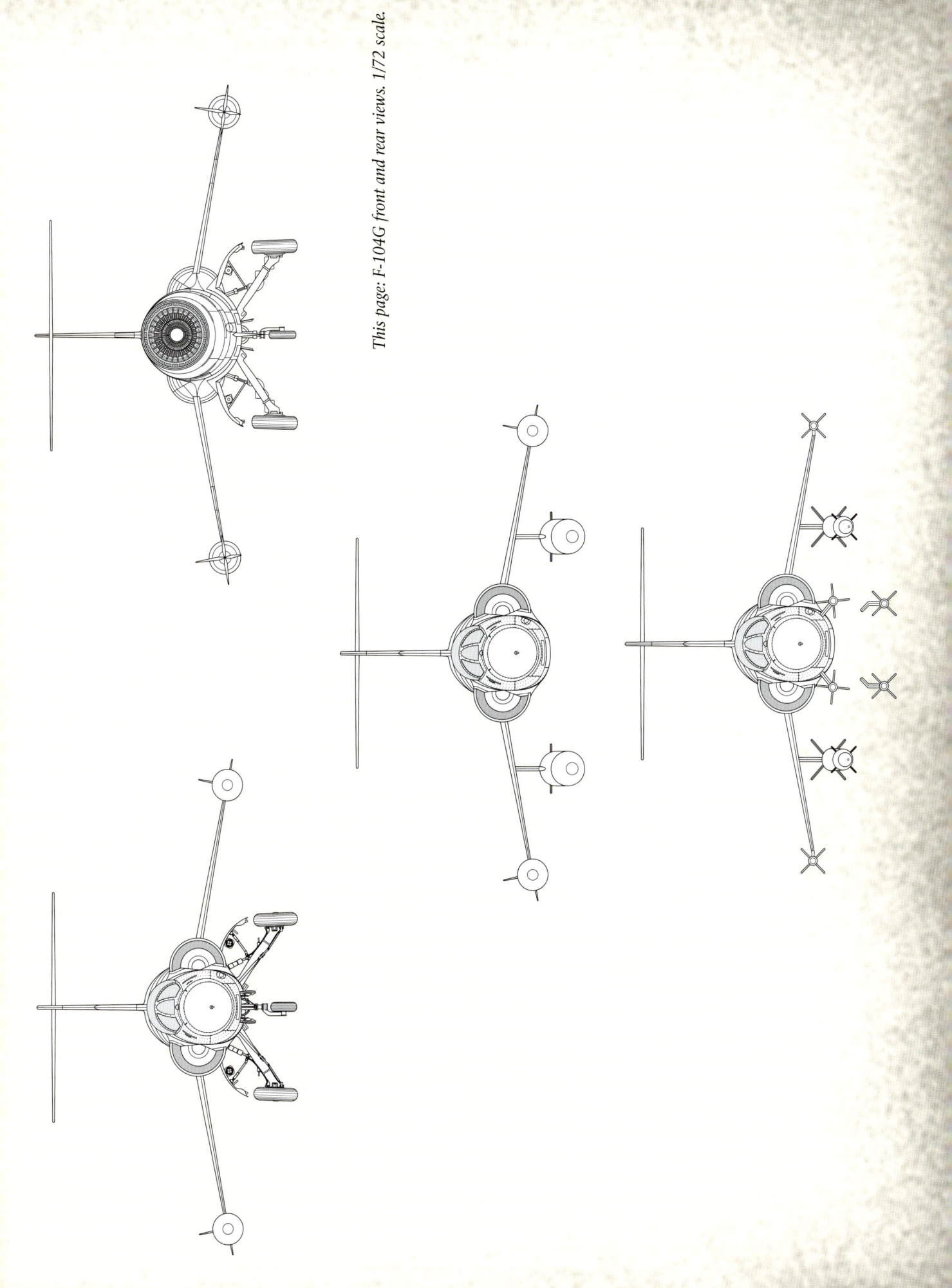

F-104G Starfighter 1/48 scale.

AS.34 Kormoran air to surface missile.

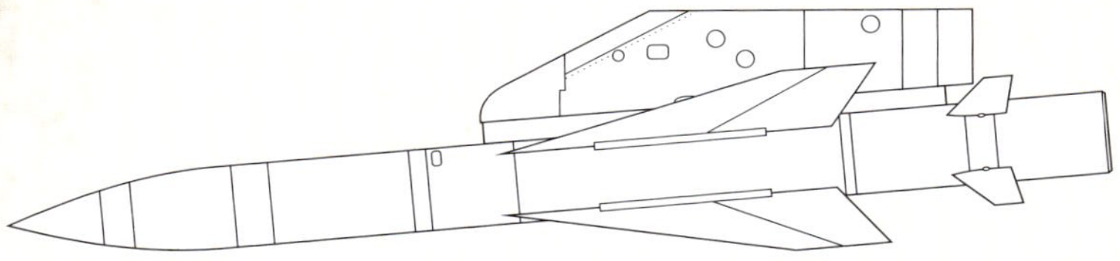

100 gal. external fuel tank

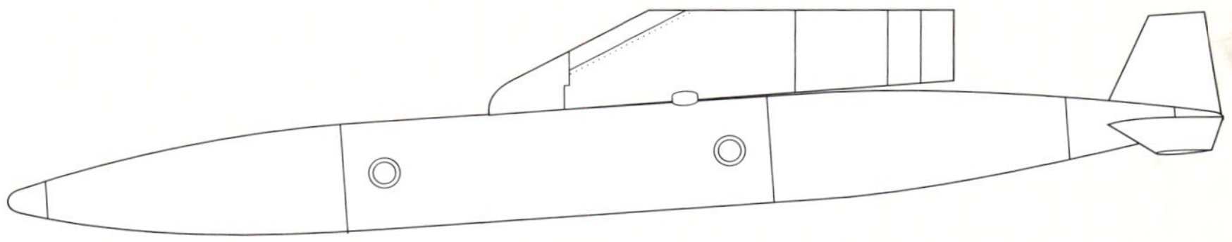

Reconnaissance pod.

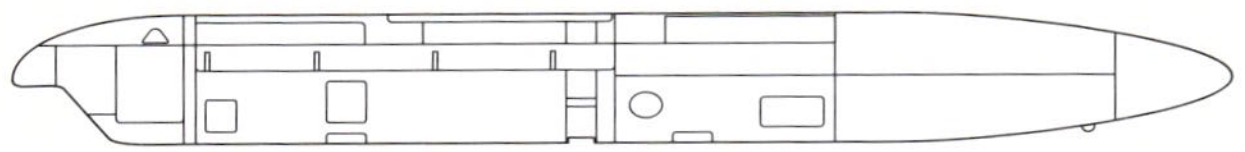

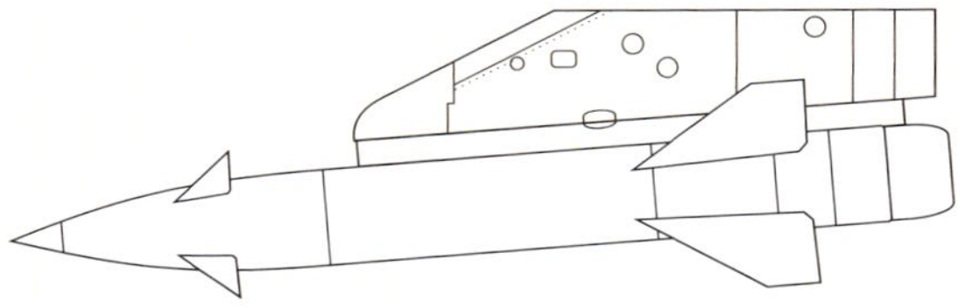

AIM-9 Sidewinder, a short range air-to-air missile.

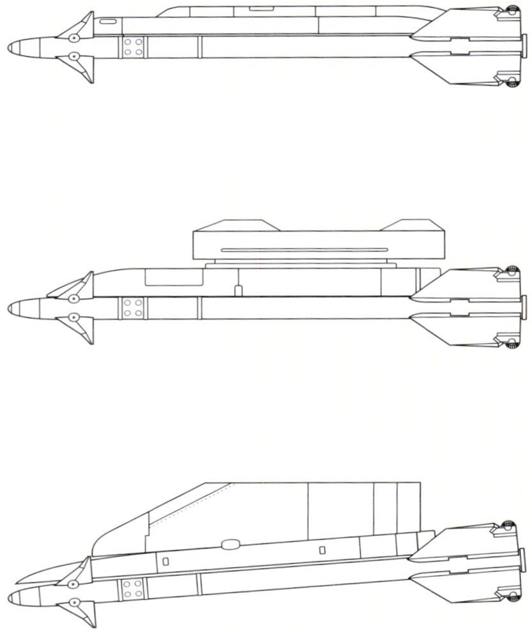

AIM-7 Sparrow, medium range air-to-air, semi-active radar homing missile.

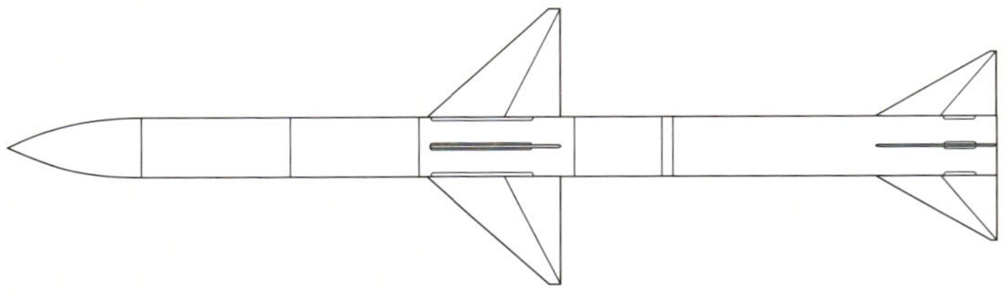

AGN-12 Bullpup air to ground missile.

34

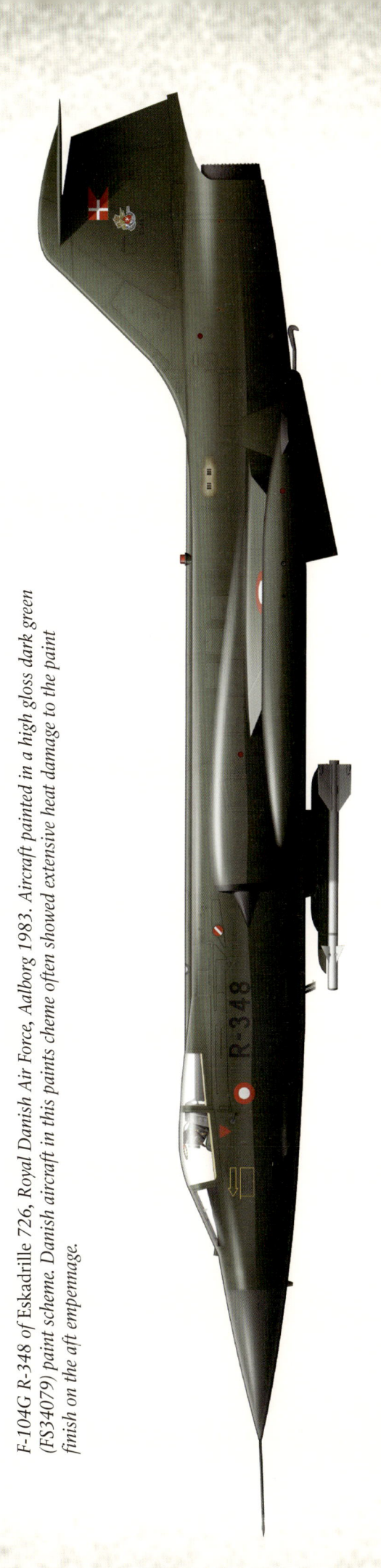

F-104G R-348 of Eskadrille 726, Royal Danish Air Force, Aalborg 1983. Aircraft painted in a high gloss dark green (FS34079) paint scheme. Danish aircraft in this paints cheme often showed extensive heat damage to the paint finish on the aft empennage.

TF-104G 27+06 of WasLw 10, Luftwaffe, Jever 1977. Aircraft in the Norm 62 camouflage. Tank markings were in bright orange called "Leuchtorange" – RAL9006. Radome is white with a green anti-glare panel.

35

F-104G 20+36 of JaboG 34, Luftwaffe, Memmingen 1984. Aircraft painted in Norm 83 wraparound paint scheme of a dark grey and two lighter greens. FS34079, RAL6003 (FS34082), RAL7021 (FS37031). Radome is white with a black or dark olive green anti-glare panel. Tip tanks are in a older paint scheme with an orange recognition band.

37

RF-104G D-8293 RNLAF 1983. Aircraft in the standard late RNLAF paint scheme, very similar to the Luftwaffe Norm 72 paint scheme. Undersides were painted a light non-metallic grey, with the Orpheus pod being a slightly different light grey.

39

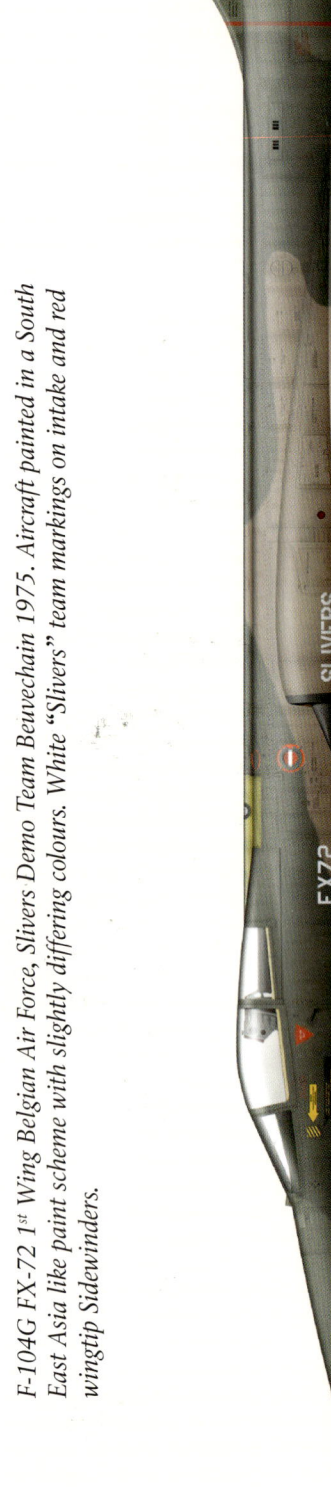

F-104G D-8090 Koniklijke Luchtmacht (Royal Netherlands Air Force), August 1963. Aircraft in the early RNLAF air defence paint scheme. Colour is called "nevelgrijs" or haze grey and is close to ADC grey but lighter, RAL7001 (FS36320).

F-104G FX-72 1st Wing Belgian Air Force, Slivers Demo Team Beuvechain 1975. Aircraft painted in a South East Asia like paint scheme with slightly differing colours. White "Slivers" team markings on intake and red wingtip Sidewinders.

F-104G 4-5 MM 6505 of 4° Aerobrigata Caccia Intercettori Ognitempo (4th All-Weather Fighter Interceptor Brigade) Aeronautica Militare Italiana, Grosseto 1963. Aircraft in natural metal finish with large full colour nationality markings. White upper wings with grey lower surfaces on wing. Radome is white with black anti-glare panel.

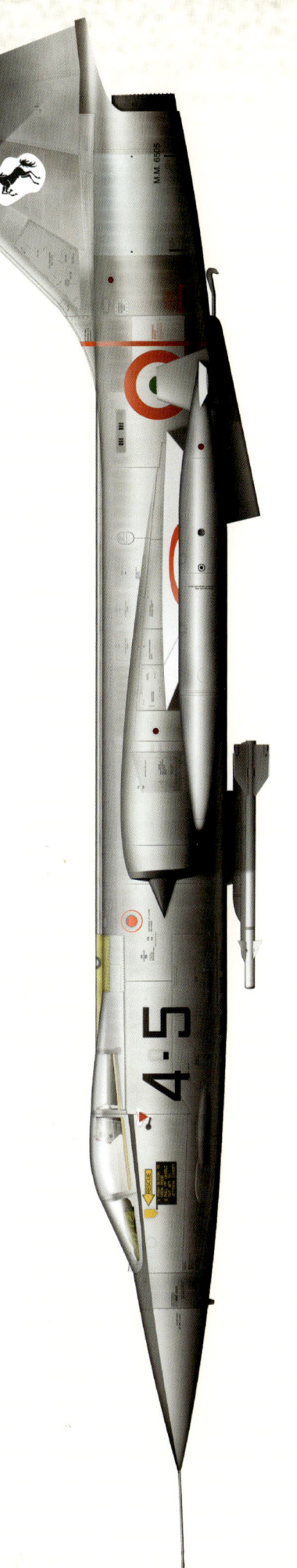

TF-104G MM 4553 of 4° Stormo 20° Gruppo Addestramento Operativo Pratica di Mare, Aeronautica Militare Italiana. Aircraft in standard late service Italian paint scheme with an overall medium grey base – FS35526 with dark grey markings. White radome with a dark grey anti glare panel.

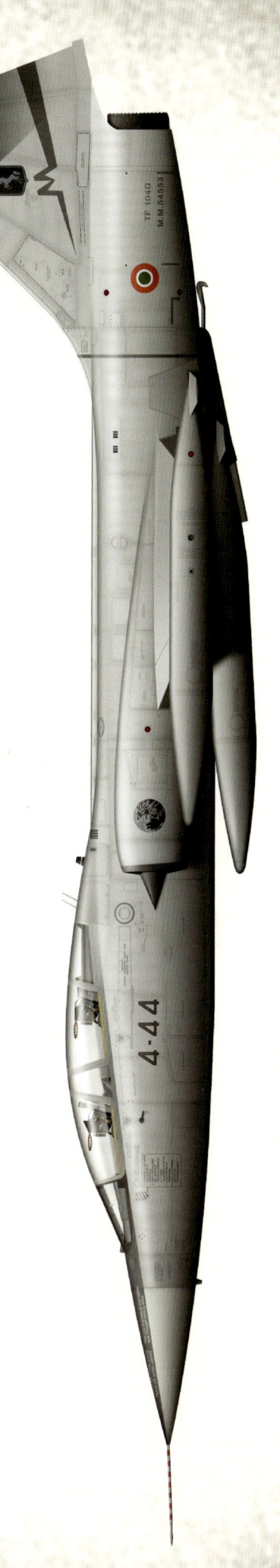

F-104G FX-52 31st Squadron Belgian Air Force, Tiger Meet Koksijde 1978. Aircraft painted in all round yellow and black tiger stripe scheme with full colour nationality markings.
More special camouflage F-104 profiles can be found in: F-104 Starfighter Special Camouflages (Spotlight On series), ISBN: 978-8363678586

43

Lockheed/Canadair F-104G of 104 Escuadrón Ejercito del Aire (Spanish Air Force) Torrejon Air Base 1968. Aircraft painted all round ADC grey with a large unpainted section on the rear fuselage starting just forward of the airbrakes. Wings painted white with light grey undersides.

F-104G D-8341 322 Squadron Koniklijke Luchtmacht (Royal Netherlands Air Force) Leeuwarden. Aircraft in the standard late RNLAF paint scheme, very similar to the Luftwaffe 72 scheme. Undersides were painted a light non-metallic grey, with the Orpheus pod being a slightly different light grey.

F-104G 61-2625 K-FN 331 Skvadron (Squadron) Luftforsvaret (Royal Norwegian Air Force), Bodø 1963. Aircraft in natural metal finish with white upper wings and light grey wing undersides. Radome is white with a black anti-glare panel running up to the forward windscreen.

Canadair CF-104 Starfighter s/n 104762 1 Canadian Air Group Canadian Forces, CFB Baden-Söllingen, Germany 1983. Aircraft painted in a olive green colour – 503-120 (FS14064) with white and red markings on the tail and tiptanks. Radome and glare panel are black.

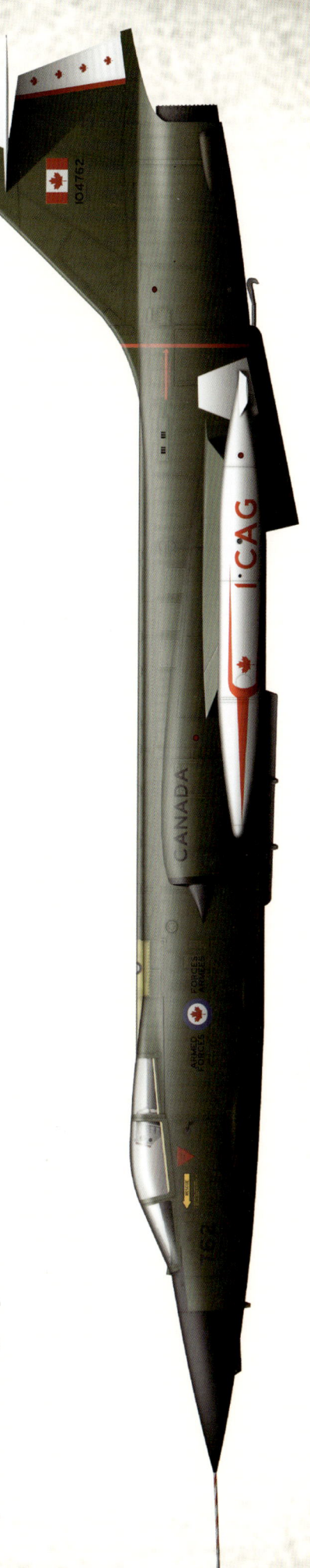

45

CF-104 s/n 4900 331 Squadron Royal Norwegian Air Force. Aircraft painted in an olive green paint scheme with light grey undersides. Radome is white with a black anti glare panel.

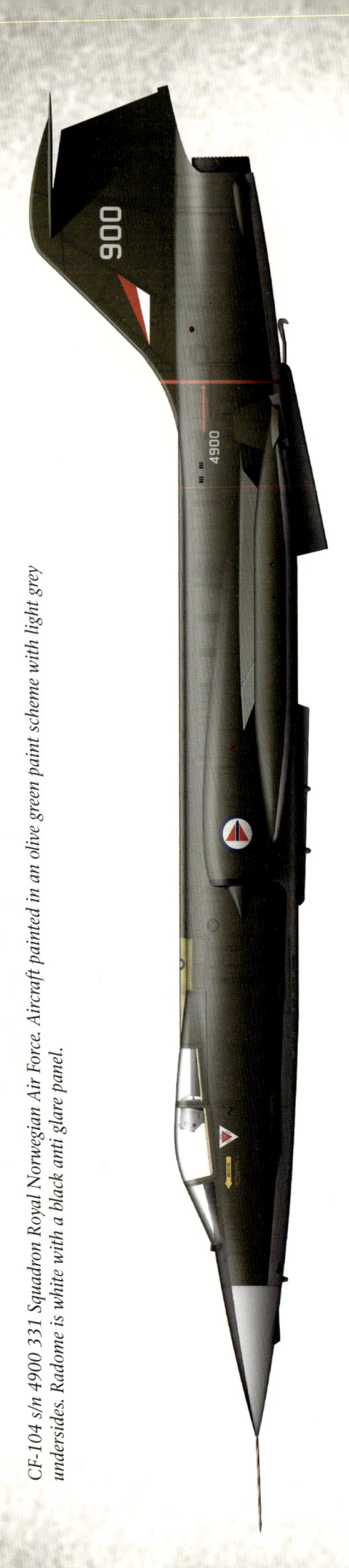

CF-104 s/n 104787 of Canadian Armed Forces, 417 Squadron Cold Lake mid 1970s. Aircraft in natural metal finish with white upper wings and light grey wing undersides. Radome is white with a black anti-glare panel running up to the windscreen. Upper part of stabiliser horn and stabiliser itself painted red.

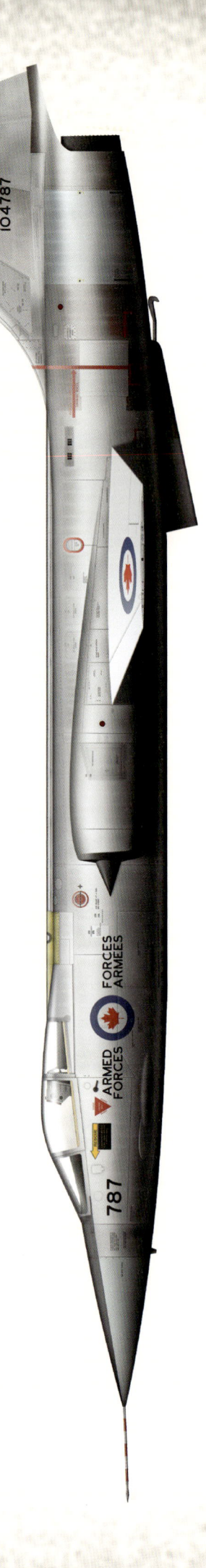

Ex-Luftwaffe F-104G 6.056 of the Turkish Air Force. Aircraft in the Norm 62 paint scheme. Radome is white with a green anti-glare panel.

Ex-Canadian CF-104 8.786 of the Turkish Air Force. Aircraft still painted in the late Canadian Air Force paint scheme - dark green over dark grey with a light grey underside. 503-120 (FS14064), 503-301 (FS34084), 501-302 (FS 36076), 101-327 (FS36300). Tip tank appears to be an ex-luftwaffe example in Norm 62 paint scheme with a orange recognition band.

47

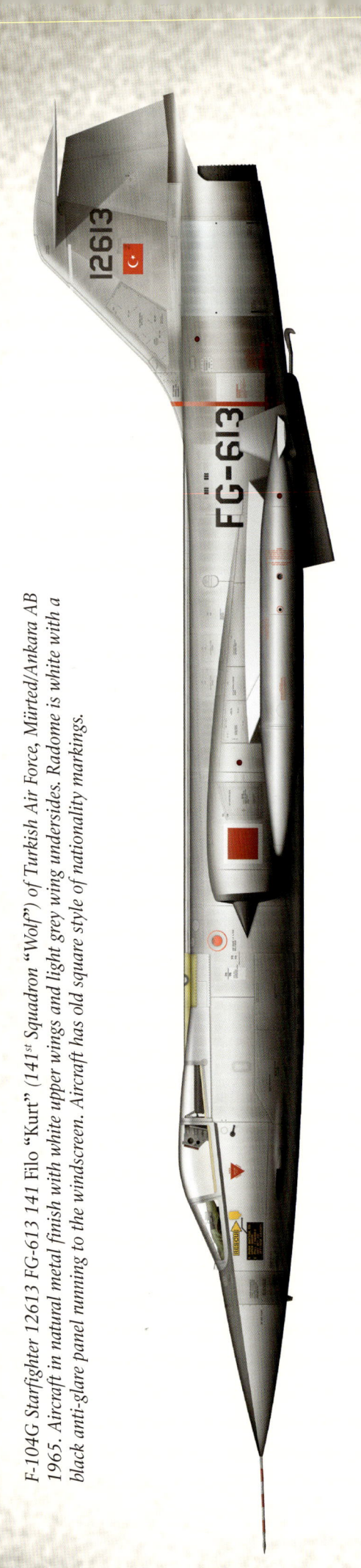

F-104G Starfighter 12613 FG-613 141 Filo "Kurt" (141st Squadron "Wolf") of Turkish Air Force, Mürted/Ankara AB 1965. Aircraft in natural metal finish with white upper wings and light grey wing undersides. Radome is white with a black anti-glare panel running to the windscreen. Aircraft has old square style of nationality markings.

F-104F BB+377, 4 Staffel WaSLw (Waffenschule der Luftwaffe) 10, Nörvenich 1962. Aircraft in natural metal finish with white upper wings and light grey wing undersides. Radome is white with a black anti-glare panel running up to the to the front fuselage.

48

RF-104 EA+121, AG (Aufklärungsgeschwader) 51 "Immelmann" Luftwaffe, Manching, mid 1960s. Aircraft in the Norm 62 paint scheme. Tank markings were in bright orange called "Leuchtorange". Radome is white with a green anti-glare panel.

F-104G DC+245 of JaboG 33, Luftwaffe, Büchel 1963. Aircraft in natural metal finish with white upper wings and light grey wing undersides. Radome is white with a black anti-glare panel running up to the to the front fuselage. Nose band is medium blue with a staffel logo.

49

F-104J Starfighter 76 – 8690 690 of 202nd Hikotai (Squadron) 5th Kokudan (Wing) Japan Air Self Defense Forces, Misawa AB 1980. Aircraft painted in a two tone blue scheme with temporary paint. Often these special paint schemes were applied for gunnery camps and non FS number paints were used.

CF-104G 770, 1st Canadian Air Group, West Germany, early 1980s. Aircraft painted in standard late paint scheme for the Canadian air force with a two-tone green upper camouflage with light grey undersurfaces. Markings are toned down.

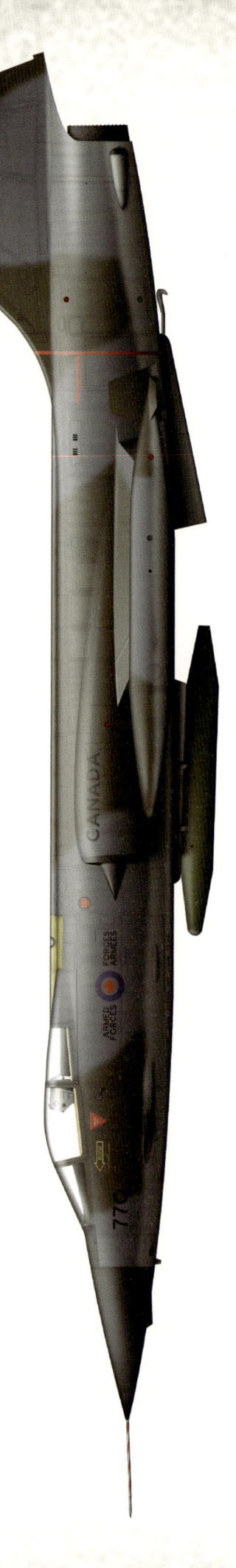

The ultimate Starfighter – F-104S

After a few years of operation of the F-104G, the command of *Aeronautica Militare Italiana* (Italian Air Force) concluded that these aircraft were insufficient to meet NATO requirements of 18 planes per squadron. Numerous crashes worsened this situation year by year. Moreover, the interceptor version F-104G CI (*Caccia Intercett'ri*) armed with only two AIM-9B Sidewinder missiles and no cannon, was not fully able to defend the country. In the mid 1960s the search for new and more capable fighter began.

The AMI evaluated the Mirage III, the Northrop F-5, the McDonnell F-4C Phantom II and a proposed upgraded and more powerful version of the Starfighter, powered by new J79-GE-19 engine. The Phantom was the best fighter, but it was very expensive and had a crew of two in a period when the AMI had no Weapon Systems Officers. Italy elected to stay with Lockheed, who offered a lot of work for the Italian industry in production of the new variant.

The new version of the Starfighter, named F-104S because it was designed to carry and fire AIM-7E Sparrow SARH air-to-air missiles, had a more powerful engine, so the air intakes were moved 23 mm aft and their diameter was increased to improve the airflow. They were supplemented by rectangular, outward-opening auxiliary intakes, much larger than those of the F-104G. They were usually used during take offs on hot summer days. Two trapezoid fins were added to the sides of the ventral fin and two additional outboard weapon pylons were added to the wings. The Martin Baker IQ 7A ejection seat was installed. Lockheed modified two Italian F-104Gs into prototypes for the F-104S. The first prototype flew on 22 December 1966, followed by the second one in March 1967. As with the F-104G two main versions of the F-104S were finally developed: the Interceptor variant (CI) and the Strike variant (CB).

The F-104S/CI was fitted with FIAR/NASARR F15G radar capable of guiding AIM-7 Sparrow missiles. The missile's guidance system occupied the space used for the cannon in the F-104G. So the CI was only armed with a maximum combination of two Sparrows and four Sidewinders. Theoretically it was a great improvement over the two Sidewinders of the G, but the need to carry auxiliary fuel tanks (on the inboard pylons) and the impossibility to use the ventral pylons (just as it was for Italian F-104G) limited the CI maximum armament to two Sidewinders on the wingtip rails and two Sparrows on the outboard pylons. During QRA duty F-104S/CI were usually lighter and the standard load was just one Sidewinder and one Sparrow plus tip tanks. F-104S/CI also had no centerline pylon.

The CI variant was operated by six fighter squadrons (*gruppi*).

The F-104S/CB had the FIAR/NASARR R21G-H radar and a radar altimeter for low level strike missions. It retained the M61A1 Vulcan cannon as its only air-to-air weapon and also had an additional

Final checks on an Italian F-104S at Bitburg AB in 1988.

internal fuel tank with a capacity of 462 liters. The F-104S/CB had nine weapon pylons and was theoretically able to carry a wide range of external stores, weighing up to 3,400 kg. The wingtips and the inner underwing pylons were always used for the tanks. Side ventral pylons were rarely used, almost only for display purpose, so bombs were usually carried on the outboard wing pylons and on the centerline station. The most frequently used configuration for this variant was with two or four tanks and a SUU-21 cluster bomb dispenser on the centerline station.

Only three strike squadrons of the AMI operated the F-104S/CB.

Fiat and Aeritalia built 206 F-104S Super Starfighters for the AMI: 118 of the CI variant and 88 of the CB variant. Deliveries to the AMI began in 1968, and the last F-104S was delivered in 1979. The only foreign operator of the F-104S variant was Turkey which ordered 40 F-104S/CB aircraft. They were delivered between December 1974 and October 1976. Total F-104S production amounted to 246 aircraft.

During the 1970s and 1980s there was a shortage of F-104S CI and sometimes a few CB F-104S were loaned to a fighter squadron by the strike squadron at the same air base in order to give fighter pilots enough flight hours to remain combat ready.

An F-104S ASA-M Starfighter of 4° Stormo takes off. (George Papadimitriou)

In the 1980s an upgrade program, called "Weapons System Upgrade" (*Aggiornamento Sistema d'Arma* – ASA), was implemented for 147 AMI F-104S Starfighters. The modifications included:

Two conical antennas were added on the upper fuselage, just behind the canopy, and below, just aft of the radome next to a blade antenna. The aircraft was also fitted with a sensor container aft of the brake chute vane. Both were part of the ALQ-70/72 ECM system. The antennas equipped all the fleet of modified aircraft, but they were active only on aircraft destined for the fighter-bomber squadrons. The aircraft was adapted to carry the AIM-9L air-to-air missiles that replaced the B version of the Sidewinder and along with the AIM-7 Sparrow the *Alenia Aspide* SARH missiles could be carried. A new radar version (the FIAR R-21G/M1 Setter) with frequency-hopping and look-down/shoot-down capability was introduced and the cockpit and console layouts were rearranged. A new weapons management panel appeared. The first upgraded aircraft flew in 1984 and service deliveries lasted from 1986 to 1991.

Two F-104S of 18° Gruppo 37° Stormo in flight. (AMI)

F-104S/CB 5-25 of 102° Gruppo 5° Stormo lands at Volkel during a squadron exchange with 306 Sqn RNLAF in October 1986. Note the cannon port. (Henk Schuitemaker)

The upgrade was intended especially for the F-104S/CI since its F15G radar was very unreliable. Pilots wished the cannon to be reinstalled, but only airframes made as CB retained the cannon, and all the others remained in the old CI configuration with a missile-only armament.

In 1984 the 156° Gruppo converted to Tornados and its F-104S/CB aircraft became available. They were converted to ASA standard and sent to Trapani-Birgi in Sicily, where they re-formed as the 18°*Gruppo* CBO, the only fighter squadron in the AMI that operated the F-104S/CB in the fighter role. They were armed only

The F-104S ASA prototype in flight. (AMI)

with the cannon and two AIM-9 Sidewinder missiles. The other unit to receive the F-104S CB/ASA was 102° *Gruppo*. The F-104S/CB were retired in July 1993, when 102° *Gruppo* was disbanded.

The pilots were not satisfied with the F-104S ASA modifications as it did not actually enhance the combat capabilities of the F-104S. This upgrade was selected basically as an interim solution until the multinational Eurofighter, in development of which Italy had also been involved, was available, but the Eurofighter development program was delayed. In the 1990s, facing the obsolescence of the Starfighter fleet,

the AMI decided to lease 24 ex-Royal Air Force Tornado interceptors, and upgrade a part of the Starfighter fleet again. The modification was called F-104S ASA-M. Within this upgrade the three ventral pylons disappeared and the corresponding cabling was removed, as well as the ALQ 70/72 ECM system. The avionics was improved: a GPS antenna was located in the third section of the canopy. The aircraft were retrofitted with the Have Quick radio for secure communication on the UHF band and a new TACAN system. In conjunction with these changes the cockpit was rearranged once again to include the new radio panel and the new navigation system. The ASA-M could carry only air-to-air missiles (AIM-9L, Aspide/Sparrow). The first flight of the ASA-M took place in 1995 and deliveries lasted from 1997 to 2002. In total 55 examples were upgraded. Fifteen TF-104Gs were also upgraded, being given the designation of "TF-104G-M".

These machines performed combat air patrols in 1999 during Operation Allied Force, the NATO air campaign against Serbia. That operation showed that despite the ASA-M modification the F-104S was no longer able to fly alongside other NATO fighters and remain in service until the arrival of the Eurofighter. As an interim solution 34 old, third-hand F-16A/B ADF were leased from Lockheed Martin to replace F-104S in three AMI squadrons in 2004. The last operational F-104S ASA-M flight, by 9° *Stormo*, took place on 31 October 2004.

F-104S ASA-M 9.99 MM 6930 of 9° Stormo "Francesco Baracca" 10° Gruppo Caccia Intercettori Ognitempo Grazzanisse AB. This aircraft took part in the F-104 vs Ducati 999F04 motorbike competition in 2004.
(George Papadimitriou)

F-104S ASA-M "Black Beauty" of 4° Stormo in special paint scheme.
(George Papadimitriou)

F-104S/CI Starfighter of 36° Stormo in flight, armed with two AIM-7 Sparrow and two AIM-9 Sidewinder air-to-air missiles.
(AMI)

F-104S ASA MM6732 36-02 of 12° Gruppo 36° Stormo lands at Twenthe AB, Netherlands on 9 June 1994. (Hans Rolink)

F-104S ASA-M Starfighter 4-20 of 4° Stormo taxis before take off. (George Papadimitriou)

F-104S ASA-M Starfighter MM6876 preserved at the Polish Aviation Museum in Krakow. This example took part in the last F-104 operational flight in the Italian Air Force on 31 October 2004 and the very last F-104 military flight in Italy on 27 July 2005. (Jarosław Dobrzyński)

F-104S with Sparrow and Sidewinder missiles. 1/72 scale.

CF-104 with Sidewinder missiles. 1/72 scale.

F-104S 4-7 MM 6711 of 4° Stormo 9° Gruppo Caccia Intercettori Ognitempo Grosseto Air Base Aeronautica Militare Italiana. Painted in the 1965 scheme of "Verde Scuro" – RAL6014 (FS24064), over "Grigio Mare Scuro" – RAL7012 (FS36152). Undersides were painted in a light metallic colour.

F-104S ASA-M 4-12 MM 6926 of 9° Stormo "Francesco Baracca" 10° Gruppo Caccia Intercettori Ognitempo Grazzanisse Air Base Aeronautica Militare Italiana, 2004. Aircraft painted in the light service light grey paint scheme for the Italian air force. Markings are dark grey.

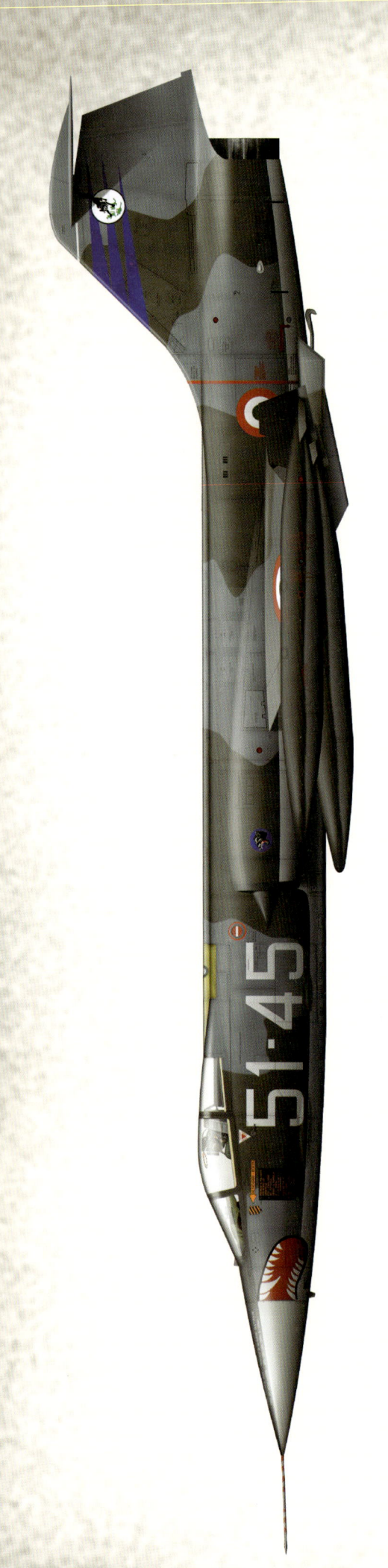

F-104S 51-45 MM 6797 of 51° Stormo 155° Gruppo Caccia Bombardieri (155th Fighter – Bomber Wing) Aeronautica Militare Italiana Treviso spring 1983. Painted in the 1965 scheme of "Verde Scuro" over "Grigio Mare Scuro". Undersides were painted in light metalic colour. Sporting a large attractive shark mouth behind the radome.

59

Operators

USA

The Lockheed F-104 Starfighter served with the United States Air Force (USAF) from 1958 until 1969 and continued in service with Air National Guard units until 1975. The USAF was not satisfied with the Starfighter and procured only 296 units in single-seat and two-seat versions. At that time, USAF doctrine placed little importance on air superiority (the fighter-to-fighter mission), and the Starfighter was deemed inadequate for either the interceptor (meaning fighter-to-bomber) or tactical fighter-bomber role, lacking both payload capability and endurance compared to other USAF aircraft. Its US service was quickly wound down after the second deployment to the SEA theatre in 1967. The National Aeronautics and Space Administration (NASA) flew a small mixed fleet of various F-104 variants in supersonic flight tests and spaceflight programs until 1994.

The F-104A entered service in a different role than originally envisioned by Lockheed. It initially served briefly with the USAF Air Defense Command/Aerospace Defense Command (ADC) as an interceptor, although due to short range, lack of all-weather capability and modest weapon load it was not well-suited for that role. The F-104 was intended as an interim solution while the ADC waited for delivery of the Convair F-106 Delta Dart. The first unit to become operational with the F-104A was the 83rd Fighter Interceptor Squadron on 20 February 1958, at Hamilton AFB, California. After three months of service, the unit's Starfighters were grounded after a series of engine-related accidents. The aircraft were then fitted with the J79-3B engine and four further Air Defense Command squadrons received the type: the 337th FIS at Westover AFB, Massachusetts in April, the 538th FIS at Larson AFB, Washington in June and the 56th FIS at Wright-Patterson AFB, Ohio in July and 319th FIS at Webb AFB, Texas. The last F-104A was delivered in December 1958. The F-104A Starfighter was USAF's first operational interceptor capable of flying with sustained Mach 2+ speed. The USAF reduced its orders from 722 Starfighters to 155. After only one year of service most of the F-104As were handed over to ADC units of the Air National Guard – 197th FIS, Arizona Air National Guard based at Tucson ANGB/Tucson International Airport, Arizona, 157th FIS, South Carolina Air National Guard based at McEntire ANGS, 151st FIS, Tennessee Air National Guard based at McGhee Tyson ANGB. The last two regular ADC units to operate the F-104A and B were 319th and 482nd Fighter Interceptor Squadrons based at Homestead AFB, Florida, which received their aircraft in 1963 and flew them until 1969. These last F-104As in regular USAF service were re-engined with more powerful

Two F-104A Starfighters of the 83rd FIS and an EC-121 AEW&C aircraft. (USAF)

General Curtis E. LeMay after a flight in F-104B 56-3720 in 1958. (USAF)

F-104B-10-LO s/n 57-1304. (USAF)

and reliable J79-GE-19 engines, used in the F-104S version developed for Italy in 1967. In 1959 three aircraft – the YF-104 55-2596 and two production F-104As 56-0740 and 56-0757 – were leased to the US Navy for AIM-9B Sidewinder missile tests at NAS China Lake, California. Both F-104As crashed (the 56-0740 on 22 September 1960 and the 56-0757 on 7 April 1961). Only the YF-104A survived to become a QF-104A drone.

USAF F-104As saw two overseas deployments: in October of 1958 12 F-104As of the 83rd FIS were sent to Taiwan in Operation Jonah Able to support the defense of the island against communist China during the Quemoy crisis and during the Berlin Crisis in 1961 60 F-104As of ANG's 151st FIS and 157th FIS were airlifted to Europe. The crisis ended in the summer of 1962 and

Lockheed F-104B and F-104A Starfighters of the 331st Fighter-Interceptor Squadron based at Webb AFB, Texas, during a TDY (temporary deployment) at Homestead AFB, Florida, in February 1964. (USAF)

the personnel returned to the United States.

The subsequent F-104C variant entered service with Tactical Air Command as a multi-role fighter and fighter-bomber. The 479th Tactical Fighter Wing, comprising 434th, 435th, 436th and 476th Tactical Fighter Squadrons, based at George AFB, California, was the only unit to equip with the type in September 1958. Although not an optimum platform for the theatre, the F-104 did see limited service in the Vietnam War, both in the air-superiority role and in the air support mission. Although they saw little aerial combat and scored no air-to-air kills, Starfighters were successful in deterring MiG interceptors and were also appreciated as close support aircraft due to their quick reaction time. F-104C-equipped squadrons made two deployments to South-East Asia. The first was to Da Nang in South Vietnam from April to December 1965, flying 2,937 combat sorties. The 476th Tactical Fighter Squadron deployed in April 1965 through July 1965; and the 436th Tactical Fighter Squadron deployed to Vietnam in July 1965 through October 1965. During that

Major Alan Boughton in the cockpit of an F-104C of the 476th Tactical Fighter Squadron, 479th TFW. (USAF)

Capt. Samuel H. Fields in front of F-104A Starfighter 56-0821 of 331st FIS, Webb AFB, 1963. (USAF)

first deployment, five Starfighters were lost – one crashed as a result of battle damage, one was shot down by ground fire, one was shot down by a Chinese MiG-19 (Shenyang J-6) over Hainan Island, and two were lost in a mid-air collision returning from the search for a downed pilot.

Starfighters returned to the theatre when the 435th Tactical Fighter Squadron was deployed to Udorn Air Force Base, Thailand from June 1966 until July 1967, in which time they flew a further 5,306 combat sorties. A further nine airplanes were lost: two to ground fire, three to surface-to-air missiles, and four in accidents. Again, in 1967, these TAC aircraft were transferred to the 198th TFS, Puerto Rico Air National Guard based at Muniz ANGB/San Juan International Airport, Puerto Rico where they served until 1975.

F-104A 56-0863 of the 157th Fighter Squadron S.C. ANG on the ramp at the South Carolina Air National Guard Base, Congaree Air Field, early 1960s. (USAF)

Lockheed F-104A-25-LO Starfighter (s/n 56-0860) assigned to the 151st Fighter-Interceptor Squadron, 134th Fighter Interceptor Group, Tennessee Air National Guard, at McGhee Tyson Air Force Base, Knoxville, Tennessee, early 1960s. (USAF)

F-104C Starfighters of 479th TFW photographed at NAS Key West, Florida during a visit by President John F. Kennedy on 26 November 1962. (Florida Keys Public Libraries)

Canada

On 2 July 1959 it was announced in the House of Commons that Canada had selected the Lockheed F-104 Starfighter as the replacement for the Sabre Mk.6 in service with the RCAF's European Air Division as a nuclear strike aircraft. Due to specific requirements of the RCAF license production of the version specialized for that role began in Canada under the designation CF-104. In late 1961 an operational conversion unit, No. 6 OTU (eventually redesignated No 417 Squadron) was established at Cold Lake, Alberta. The other RCAF CF-104s were all committed to the support of NATO's nuclear deterrent mission in Europe. In December of 1962, the RCAF began to equip eight Europe-based squadrons of its No. 1 Air Division with CF-104s. The CF-100-equipped squadrons were disbanded and the pilots of the Sabre squadrons began conversion to the CF-104. The first were No. 427 and 434 Squadrons of 3 Wing based at Zweibrücken, in Rhineland-Palatinate followed by 422 and 444 Squadrons of 4 Wing based at Baden-Söllingen in Baden-Württemberg, Germany as well as 430 and 421 Squadrons of 2 Wing based at Grostenquin, France. The last to convert were two squadrons based at Marville, Nos. 439 and 441, tasked with tactical reconnaissance duties.

CF-104 Starfighter 751 in flight at low altitude over CFB Baden – Söllingen, Germany. (CAF)

On 12 October 1962 operation Rho Delta began – transport of the CF-104s for service in Europe. A total of 139 aircraft were disassembled and airlifted across the Atlantic by Lockheed C-130 Hercules. The first unit to become operational on the CF-104 was No. 427 Squadron on 17 December 1962, followed by No. 434 Squadron in April 1963. Nos.444 and 422 Squadrons received the Starfighters in May and July 1963. In 2 Wing No. 430 Squadron received the CF-104s in September 1963 while No. 421 Squadron had to wait until December. Since France did

CF-104 Starfighters at a 441 "Silver Fox" Squadron parade at CFB Baden – Söllingen. (CAF)

Three CF-104s over Germany: 104805 "Toothbrush" of 421 "Red Indian" squadron, 104838 of 439 "Tiger" squadron and 104880 "Tijuana Taxi" of 441 "Silver Fox" squadron. (CAF)

not want NATO nuclear weapons on its territory, in February 1964 No. 2 Wing at Grostenquin was disbanded, and its two CF-104 squadrons were transferred elsewhere, No 421 moving to 4 Wing at Baden-Söllingen and No. 430 moving to Zweibrücken. By the end of 1964 Grostenquin air base returned under French command. The last to re-equip was 1 Wing at Marville. No. 441 Squadron completed re-equipping in January and No. 439 Squadron in March 1964. Aircraft of these units were equipped with Vinten VICON ventral reconnaissance pods. With the acquisition of the CF-104 the "Fighter" prefix vanished from Wing designations as the squadrons were classified as Strike/Attack and Strike/Reconnaissance Squadrons.

When the re-equipment and necessary construction work to adapt the bases to house nuclear weapons were completed the Strike/Attack squadrons of 3 Wing at Zweibrücken and 4 Wing at Baden-Söllingen achieved combat readiness. In each base two to four fully fueled CF-104s armed with Mk 28 nuclear bombs were held in Quick Reaction Alert, ready to take off within minutes and attack indicated targets. Maximum security measures were undertaken. The nuclear-armed aircraft could never leave the QRA area, access to which was strictly limited. Bombing runs were practiced with dummy bombs with the same ballistic characteristics as the "real" ones at ranges at Capo Frasca in Sardinia and Suippes in France. The pilots were aided by LABS (Low Altitude Bombing System) which maintained the flight profile. The bomb could be released either "over the shoulder" from a half-loop onto a target which was behind the aircraft or on a parachute (Low Angle Drogue Delivery). In 1965 the Mk 28 bombs were gradually replaced by more modern Mk 57 and Mk 43 types. A limited number of twin-seat CF-104Ds was also modified to carry nuclear bombs in order to enable training pilots of 3 and 4 Wing in radar navigation and low-level ground attacks to prepare them to strike targets in Eastern Europe in poor weather.

In March 1966 President Charles de Gaulle announced the withdrawal of France from the military structures of NATO. All foreign military forces had to leave France within a year. The RCAF's base at Marville was closed by March 1967, and its two CF-104 reconnaissance squadrons (439 and 441) moved to the ex-French air base at Lahr, Baden-Württemberg in Germany. Nos 434 and 444 Squadrons were disbanded in 1967–68, reducing CF-104 strength to four nuclear strike squadrons and two tactical reconnaissance squadrons.

By 28 February 1968 all branches of the Canadian military were integrated into Canadian Armed Forces. In May of 1969, 3 Wing at Zweibrücken was disbanded. No 427 Squadron was relocated to Baden-Söllingen and No 430 to Lahr and the base was handed over to USAFE (US Air Force Europe).

In 1970, the Canadian government decided to reduce the strength of the Air

Division to only three squadrons and to relinquish its nuclear strike role in favor of conventional attack by 1972. By January of 1972, the CF-104s had been converted from their nuclear role to that of conventional ground attack, thus becoming similar to the F-104G standard. The Vulcan cannon was installed, and the fairing was removed from the cannon port. Twin bomb ejector rack carriers and multi-tube rocket launchers were installed.

In 1972, 1 Air Div was redesignated 1 Canadian Air Group with headquarters at Baden-Söllingen. Lahr was closed, and Nos. 422, 427, and 430 Squadrons were disbanded. Nos. 439 and 441 replaced all but 421 Squadron in Nos 3 and 4 Wings at Baden. Of the remaining three squadrons, 421 was committed to converting to ground attack roles, together with No. 431 Squadron, leaving only No. 441 Squadron to continue tactical reconnaissance missions with the Vinten VICON camera pod.

A number of former Canadian Forces single-seat CF-104 fighter-bombers and CF-104D two-seat trainers were transferred to Denmark and Norway after having been brought up to F-104G/TF-104G standards. By the end of 1980, these transfers along with attrition had brought Europe-based RCAF strength down to only three Starfighter squadrons. These were Nos. 421, 439, and 441, all based at Baden-Söllingen. At that time, No. 417 Squadron at Cold Lake was still functioning as a CF-104 Operational Conversion Unit.

Beginning in 1983, the CF-104 Starfighters were replaced in Canadian Armed Forces service by McDonnell Douglas CF-18 Hornets. The last CF-104 was phased out by No. 441 Squadron on 1 March 1986. Canada then offered Turkey an initial batch of 20 CF-104s, later increased to 52, including six CF-104Ds. Thirty of them were sent to MBB at Manching in Germany in March of 1986 for overhaul before being transferred to Turkey. The remaining ones were broken down for spares.

About 110 out of 239 delivered CF-104/CF-104Ds were lost in accidents – a loss rate of 46%. A Canadian CF-104 was involved in the most tragic Starfighter accident on 22 May 1983 when an aircraft of 439 Sqn, piloted by 27-year old Captain Alan Stephenson, became uncontrollable when performing a formation flight display during an air show at Rhein-Main air base near Frankfurt.

The pilot ejected and the aircraft crashed beside a nearby motorway, hitting a car carrying six passengers. Five of them – pastor Martin Jürges, his mother Erna, his wife Irmtraud and their children Jan und Katharina – were killed instantly. The sixth victim, 19-year old Gesine Wagner, the niece of pastor Jürges suffered severe burns and died in hospital later in August that year.

CF-104 104838 of 439 Squadron "Tiger" based at CFB Baden – Söllingen, passing Hohenzollern castle in 1977. (CAF)

Federal Republic of Germany

West Germany was the primary user of the Starfighter, operating over 35% of all F-104s built. In total this country received a total of 916 F-104s, comprising 613 F-104Gs, 136 RF-104Gs, 137 TF-104Gs and 30 F-104Fs, forming the mainstay of the combat equipment of both the *Luftwaffe* (Air Force) and *Marineflieger* (Naval Aviation). At its peak in the early 1970s, the F-104 equipped five fighter-bomber wings, two interceptor wings and two tactical reconnaissance wings. The *Marineflieger* operated a further two wings of F-104s in the maritime strike and reconnaissance roles. The German Starfighter units were as follows:

Luftwaffe:

Jagdbombergeschwader (Fighter-Bomber Wing) 31 "Boelcke" based at Nörvenich, North Rhine-Westphalia

Jagdbombergeschwader 32 based at Lechfeld, Bavaria

Jagdbombergeschwader 33 based at Büchel, Rhineland-Palatinate

Jagdbombergeschwader 34 based at Memmingen, Bavaria

Jagdbombergeschwader 36 based at Rheine-Hopsten, North Rhine-Westphalia

Jagdgeschwader (Fighter Wing) 71 "Richthofen" based at Wittmundhafen, Lower Saxony

Jagdgeschwader 74 "Mölders" based at Neuburg, Bavaria

Aufklärungsgeschwader (Reconnaissance Wing) 51 "Immelmann" based at Manching – Ingolstadt, Bavaria until 1969 and then Bremgarten, Baden-Württemberg.

Aufklärungsgeschwader 52 based at Leck, Schleswig-Holstein

Waffenschule 10 (WaSLw 10) operational conversion unit based initially at Nörvenich and later at Jever, Lower Saxony.

Luftwaffenversorgungsregiment 1 (LVR 1) maintenance and technical support unit, based at Erding, Bavaria from 1962 till 1988.

Wehrtechnische Dienststelle 61 (WTD 61) Bundeswehr Technical and Airworthiness Center for Aircraft at Manching – Ingolstadt

Lockheed F-104F Starfighter BB+365 of the Luftwaffe *in 1960. This aircraft was lost on 19 June 1962 when four planes crashed into a brown coal quarry near Knapsack, Germany, during formation aerobatics training after disorientation of the leader. All the pilots, three Germans and one American, were killed. (USAF)*

F-104F 29+06 of WaSLw 10 preserved at Luftwaffenmuseum der Bundeswehr Berlin – Gatow. The aircraft tactical number system in Germany was changed from two letters and three digits to four digits in November 1967. (Jarosław Dobrzyński)

Marineflieger

Marinefliegergeschwader 1 based at Schleswig-Jagel

Marinefliegergeschwader 2 based at Eggebeck, Schleswig-Holstein

The German F-104Gs came from all five production lines of the Starfighter consortium. West Germany received 30 F-104Fs, 96 F-104Gs, and 136 TF-104Gs from Lockheed, 255 F/RF-104Gs from ARGE-Nord, 210 F-104Gs from ARGE-Sud, 88 F-104Gs from ARGE-West, 50 F/RF-104Gs from the Italian Group, plus 50 F-104Gs from MBB to replace some of those lost in crashes.

The first Starfighters which Germany received were the Lockheed-built two-seat F-104Fs which were initially used in the USA to train German instructors. At that time, the F-104Fs were painted with standard USAF insignia and carried USAF serial numbers. These machines were subsequently shipped to Germany and assigned to *Waffenschule* 10, which was then based at Nörvenich in Germany (later it moved to Jever). After handover, they were repainted in *Luftwaffe* colours and received German serial numbers. They conversion of pilots for *JaboG* 31 began in July of 1960.

The first operational unit equipped with the F-104G was *Jagdbombergeschwader* 31 "Boelcke" (JaboG 31), also

Formation of four F-104Gs of JG 74 in flight over the Bavarian Alps in June 1965. (Bundesarchiv)

Two F-104Gs 26+89 and 26+83 of MFG 2 at RAF Greenham Common during IAT'83, 23 July 1983. (Hans Rolink)

F-104G 22+77 of the Marineflieger *in flight over the North Sea. (WTD 61)*

based at Nörvenich. *JaboG* 31 became operational in June 1962. Other fighter-bomber, fighter and reconnaissance wings followed. The next to convert were *JaboG* 33 (August 1962), *JG* 71 (April 1963), *MFG* 1 (September 1963), *AG* 51 (November 1963), *JG* 74 (May 1964), *JaboG* 34 (July 1964), *AG* 52 (November 1964), *JaboG* 32 (January 1965), *JaboG* 36 (February 1965), *MFG* 2 (March 1965). In fighter-bomber wings the Starfighter replaced the F-84F Thunderstreak, in fighter interceptor wings the F-86 Sabre and in reconnaissance wings the RF-84F Thunderflash.

With the high rate of new aircraft deliveries, a massive pilot training programme was required in order to get them into service quickly. The weather and operational restrictions in Northern Europe limited severely the amount of training that could be done in Germany. The immediate answer was to set up a *Luftwaffe* training facility at Luke AFB in Arizona where vast spaces and fair weather for most of the time made it easier. The host unit was 4510th Combat Crew Training Wing (CCTW) at Luke, comprising 4540th Combat Crew Training Group (CCTG) with 4512th, 4518th, and 4443rd Combat Crew Training Squadrons, tasked with providing the advanced flying training. These units received many of the *Luftwaffe* Starfighters which were stationed in the United States and used for pilot training. Although remaining *Luftwaffe* property, these aircraft carried USAF insignia and were assigned USAF serial numbers. On 1 September 1966 the 4540th CCTG and 4443rd CCTS were deactivated at Luke and the F-104 training program was conducted by the two remaining squadrons, the 4512th CCTS and the 4518th CCTS. On 1 October, 1969 the 58th Tactical Fighter Training Wing (TFTW) was activated, replacing the 4510th CCTW as the host unit at Luke. Concurrently, the 69th Tactical Fighter Training Squadron (TFTS) and the 418th Tactical Fighter Training Squadron (TFTS) were activated as F-104 training units, replacing the 4512th CCTS and 4518th CCTS. Final F-104G training for the European environment was done at *Waffenschule* 10 (*WaSLw* 10) at Jever.

Phasing out of the Starfighters began in the early 1970s. The first to be retired was the RF-104G tactical reconnaissance version. In April and September of 1971 *AG* 51 and *AG* 52 respectively converted to the McDonnell RF-4E Phantom II. In 1974 the interceptor wings followed. In July and September *JG* 71 and *JG* 74 respectively converted to the F-4F Phantom II. The first fighter-bomber wing to retire the F-104 was *JaboG* 36, which in January of 1975 also converted to the F-4F. In early 1980s a new strike aircraft, the Panavia Tornado IDS, designed and built jointly by Great Britain, West Germany and Italy, entered service. The first unit to convert to the new type was *MFG* 1 in October of 1981, followed by *JaboG* 31 in May 1983, *JaboG* 32 in April 1984, *JaboG* 33 in May 1985, and *MFG* 2 in September 1986. The last operational Starfighter unit was *JaboG* 34, which retained them until October 1987.

In the 1970s and 1980s *MFG* 2 maintained a two-aircraft display team, the Vikings, which occasionally performed at air shows in Germany and abroad. The last display of the Vikings took place on 27 September 1986 at Neuburg.

Most of retired German Starfighters were transferred to Turkey, Greece and Taiwan. The last *Luftwaffe* unit to operate the Starfighters was *WTD* 61 at Manching which used a few F-104Gs and TF-104Gs for various avionics trials and systems development programs. The last flight of a German Starfighter (98+04) took place from Manching on 22 May 1991.

From 1961 to 1989 a total of 298 German Starfighters were lost in accidents, losses on the ground and damaged beyond repair (including MAP F-104G serial number 62-12312) claiming the life of 116 pilots (including eight USAF pilots). However, 171 pilots ejected safely, eight pilots ejected twice.

F-104G 26+53 of WTD 61 in "lizard" camouflage scheme photographed at Münster-Osnabrück airport during Montgolfiade Air Show on 23 May 1988. (Hans Rolink)

69

Above: Four fighters participating in the REFORGER '82 exercise fly over the cloud-shrouded Neuschwanstein Castle in Bavaria. The flight of three F-15 Eagles from Eglin Air Force Base, Florida is led by a Luftwaffe F-104 Starfighter. (USAF)

F-104G 26+49 *of the* Luftwaffe *in "lizard" camouflage scheme, preserved at* Luftwaffenmuseum der Bundeswehr Berlin – Gatow. *(Jarosław Dobrzyński)*

RF-104G 24+01 *of AG 51 in flight over Germany with a USAF McDonnell RF-101C Voodoo. (USAF via DoD)*

70

West German-owned TF-104G 61-3631 of the 58th TFTW at Luke AFB, Arizona in 1982. (USAF)

West German-owned F-104Gs of the 58th TFTW at Luke AFB, Arizona in 1982. (USAF)

TF-104G 61-3622 of the 58th TFTW taxis out for a training sortie at Luke AFB, Arizona in 1982. (USAF)

Oberleutnant zur See *Reinhard Dresbach* of the *Marineflieger* sits in the F-104 Starfighter aircraft simulator during the training of German pilots conducted by the 69th Tactical Fighter Training Squadron at Luke AFB, Arizona in 1982. (DoD)

Two F-104G Starfighters of the 69th TFTS, 58th TFTW parked on the flight line at Luke AFB, Arizona, November 1982. (USAF)

A right side view of an F-15 Eagle, F-4C Phantom II, F-104 Starfighter, and F-5 Tiger II aircraft, top to bottom, on a Tactical Training Luke training mission. The aircraft are, respectively, from the 550th, 310th, 69th, and 425th Tactical Fighter Training Squadron, all under the 12th Air Force, photographed on 8 January, 1979. (USAF)

72

The Netherlands

The Netherlands was another major European Starfighter user and manufacturer. The type replaced the F-84/RF-84, as well as Lockheed RT-33s, in *Koninklijke Luchtmacht* (Royal Netherlands Air Force). The Dutch acquired 95 F-104Gs, 25 RF-104Gs, and 18 TF-104Gs from Fokker (ARGE-Nord), Fiat (Arge Italy), and Lockheed production. This gave a total of 120 single-seaters and 18 two-seaters. Dutch RF-104Gs initially had a trimetrogon camera system, quickly replaced by the NVOI Orpheus centerline reconnaissance pod. Twenty-five aircraft were delivered under the Military Assistance Program (MAP).

The following units of the *KLu* operated the Starfighter:

306 Squadron: 1962 until 1983.
311 Squadron: 1964 until 1982
312 Squadron: 1965 until 1984
322 Squadron: 1963 until 1979
323 Squadron: 1964 until 1980
Training and Conversion Unit: 1964 until 1978
Conversie Afdeling Volkel: 1969 until 1984.

The Royal Netherlands Air Force received its first two F-104s 12 December 1962 when D-8013 and D-8022 were delivered to 306 Squadron at Twenthe Air Base.

No. 306 Squadron served as the operational conversion unit for the training of Starfighter crews from all other *KLu* F-104G squadrons that were being formed at that time. In January 1964, this unit converted from F/TF-104Gs to RF-104G reconnaissance aircraft. The task of Starfighter crew training was assumed by the "Dutch Masters" operational conversion unit based at Leeuwarden. The F-104Gs were operated in the interceptor role by 322 and 323 Squadrons based at Leeuwarden and in the fighter-bomber role by 311 and 312 Squadrons based at Volkel. The reconnaissance unit, 306 Squadron was also based at Volkel.

In the early 1980s, the Royal Dutch Air Force began replacing the Starfighters with European-built F-16A/B Fighting Falcons. The first to convert were the two interceptor squadrons.

On 15 March 1978, after the last Starfighter conversion at Leeuwarden, the TCA was the first squadron which retired the F-104. On 16 May 1979 645 Squadron (combined 322 and 323) was formed. This squadron received some Starfighters and operated them until 322 and 323 became operational on the F-16.

The remaining F-104s were transferred to Volkel. Turkey was interested in purchase of 25 surplus F-104s from the *KLu*. They were delivered on 25 August 1980 (12), 15 December 1980 (11) and the final two in 1982. Meanwhile the US decided that the remaining 16 MAP-delivered F-104Gs had to be transferred to Greece (10) and Turkey (6). The Greek Starfighters were delivered on 7 May 1982 (4) and 23 June 1982.

In June 1984, No. 312 Squadron was the last *KLu* operational F-104G unit. When No. 312 Squadron disbanded, its 18 F-104Gs and two four TF-104Gs were transferred to the CAV at Volkel until their last formal flypast on 21 November 1984. That day the D-5803, D-5810, D-5804, D-8258 and D-8256 made a final flight pass along all *KLu* airbases.

During 22 years the Klu flew 345,500 hours with the F-104, losing 43 aircraft (35.8% of the fleet) in accidents.

RF-104G D-8119 of the 306 Squadron RNLAF with Orpheus reconnaissance pod. (Hans Rolink)

F-104G D-8048 of CAV with practice weapons dispenser taxis at Volkel on 20 October 1982. (Hans Rolink)

Two F-104Gs of the 323 Squadron RNLAF fly in formation with two USAF F-4E Phantoms of 32nd TFS "Wolfhounds" based at Soesterberg AB. (USAF)

Belgium

Following Germany and the Netherlands Belgium selected the F-104G Starfighter as the mainstay of its air force and joined the F-104 manufacturing consortium. A total of 112 Starfighters were ordered by the Belgian Air Force: 100 F-104G (serial numbers FX-01 to FX-100) and 12 TF-104G trainers (serial FC-01 to FC-12). Of these, 25 F-104Gs were MAP-funded, and the remainder was paid for by the Belgian government. With the exception of the very first ones, shipped as assembly kits to Belgium, all Belgian F-104Gs were built and assembled by the SABCA Gosselies plant (ARGE – West), which also built a further 88 units for the *Luftwaffe*. The initial three TF-104Gs were built by Lockheed Palmdale as TF-104Fs (without sophisticated electronic systems as in the TF-104G) and the remaining nine two-seaters were assembled by SABCA from Lockheed-built kits. Later the initial three TF-104Fs were upgraded to the TF-104G standard. One aircraft crashed before being taken on charge by the Belgian Air Force, and was later replaced by another similarly numbered example (FX-47).

The following units of the *Force Aérienne Belge* (FAéB) – *Belgische Luchtmacht* (Belgian Air Force) operated F-104G and TF-104G Starfighters:

1 *Wing de Chasse Tous-Temps* (1 W Ch TT) – 1° *Jacht Wing Alle Weer* (1 JW AW) – 1st All-Weather Fighter Wing based at Beauvechain – Bevekom:
349 *Smd* "Goedendag" Air Defense October 1963 till February 1980
350 *Smd* "Ambiorix" Air Defense April 1963 till April 1981
Flight TF-104G Conversion and Air Defense training June 1965 till March 1980
10 *Jacht Bommenwerpers* Wing (10 JBW) – 10th Fighter-Bomber Wing based at Kleine Brogel:
23 *Smd* "Duivel" (Devil) Fighter-Bomber/(Nuclear) Strike January 1965 till October 1982
31 *Smd* "Tijger" (Tiger) Fighter-Bomber/(Nuclear) Strike June 1964 till October 1983
OCF Conversion & Fighter-Bomber training January 1968 till July 1983

The Starfighters replaced Avro Canada CF-100 Canucks Mk.5 of N°1 All-Weather Fighter Wing at Beauvechain air base, and the Republic F-84F Thunderstreaks of N°10 Fighter-Bomber Wing at Kleine Brogel air base.

The F-104Gs with numbers FX-01 to FX-40 were assigned to No. 1 Wing and the F-104Gs with numbers FX-41 to FX-80 were assigned to No. 10 Wing. Airplanes with numbers FX-81 to FX-100 were held in storage as attrition replacements.

No.1 Wing started receiving its Starfighters in April 1963. 350 Squadron was re-equipped as the first, 349 Squadron followed suit in October of that year. The aircraft remained assigned to squadrons until 25 April 1966, when Wing pooling was instated. For No. 10 Wing the Starfighter era began in June 1964. No. 31 Squadron re-equipped first. Initial operations were carried out from Beauvechain air base, where assistance for the type conversion could be given by No. 1 Wing. Most aircraft left for Kleine Brogel air base in July. The 31 Squadron received all Starfighters earmarked for No. 10 Wing; 23 Squadron kept operating F-84F Thunderstreaks, sending its pilots to 31 for conversion. Effective on 1 January 1965, the aircraft were pooled in the Wing, the remaining F-84Fs going to the No.10 Wing F-84F Base Flight before being retired.

Deliveries largely went as planned but due to the non-delivery of FX-01, kept

Belgian F-104G FX20 of No.1 Wing based at Beauvechain. This aircraft flew with the "Slivers" aerobatic team. (BAF)

as an instructional airframe, and to early crashes, two aircraft from the attrition batch were delivered to each wing as early as in 1965 – FX-82 and FX-83 to No. 1 Wing and FX-91 and FX-92 to No. 10 Wing. All the others were kept in storage, and gradually issued to units as older airframes went back to SABCA Gosselies for overhaul. During their operational life the F-104Gs were swapped between the two Wings in order to balance airframe fatigue between medium to high altitude fighter missions and low altitude fighter-bomber missions.

No.1 Wing's main mission was air defense. Therefore between 1957 and 1996, Beauvechain air base hosted a NATO 24 hours alert section. The F-104 became operational in this role in August 1964. The 24 hours alert section, with two aircraft (one ready at 15 minutes, one ready at 30 minutes), became the Quick Reaction Alert (QRA) section. In 1967 this section was enlarged to four, two pairs of aircraft. In the interceptor role the F-104Gs were replaced by F-16A Fighting Falcons in September 1980.

From late 1968 to 1975 No. 1 Wing maintained an F-104 aerobatic team, called "The Slivers". The team's pilots were Captain Steve Nuyts and *Adjudant-Chef* (warrant officer) Palmer de Vlieger. The Slivers specialized in very spectacular synchronous flying displays at very low level. Their first public display took place on 14 May 1969 and the last during Florennes Air Show on 21 June 1975. During that period they performed 68 flight displays in Belgium, the Netherlands, Germany, Italy and France. Their last "private" display in front of friends and colleagues took place on 11 July 1975 at Beauvechain air base.

Initially No. 10 Wing operated the F-104Gs only in the fighter-bomber strike role. The F-104G replaced the F-84F in this role in 1965 at Kleine Brogel and by December 1966 all F-104Gs of Kleine Brogel became operational. From the early sixties Kleine Brogel air base hosted a 24-hours nuclear Quick Reaction Alert within NATO Nuclear Quick Reaction Alert Force. The nuclear ordnance were US nuclear B61 tactical free-fall bombs, controlled and maintained in special storage facilities by the 52nd Special Ammunition Group based at Meeuwen. The US forces retained custody of all US nuclear weapons and would have released US nuclear weapons to the Belgian Air Force only in accordance with NATO defense plans, SACEUR directives, and US national control procedures. The QRA area was a maximum security hardened shelter complex near the Kleine Brogel eastern runway end. In 1972 smaller, more sophisticated and flexible nuclear bombs were introduced. These bombs were stored in special vaults in the aircraft shelters. In 1968 No. 10 Wing switched to the dual role FBS/FBA (Fighter Bomber Attack) missions which involved the use of conventional weapons. In this role the F-104G was armed with the M61 Vulcan cannon, three napalm canisters or two Snakeye bombs or two LAU rocket launcher pods, each with nineteen 2.75" FFAR rockets. The Starfighter phase-out started in late 1979. Older aircraft were sent to Saffraanberg Technical Training School. No. 349 Squadron was first to replace its Starfighters with the General Dynamic F-16A Fighting Falcon, allowing No. 1 Wing F-104G/TF-104G operations to be centralized within 350 Squadron from 1 April 1980. At the same time Flight TF-104G was disbanded and replaced by the F-16 Conversion Flight. This lasted until 14 April 1981, when all remaining 350 Squadron Starfighters were flown to Koksijde air base storage park. At Kleine Brogel air base things were fairly similar. N° 23 Squadron replaced the F-104Gs with F-16s in 1982, leaving the 31st alone to operate Starfighters from 1 July 1982 until October 1983. Withdrawn aircraft were sent from Kleine Brogel to Koksijde air base for storage. Sixteen aircraft were delivered to the Turkish Air Force. The last two Belgian Starfighters (FX-99 and FC-11) flew into retirement from Kleine-Brogel on 26 September 1983. In 1990 15 aircraft were taken out of storage and sent to Taiwan via the USA. Several other aircraft were donated to various museums.

A total of 41 Belgian Starfighters, including three TF-104Gs, (nearly 37%) were lost in accidents.

Belgian TF-104G FC05 in flight. (BAF)

Italy

Italy was the longest operator and manufacturer of the Starfighter, with a purpose-developed version – the F-104S – which after two upgrades remained in service as late as 2005.

The first F-104G for Italy, built by Lockheed, first flew at Palmdale on 3 April 1962 with Italian test pilot, Capt. Franco Bonazzi at the controls. It was then dismantled and airlifted to the Fiat factory at Turin, where it made its first flight in Italian airspace on 9 June 1962. It received AMI serial number MM (*Matricola Militare*) 6501. Beginning in March 1963, the *Aeronautica Militare Italiana* (AMI) received 125 Fiat-built F-104Gs (including 11 RF-104Gs) plus 12 Lockheed-built TF-104Gs and 16 Fiat-built TF-104Gs. The F-104Gs and TF-104Gs first entered service at Grosseto with 4° *Stormo* in 1963. These aircraft ultimately equipped four interceptor/fighter-bomber squadrons (*gruppi*), two reconnaissance squadrons, and one training squadron. One of these machines was a pattern aircraft supplied by Lockheed. The first Fiat-built F-104G performed its initial flight on 9 June 1962, with the first operational Starfighter squadrons coming online in 1965. The Starfighter replaced the F-86 and F-84/RF-84 in AMI service. Of the 125 F-104Gs for the AMI, 51 were configured as interceptors F-104G/CI (*Caccia Intercettori*) without cannon and only two AIM-9B Sidewinder missiles and 54 were configured for the strike role (F-104G/CB – *Caccia Bombardiere*) with cannon and external stores, and 20 were configured as RF-104Gs, with the built-in trimetrogon camera arrangement. A number of RF-104Gs were later modified to carry the Dutch Orpheus pod.

In late 1965, the 154° *Gruppo* based at Ghedi received a NATO Flight Safety Award after it had flown more than 5,000 hours on the F-104G without a single accident. However, like the air forces of other European operators of the Starfighter, the accident rate of AMI single-seat F/RF-104Gs and two-seat TF-104Gs was fairly high – around 37.5% of the fleet was lost.

The following AMI units operated the F/RF-104G:

9° *Gruppo*/4° *Stormo*, Grosetto (from March 1963)
10° *Gruppo*/9° *Stormo*, Grazzanise (from January 1967)
12° *Gruppo*/36° *Stormo*, Gioia del Colle (from 1965)

F-104G 3-34 of 3° Stormo of the Italian Air Force in flight over Alps. (AMI)

20° *Gruppo*/4° *Stormo*, Grosseto (from late 1963 to June 1994)
21° *Gruppo*/53° *Stormo*, Cameria/Novara (from April 1967)
22° *Gruppo*/51° *Stormo*, Treviso/Istrana (from June 1969)
23° *Gruppo*/5° *Stormo*, Rimini/Miramare (formed as 101° *Gruppo*/ 5° *Aerobrigata*) from September 1967.
28° *Gruppo*/3° *Stormo*, Villafranca, RF-104G from 1964 to June 1993)
102°*Gruppo*/5° *Stormo*, Rimini (from May 1964)
132° *Gruppo*/3° *Stormo*, Villafranca (1965 to October 1990)
154° *Gruppo*/6° *Stormo*, Ghedi (1964 to early 1993)
155° *Gruppo*/51° *Stormo* F-104G until 1974 (formerly in 50° *Stormo* at Piacenza, then Istrana).
156° *Gruppo*/36° *Stormo*, Gioia del Colle, 1966 to 1970.

The AMI continued to use the F/RF-104G in large numbers long after other European air forces had replaced their Starfighters with more modern types. Beginning in 1968, the F-104G was supplemented by the much improved F-104S variant, developed specially for Italy. 206 airplanes in two variants – the F-104S/CI interceptor and F-104S/CB fighter-bomber – were built for the AMI.

The CI variant was operated by six fighter groups:
9° *Gruppo* (from 1970)
10° *Gruppo* (from 1974)
12° *Gruppo* (from 1970)
21° *Gruppo* (from 1972)
22° *Gruppo* (from 1969)
23° *Gruppo* (from 1973)

The F-104S/CB variant was operated only by three groups:
102°*Gruppo*, specialized in the nuclear strike role (from 1973)
155°*Gruppo* specialized in the conventional strike role (from 1971)
156°*Gruppo* specialized in the anti-shipping role (from 1970)

The AMI's last F-104G fighter-bomber unit (154° *Gruppo*/6° *Stormo*) replaced its Starfighters with Panavia Tornados from early 1983, leaving 28° *Gruppo*/3° *Stormo* as the last operator of earlier-generation Starfighters, with Orpheus reconnaissance pod-equipped RF-104Gs. These were finally retired in June 1993. During the Gulf War in 1991 they flew reconnaissance missions over Iraq from Turkish bases.

During the crisis with Libya in the early 1980s a pooled fleet of F-104S/CI was sent to Trapani-Birgi in Sicily for QRA duty to provide protection for the south-western flank of Italy. Each fighter squadron had to send four to six fighters for three/four weeks on a rotational basis.

In the 1980s an upgrade program, called "Weapons System Upgrade" – *Aggiornamento Sistema d'Arma* (ASA) – was implemented for 147 AMI F-104S Starfighters. The first upgraded aircraft flew in 1984 and service deliveries lasted from 1986 to 1991. During 1997–2002 55 aircraft underwent another upgrade, called F-104S ASA-M, in order to enhance their combat capabilities and extend their service life. Fifteen TF-104Gs were also upgraded, being given the designation of TF-104G-M.

The F-104S ASA-M interceptors flew combat air patrols during Operation Allied Force, the NATO air campaign against Serbia. During that operation the Starfighters showed their age and inability to fly alongside more modern NATO aircraft. In the early 2000s the final phase-out of the Starfighters began. As an interim solution before the Eurofighter was available AMI leased 34 old F-16A ADF fighters.

The last operational flight of the F-104S ASA-M took place on 31 October 2004. Five aircraft – MM6850 4-16, MM6876 9-39, MM6890 4-50, MM6930 9-99, MM6934 9-31 – made the last operational sortie from Grazzanise AB. After that the last four Italian F-104s (two TF-104M and two F-104ASA-M) were operated by 311°*Gruppo Reparto Sperimentale di Volo* (Italian Air Force Test Center) at Pratica di Mare. The very last F-104 military flight was made by TF-104G-Ms MM54260 RS-08 and MM6876 RS-05 of 311°*Gruppo* in support of the Eurofighter tests by the RSV on 27 July 2005 at Pratica di Mare.

Between 1964 and 2002 AMI lost in accidents 156 Starfighters, with the death of 78 pilots.

F-104S/CB 5-06 of 102° Gruppo 5° Stormo taxis at Volkel during a squadron exchange with 306 Sqn RNLAF in October 1986. (Henk Schuitemaker)

TF-104G 4-40 of 4° Stormo taxis before take-off. (George Papadimitriou)

An A-7D Corsair aircraft, lower left, from the 127th Tactical Fighter Wing flies in formation with an Italian F-104S Starfighter, an Italian Tornado and a Turkish TF-104G Starfighter, during the NATO exercise Dragon Hammer '87. (USAF)

Two Italian F-104S Starfighters taxi past a Turkish Air Force Transall C-160 at Bitburg AB, Germany in 1988. (USAF)

F-104S ASA-M Starfighters during engine startup. The number of fingers shown by the pilots and crew chiefs indicates the percent rate of the turbine RPM. (AMI)

F-104S ASA-M 4-59 of 4º Stormo taxis in front of spectators during an air show with MB-339 aircraft of the Frecce Tricolori aerobatics team in the background. (George Papadimitriou)

Japan

In November 1960, the Japanese government announced that it would acquire the F-104 Starfighter as its standard air superiority fighter. An industrial cartel headed by Mitsubishi Heavy Industries was given the responsibility for the license manufacture of the Starfighter in Japan.

The Japanese Starfighter was given the designation F-104J, the J standing for Japan. It was similar to the F-104G, but specialized as an all-weather interceptor because of post-war treaty restrictions, allowing Japan to possess combat aircraft with defensive capabilities only. It featured the Autonetics NASARR F-15J-31 fire control system optimized for the air-to-air mode only, and was armed with a 20-mm M61A1 cannon and four AIM-9 Sidewinder air-to-air missiles.

From late 1961 to March 1965 the *Koku Jietai* (Japanese Air Self Defence Force, or JASDF) took delivery of three F-104Js (Model 683-07-14) built by Lockheed and a further 29 assembled by Mitsubishi from components delivered by Lockheed. A total of 178 F-104Js built by Mitsubishi were delivered from March 1965 to 1967. JASDF also acquired 20 F-104DJ (Model 583B-10-17) two-seat trainers, built by Lockheed and reassembled in Japan between July 1962 and January 1964.

The first Lockheed-built F-104J (Model 683-07-14) flew on 30 June 1961. Deliveries of Mitsubishi-assembled F-104Js extended from March 1962 to March 1965. The delivery of Mitsubishi-manufactured F-104Js extended from March 1965 to 1967.

The following units of the JASDF operated the F-104J/DJ:
201st *Hikotai*, 2nd *Kokudan*, Chitose Air Base, October 1963 to 1975
202nd *Hikotai*, 5th *Kokudan*, Nyutabaru Air Base, 1964 to 1982
203rd *Hikotai*, 2nd *Kokudan*, Komatsu Air Base, 1964 to 1984
204th *Hikotai*, 5th *Kokudan*, Tsuiki Air Base, 1964 to 1984
205th *Hikotai*, 6th *Kokudan*, Komatsu Air Base, 1965 to 1981
206th *Hikotai*, 7th *Kokudan*, Hyakuri Air Base, 1965 to 1978
207th *Hikotai*, 7th *Kokudan*, Hyakuri Air Base, 1966 to 1972
Naha Air Base, to 1986
Air Proving Wing, Gift Air Base 1962 to 1986
UF-104, Iwo Jima 1992 to 1997

Beginning in December 1981, the Japanese Starfighters were replaced by Mitsubishi-built F-15J/F-15DJ Eagles. The last JASDF F-104J was retired by the 207th *Hikotai* in March 1986. Thirty-one F-104Js and six F-104DJs were sold to Taiwan. After their retirement from the front line operation, some F-104s were used by the Air Development and Testing Wing.

The last 16 Japanese Starfighters were converted to UF-104JA target drones and shot down at the firing range located near Iwo-Jima.

F-104J 36-8524 of the JASDF with USAF F-15 Eagles in the background.

Above: F-104J 76-8705 of the JASDF.

Right: Crewmen from the Japanese Air Self Defense Force carrying out maintenance work on a JASDF F-104 Starfighter aircraft, during Exercise Cope North '81. (DoD)

Bottom: F-104J 36-8541 of the JASDF, armed with AIM-9 Sidewinder missile, taxis after landing. (DoD)

Denmark

Between November 1964 and September 1965, the *Kongelige Danske Flyvevåbnet* (Royal Danish Air Force) received 25 F-104Gs built by Canadair and four Lockheed-built TF-104Gs through the US Mutual Aid Program. These equipped the *Eskadrille* 723 and *Eskadrille* 726, both based at Aalborg. During 1972–74 fifteen ex-Canadian Forces CF-104s and seven CF-104Ds were transferred to Denmark, following the conversion of the single seaters to F-104G standard. The CF-104Ds were specially modified for use by *Esk* 726 in the electronics countermeasures role.

In the 1980s Danish Starfighters began to be replaced by the F-16A and Bs. *Eskadrille* 723 was disbanded on 1 January 1983 and *Eskadrille* 726 on 30 April 1986. The Starfighters were then retired from Danish service, except for four aircraft retained as target tugs. Twelve of the 51 Starfighters operated by the RDAF between 1965 and 1986 were lost in accidents, a rate of 23.5%.

The surviving MAP-funded F-104Gs and three TF-104Gs were transferred to Taiwan in 1987.

TF-104G RT-684 of the Royal Danish Air Force. (RDAF)

CF-104 R-814 of the Royal Danish Air Force. (RDAF)

Norway

In 1963 the *Kongelige Norske Luftforsvaret* (Royal Norwegian Air Force) received 16 Lockheed-built F-104Gs, and two TF-104Gs. The first 13 F-104Gs were delivered to Bodø harbor on 7 August 1963. The two-seaters were airlifted from the USA on 6 September 1963. A further three F-104Gs were delivered by sea on 26 October 1963. The single-seaters were designated RF-104G, but they were armed with the M61A1 Vulcan 20mm cannon, powered by the J79-GE-11A engine and fitted with AN/ARC-552 radio sets, AN/ARN-52 TACAN navigation systems and F-15A-M-11 NASARR radars.

Two Canadair-built F-104Gs were delivered on 23 June 1965 and a third one in February 1966. They all served with No. 331 *Skvadron* at Bodø.

After one TF-104G had been lost in 1970 a need for additional trainers emerged, so two used TF-104Gs from the German training centre in the USA were bought in June 1975.

No. 331 *Skvadron* operated solely as an air-to-ground unit until August 1967, when this role was changed to All-Weather Interceptor. This was also the start of period of numerous interceptions of Soviet reconnaissance planes patrolling along the Norwegian coastline.

In 1973, 334 *Skvadron*, which had been flying the Northrop F-5s since the summer of 1967, converted to the F-104. The squadron was equipped with eighteen ex-Canadian Forces CF-104s and four CF-104Ds. The first plane, the two-seater 637, landed at Bodø in the spring of 1973. Since in Canadian service the planes were configured in the nuclear strike role, with the cannon replaced by an extra fuel tank, it was decided to modify the aircraft to a weaponry standard equal to the G models, which meant reinstalling the M61A1 cannon. Later, ALR-46 radar warning receivers were fitted. The modification was made by Scottish Aviation Ltd, beginning in December 1974. The radar was upgraded in Norway to improve its performance in the air-to-air combat and the aircraft were also modified to carry Martin Bullpup air-to-surface missiles and were employed in the anti-shipping role.

Norway was one of the original European customers for the new American combat aircraft, the F-16, which was to replace both the F-104 and the F-5. In January 1981 the first Norwegian pilots were sent to Rygge for conversion to the new fighter. No. 331 *Skvadron* received its first F-16s in June the same year.

The Starfighters originally delivered via the MAP program were formally US property and after being retired from Norwegian service within the new military aid program, they were delivered back to the Turkish Air Force.

From 1981 334 *Skvadron* was the only RNoAF unit equipped with Starfighters. Later this squadron was also to convert to the F-16. In January 1982, conversion to the F-16 gathered momentum, and the Starfighters only received maintenance-flights to uphold their readiness. On 13 June 1982, the first plane was retired. The final flight of a Norwegian Starfighter took place on 22 April 1983. During 20 years of operations in the RnoAF the Starfighters accumulated over 100,000 flight hours. Twelve were lost in crashes, claiming the life of seven pilots.

After retirement the Norwegian Starfighters were ferried to Sola for storage. From there most of them found their way to various museums or to private owners.

CF-104 4889 of the Royal Norwegian Air Force. (Nils Mosberg)

Turkey

After Germany, Turkey was the second largest Starfighter operator, with 421 aircraft in service from 1963 to 1996. As an important US ally, guarding the south-eastern flank of NATO, Turkey was one of the first countries to receive Starfighters through MAP funding. In May 1963, the *Türk Hava Kuvvetleri* (THK) received 32 F-104Gs built by Lockheed and Canadair, plus four TF-104Gs built by Lockheed. These aircraft equipped 141 and 142 *Filo* (squadron), plus an OCU, in AJU 4 (4th Fighter Wing) at Mürted. In 1972, 9 Wing at Balikesir received nine F-104Gs and two TF-104Gs previously operated by the Spanish Air Force.

Eighteen F-104S/CB fighter-bombers were purchased new from Italy in 1974 and delivered between 18 December 1974 and 10 February 1975. The remainder followed at a rate of three per month. The THK F-104S order was finally increased to 40. Deliveries from this order lasted from March to October 1976. These aircraft took part in the 1974 Turkish invasion of Cyprus, but Greek and Turkish Starfighters never faced off against each other. From 1980, large numbers of Starfighters retired by the Belgian, Canadian, German, Norwegian and Dutch air forces began to be transferred to Turkey. Seventeen F-104Gs were transferred from Belgium during 1981–83 and were retired by 1987. Forty-three F-104Gs (including 22 RFs) and ten TF-104Gs were delivered from the Netherlands from August 1980 to March 1984. Nine RF-104G, 3 CF-104s, and one TF-104G were delivered from Norway in June and July of 1981. During 1980–1988 the THK received 165 ex-German F-104Gs and 36 TF-104Gs. In total THK operated 275 F-104Gs and 56 TF-104Gs. In 1986 44 ex-Canadian CF-104s and six CF-104Ds were transferred to Turkey after an extensive overhaul in Germany. The Turkish F-104s fulfilled both air defense and ground attack roles. Over the years, many THK Starfighters were cannibalized for spares to keep the others flying and, as in other countries, many were lost in crashes.

Starfighters equipped the following squadrons of the THK:
4 *Ana Jet Us* (Mürted)
141 *Filo* (late 1963 to 1988)
142 *Filo* (late 1963 to early 1989)
Once l Flight (OCU) (1963 to 1987)
6 *Ana Jet Us* (Bandirma)
161 *Filo* (to 1989)
162 *Filo* (1982 to 1990)
8 *Ana Jet Us* (Diyarbakir)
181 *Filo* (1985 to 1995)
182 *Filo* (1985 to 1995)
9 *Ana Jet Us* (Balikesir)
191 *Filo* (1975 to 1993)
192 *Filo* (F-104S until 1987, then F-104G to 1992)
193 *Filo* (OCU) (1987 to 1993)

In 1987, the F-16C/D Fighting Falcon began to replace the F-104G in THK service. First to convert were 141 *Filo* and 142 *Filo* at Mürted, which exchanged their F-104Gs for F-16s beginning in 1987. 161 and 162 *Filo* at Bandirma and 191 and 192 *Filo* at Balikesir exchanged their Starfighters for F-16s by the early 1990s. *Filo* 181 finally relinquished its F-104Gs in favor of F-16s in April of 1994, marking the final departure of the F-104G from THK service. During 1996 *Filo* 182 exchanged the CF-104Ds for F-16C/D Block 40s, which marked the ultimate end of the Starfighter service in the Turkish Air Force.

Above: Lockheed F-104G Starfighter 12619 FG-602 of the Turkish Air Force, preserved at TuAF Museum at Yesilkoy near Istanbul. Note the old type (square) national markings, used until 1972. (George Papadimitriou)

Left: Lockheed TF-104G Starfighter 9-725 of the Turkish Air Force, preserved at TuAF Museum at Yesilkoy near Istanbul. (George Papadimitriou)

Greece

Greece was another major F-104 user, operating a large number of both new and second-hand aircraft from 1964 until 1993. The Royal Hellenic Air Force was initially allocated 35 Canadair-built F-104Gs plus four Lockheed-built TF-104Gs under the MAP program to replace F-86 Sabres. A further ten MAP-funded Lockheed-built F-104Gs and two TF-104Gs were later delivered to Greece from USAF stocks. The Starfighters were first issued to 335 *Mira Anachaitisis* (Interceptor Squadron) "Tiger" in the 114th *Pterix* (Wing), based at Tanagra. In 1965 deliveries to 336 *Mira Diokseos Bombardismou* (Fighter-Bomber Squadron) "Olympus" of the 116th Wing at Araxos began. A part of the squadron had been equipped with the Starfighters and moved to the 114th Wing at Tanagra and another part remained at Araxos and kept operating the F-84F. On 21 December 1966, the 336 *Mira* returned to the 116th Wing at Araxos AB. The 335 *Mira* kept flying from Tanagra AB until 1 June 1977 when it joined the 336 *Mira* at Araxos AB. These two squadrons were initially dedicated to nuclear strike roles within the 1st Tactical Air Force as a part of Greece's commitment to NATO, but they reverted to the conventional strike role in the early 1970s. 335 "Tiger" squadron retired the Starfighters in May 1992. It was renamed 335 Bomber Squadron and converted to LTV A-7E Corsairs. 336 "Olympus" Squadron retired their Starfighters on 31March 31, 1993, which marked the end of the Starfighter's service in the Hellenic Air Force. HAF's F-104 fleet was expanded with a number of second-hand airplanes acquired from Spain, the Netherlands, Belgium and Germany, but many of them never entered service and were used as spare parts sources. Of 149 Starfighters delivered, a maximum of 60 aircraft was active at any one time. Attrition was made up by the transfer of nine F-104Gs from Spain in 1972 and two TF-104Gs from Germany in 1977. In 1982, ten Fiat-built F-104Gs were transferred from the Netherlands to Greece. Throughout the 1980s, the Federal Republic of Germany transferred 22 RF-104Gs, 38 F-104Gs, and 20 TF-104Gs to Greece.

Lockheed F-104G Starfighter 7151 of the 336th Olympos Squadron of the Hellenic Air Force. (HAF)

F-104G Starfighter 32720 of the 335th Tigris Squadron of the Hellenic Air Force. (HAF)

Spain

In the 1960s, the *Ejercito del Aire* was looking for ways to upgrade its inventory but was restricted by the available budget and chose the F-104 within the US Military Aid Program because it was already operated by the air forces of several other European NATO countries.

The MAP agreed to supply 18 F-104Gs and two TF-104Gs. The Spanish air force bought a third TF-104G. The F-104s were delivered to Spain by two American aircraft carriers.

They were delivered in three groups:

First Group: On 15 January 1965, five single seaters and two twin-seaters.

Second group: On 12 June 1965, 13 single seaters.

On 5 January 1966, the two-seater bought by Spain was delivered and flown to the Torrejon Air Base on 26 January.

Once the first seven F-104s had arrived at Torrejon, the official presentation of the squadron took place on 5 March 1965. On 24 September 1965, the unit was fully operational.

The Starfighters replaced the F-86F Sabres of 61 *Escuadron* (squadron) in *Ala* (wing) 6 at Torrejon. In Spanish service, they were designated C.8 (serials C.8-1 to C.8-18) and CE.8 (serials CE.8-1 to CE.8-3).

The *Ala* 6 was later renumbered *Ala* 16 and the squadron 61 became 161 *Esc* and 104 *Esc* in 1967.

The F-104s were formally withdrawn from EdA service in May of 1972, and replaced by the F-4C Phantom. All of the EdA Starfighters were returned to the USAF for transfer to Greece and Turkey.

On 21 May 1972, 104 Squadron was disbanded, which ended the brief history of the F-104 with the Spanish Air Force. The EdA Starfighters had the distinction of operating without a single accident during their seven years of service.

Two Spanish F-104Gs in flight. (EdA)

Pakistan

Pakistan, which was an important ally of the United States during the cold war, was the first country from outside NATO to equip with the F-104 Starfighter. Under the US Mutual Defense Assistance Program the Pakistani Air Force (PAF) received 12 F-104 As and two F-104Bs retired from the USAF beginning in June 1961, when ten single-seaters and both two-seaters were delivered. Two further F-104As arrived in June 1964 and April 1965 as replacements for aircraft lost in crashes. Four airplanes were lost in accidents up to 1972, when dwindling spares support forced their early retirement.

The Pakistani F-104As were somewhat unique, since at PAF's request, they were refitted with the 20 mm M61A1 Vulcan cannon and the newer J79-GE-11 engine of the F-104G was also installed on the aircraft. Being the lightest of the F-104 series with a more powerful engine they had higher thrust-to-weight ratio than other F-104 models.

The only PAF unit equipped with the F-104 was No 9 Air Superiority Squadron based at Sargodha. The F-104 was employed primarily in the air-to-air role by the PAF. It was in Pakistani service that the Starfighter saw the most extensive combat in its originally intended role as a fighter, during wars with India in 1965 and 1971. During the 1965 war Starfighter pilots claimed two Indian aircraft shot down. Two aircraft were lost in combat. Due to the poor economic situation and Western arms embargoes imposed after the war in 1965, in the early 1970s the condition of the PAF F-104 fleet was so poor that most of the aircraft were not airworthy and No.9 Squadron received some old F-86Fs to provide flight training for pilots. The situation improved significantly in March 1971, when the USA delivered a batch of spare parts to Pakistan, enabling the PAF to make the remaining seven F-104As and two F-104Bs operational again. It allowed them to participate in the war with India that broke out in December 1971. PAF Starfighters claimed four Indian aircraft shot down at the cost of two airplanes. During the war in 1971 the Pakistani Starfighters were supported by nine Jordanian aircraft, in return for the assistance of Pakistani pilots in Jordanian conversion for the type. One Jordanian F-104 was lost during the hostilities.

After the war in 1972 the surviving aircraft were phased out. Six are preserved at various locations in Pakistan.

The F-104 Starfighter were operated by Pakistani Air Force for twelve years and flew 11,690 hours. Apart from combat losses, four other PAF F-104s were lost in accidents during the whole period of operation.

F-104A 56-803 of the Pakistani Air Force. (PAF)

Jordan

Jordan became an independent country in 1946. In 1950 the Royal Jordanian Air Force was established. The first jet-powered aircraft were de Havilland Vampires delivered by Great Britain and Egypt. In 1958 12 Hawker Hunter F.Mk.6s and in 1964 an additional 23 Hunter F.Mk.73s and FGA.9s were supplied to the RJAF. However the Hunters were mainly ground attack aircraft and the Royal Jordanian Air Force needed a pure interceptor fighter. Due to insufficient financial resources RJAF decided to acquire second-hand aircraft via the American MAP program.

In 1966, Jordan signed a deal to acquire 18 ex-USAF F-104As and five F-104Bs. Deliveries began just before the outbreak of the Six Day War in June 1967. Early in 1967 a USAF training detachment with F-104Bs and F-104As arrived at Amman IAP to familiarize RJAF personnel with the type.

During the Six Day War most of Jordan's combat aircraft were destroyed on the ground, but the Starfighters survived. As they were technically still US property they had been flown to Turkey a few days before hostilities began.

After the war the deliveries of ex-USAF Starfighters were completed. Eighteen refurbished F-104As and five two-seat F-104Bs were delivered in 1967 and a further four F-104As during 1972–1973. Jordanian F-104s were operated by No. 9 Squadron RJAF based at Prince Hassan Air Base from 1967 until 1983.

Apparently the Jordanians were instructed by Pakistani pilots, and as mentioned above in return for the courtesy, nine Jordanian Starfighters were deployed to Pakistan to take part in the 1971 Indo-Pakistani War. One aircraft, number 56-767, was shot down by a MiG-21 of the Indian Air Force on 17 December 1971.

Jordanian Starfighters were retired from operational service in 1983, replaced by French Dassault Mirage F1 fighters. Some of them were converted to airfield decoys, disguised as Mirage F1s.

Republic of China (Taiwan)

The Republic of China Air Force was the second air force to convert to the F-104 Starfighter, just after the USAF. The F-104 was the longest serving combat aircraft in ROCAF history and, after the Italian Air Force, the ROCAF was the second longest operator of the F-104 Through 38 years, the ROCAF operated almost all models of the F-104, having acquired all of them, new and used, under the code name Project "*Ali Shan*" (Ali Mountain), from *Ali Shan* 1 to *Ali Shan* 11.

The ROCAF acquired 247 F-104s in F-104A, B, D, G, J, DJ, RF-104 and TF-104G versions. The majority were second-hand aircraft from the USA, Germany, Japan, Denmark and Belgium. Some of these aircraft were not airworthy and were cannibalized for spare parts.

The following units of the ROCAF operated the Starfighters:
427th Tactical Fighter Wing, ROCAF, based at Ching Chuang Kang AB 7th Tactical Fighter Squadron, ROCAF
8th Tactical Fighter Squadron, ROCAF
28th Tactical Fighter Squadron, ROCAF
35th Tactical Fighter Squadron, ROCAF
499th Tactical Fighter Wing, ROCAF based at Hsinchu AB
41st Tactical Fighter Squadron, ROCAF
42nd Tactical Fighter Squadron, ROCAF
48th Tactical Fighter Squadron, ROCAF
401st Tactical Combined Wing, ROCAF based at Tao Yuan AB
12th Tactical Reconnaissance Squadron

The first versions to equip the ROCAF were the F-104A and B. After the ROCAF had expressed interest in the F-104, advertised as a true interceptor to answer the Chinese mainland threat, it took delivery of 22 F-104As and five F-104Bs from the USAF Air Defence Command in May 1960 under Project "*Ali Shan* No.1".

All these aircraft were delivered to the Ching Chuan Kang-based 8th TFS operating under 3 TFW (3 Air Group). They received serials from 4101 to 4222.

These aircraft served with the Taiwanese Air Force until 1966 when all surviving Starfighters (in total six F-104As were lost in accidents) were transferred back to the USA after being replaced by the more modern F-104G version.

To strengthen the interception capability, in 1970 Taiwan decided to order

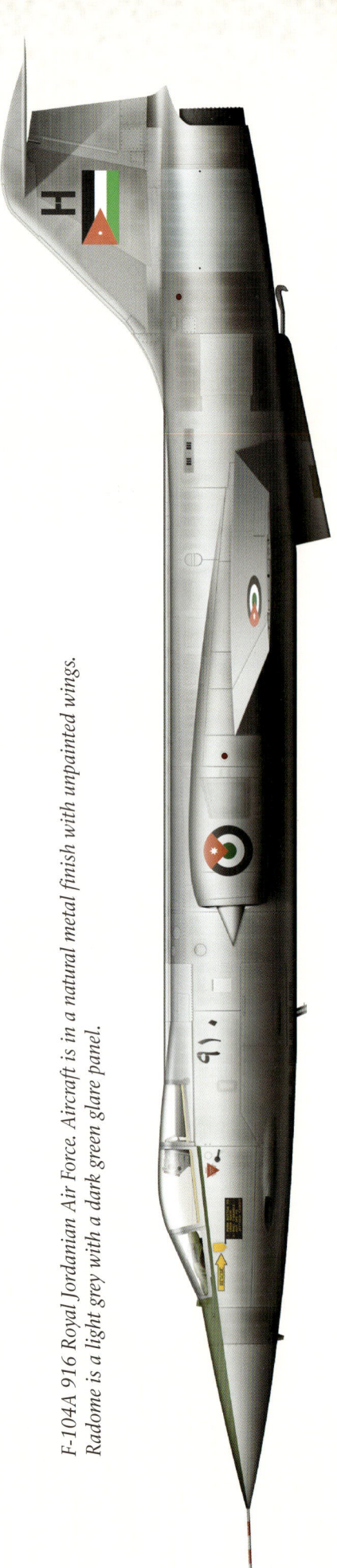

F-104A 916 Royal Jordanian Air Force. Aircraft is in a natural metal finish with unpainted wings. Radome is a light grey with a dark green glare panel.

F-104G Starfighters of the Republic of China Air Force. (RoCAF)

again a number of F-104A fighters and F-104B traers from the USA. All (again 22) F-104As had been fully modified to the latest standards, including the more powerful GE J79-19 engine from the F-104S variant and were painted in Taiwanese camouflage colours. All 22 aircraft were delivered to the Hsinchu-based 41st TFS operating under 2 TFW (11 Air Group).

In 1974 the surviving aircraft were transferred to the CCK-based 8th TFS of 3 TFW (3 Air Group) and so, the career of the F-104A once again started but also ended with the 8th TFS at CCK AB. In the mid 1980s the aircraft were painted light grey while receiving IRAN (Inspect Repair as Necessary). F-104A operations ended officially on 3 March 1988.

For pilot conversion eight F-104B and six F-104D Starfighters were operated by the ROCAF. In 1960 the 8th TFS of the 3rd TFW (3 Air Group) received five F-104Bs. They were operated until 1966 when three surviving F-104Bs were returned to the USAF after being replaced by the more modern TF-104G version. Two F-104Bs were lost in accidents during the 7seven years of operations at Ching Chuan Kang AB.

When in 1970 Taiwan again introduced F-104A interceptors under project "*Ali Shan* No.6", with these F-104As two F-104B training aircraft were also received. These second batch trainers had also the more powerful GE J79-19 engine, which was part of the USAF Cuban crisis plan to improve the F-104A/B interceptor capability in the late 1960s.

When Taiwan lost one of these two F-104B aircraft they received a replacement aircraft in 1972. They were operated by the Hsinchu-based 41st TFS under 2nd TFW (11 Air Group) until 1974 when they moved, together with all remaining F-104A aircraft, to the 8th TFS at CCK, under the 3rd TFW (3 Air Group). All aircraft stayed in service until their retirement in 1988.

In 1975 the ROCAF received six ex-USAF F-104Ds to increase its training capacity under project "*Ali Shan* No.7". These D trainers were used until their official retirement ceremony on 15 November 1988 and were only operated by the Ching Chuan Kang-based 8th TFS under the 3rd TFW (3 Air Group).

During 1963 to 1965, under Projects "*Ali Shan* Nos. 2, 4 and 5", 3 Wing received 61 new (34 Lockheed-built and 27 Canadair-built) F-104Gs and nine Lockheed-built TF-104Gs to equip 7th Squadron, 8th Squadron and 28th Squadron. After ten years of service, the survivors were regrouped into two squadrons as the 7th Squadron and 28th Squadron. 8th TFS disbanded 1975. In August 1963 12th Squadron (SMS) received eight Lockheed-built RF-104Gs under Project "*Ali Shan* No.3".

From 1984, under Project "*Ali Shan* No.8" the 41st Sqn, 42nd Sqn and 48 Sqn of 2nd Wing received 39 ex-Luftwaffe F-104Gs and 27 TF-104Gs, previously used to train German pilots at Luke AFB, Arizona.

Under Project "*Ali Shan* No.9" the 7th Sqn and 28th Sqn of 3rd Wing received 31 ex-JASDF F-104Js and six F-104DJs as attrition replacements. They were both operational and intended as spare part sources. The first batch of 17 F-104Js was delivered in July 1987.

From 1988, ROCAF took delivery of 15 ex-Royal Danish Air Force F-104Gs and three TF-104Gs under Project "*Ali Shan* No.10" and 13 ex-Belgian Air Force F-104Gs and nine TF-104Gs for use as spare parts sources.

The most important day of the ROCAF F-104's service came on 13 January 1967, when Maj Shih-Lin Hu and Capt Bei-Puo Shih each shot down one People's Liberation Army Air Force MiG-19. These were the only aerial victories scored by the F-104G. As in other countries the F-104's service history with the ROCAF was plagued with numerous accidents.

In the 1990s the F-104s were no longer modern aircraft and as they aged they became more and more difficult to maintain, so they were gradually removed from service. First to go were F-104s of the 427th TFW, which started to convert to F-CK-1s in 1993. Then, in 1997, the 499th TFW at Hsinchu AB replaced its Starfighters with Mirage 2000-5s for the interceptor role.

After 38 years of service with the ROCAF, the F-104 was officially withdrawn from service in a decommissioning ceremony held at Ching Chuang Kang (CCK) Air Base on 22 May 1998.

NASA

F-104s were destined to serve NASA for high speed and altitude flight research, and as chase and support aircraft at Dryden Flight Research Center, located at Edwards Air Force Base in California. A mixed fleet of 12 F-104As, F-104Bs, F-104Ns and TF-104Gs was operated from 1956 until 1994. NASA Starfighters provided flight research data on everything from aircraft handling characteristics, such as roll coupling, to reaction control system research. Also the durability of Space Shuttle thermal protection tiles was tested in flights aboard a Starfighter.

Another important role for NASA's Starfighters included flying many safety chase missions in support of advanced research aircraft over the years, including the wingless lift body vehicles flown at Dryden during the late 1960s and early 1970s. They served also as launch platforms for sounding (research) rockets.

In August 1956, the seventh YF-104A (55-2961) was transferred to NACA (later reorganized as NASA) as a JF-104A. Before the X-15 rocket-powered research aircraft program had started in the late 1950s, test pilots needed experience in flying with the reaction control system (RCS), which is essential for spacecraft control and maneuverability. Therefore this plane was fitted with the RCS, comprising hydrogen peroxide-powered thrusters mounted in the nose and wingtips. The reaction control system trials lasted from 1959 to 1961 and provided the necessary experience for the future rocket pilots. Then the aircraft was used by NASA for other test flight purposes until it was finally retired in November 1975. It was initially numbered 818, but later received the civil registration N818NA (the "NA" standing for NASA).

In October 1957, NASA acquired two ex-USAF F-104A single-seaters (56-0734 and 56-0749) for use in flight testing. The latter crashed in 1962. These planes were never assigned NASA serial numbers. In December 1959, F-104B 57-1303 was transferred to NASA and assigned the NASA number of 819. It was retired in 1978.

Between August and October 1963, Lockheed delivered three single-seat F-104G Starfighters to NASA, designated F-104N (N for NASA) for use as high-speed chase aircraft. Those three were the only purpose-built Starfighters produced by Lockheed for NASA – all other Starfighters operated by NASA were transferred from the USAF. Those F-104Ns were initially numbered 011 to 013. The 013 was lost on 8 June 1966, in a mid-air collision with the second North American XB-70A Valkyrie supersonic bomber prototype during a General Electric-sponsored publicity photographic flight. The pilot of the F-104N, Joseph A. Walker, was killed. The XB-70A pilot, Alvin S. White, ejected with injuries, but his copilot, Maj Carl S. Cross, was killed. The two other F-104Ns later received the civilian registrations N811NA and N812NA.

In December 1966 another ex-USAF F-104A (56-0790) was acquired by NASA as a replacement for 013. It was registered as N820NA and served until 30 October 1983.

In 1975 NASA also received two ex-*Luftwaffe* TF-104Gs and one F-104G, giving them civilian registrations N824NA, N825NA and N826NA respectively. After removal of their military equipment, they were used by NASA for various flight test purposes.

The F-104G N826NA was equipped with a pylon called a flight test fixture (FTF) mounted on the fuselage centerline. Articles to be tested were attached to or installed in the FTF, which was instrumented to record the research data aboard the aircraft and transmit the data in "real time" to engineers in Dryden's mission control room.

One of the applications of the FTF was testing of the heat-resistant tiles, covering the lower surface of the Space Shuttle. The tiles were flown on the fixture in a position similar to the environment on the orbiter to determine if their bonding was sufficient. They were also flown through rain to study how moisture would affect them.

N826NA flew the last of these missions on 31 January 1994. By then the 12 F-104s had accumulated over 18,000 flights at Dryden in wide variety of missions.

F-104A 56-0734 operated by NASA on the lakebed at Edwards AFB in 1960. Note the pitot tube relocated from the nose to the port wingtip. (NASA)

F-104A 56-0749 operated by NASA with ALSOR sounding rocket mounted on fuselage centerline in 1961. The 114 kg (253 lb) rocket reached an altitude of 116,730 m (383,000 ft) after the launch from the F-104. (NASA)

F-104A N818NA of NASA flown by Einar Enevoldson on 11 April, 1975. (NASA)

F-104G N826NA with the Flight Test Fixture (FTF) mounted on the fuselage centerline. (NASA)

Three F-104N Starfighters of NASA in flight. (NASA)

Two F-104Ns of NASA in flight. (NASA)

TF-104G N824NA flies chase on the NB-52 during DAST ARW-1 captive flight on 14 September 1979. (NASA)

F-104A 56-0763 operated by NASA flies chase on the X-15 rocket research aircraft. (NASA)

F-104G 826 and F-15 281 of NASA in flight during Space Shuttle tile testing in 1980. Note the tiles mounted on the right wing of the F-15. (NASA)

F-104N 812 flies chase on the X-24B research aircraft simulating future Space Shuttle landings at Dryden Flight Research Center, Edwards AFB on 24 October 1975. (NASA)

93

Starfighters Aerospace

The world's last F-104 operator is Starfighters Aerospace company, founded and presided by Rick Svetkoff, based at Cape Canveral, Florida. The company began with airshow appearances, but later specialized in high-speed, high – altitude testing of various avionic devices and missiles as well as macro – and microgravity training. It employs experienced ex-military Starfighter pilots, like Wolfgang Czaja from Germany and Piercarlo Ciacchi from Italy. Currently the company operates two ex-RNoAF CF-104s and one CF-104D and three ex-AMI F-104S ASA-Ms and one TF-104G-M and plans to expand the fleet by four more ex-AMI aircraft.

F-104 Starfighters of the world's last F-104 operator, Starfighters Aerospace. (Starfighters Aerospace)

Aircraft of Starfighters Aerospace in a hangar. Recent acquisitions still sport AMI paint schemes. (Starfighters Aerospace)

F-104DJ 25-5010 Japan Air Self Defense Forces. Aircraft is unpainted and in a natural metal finish. Wings are white on the upper surfaces and light grey below. The radome is white with a black glare panel on top that runs unto the front windscreen.

F-104A 56-800 of Pakistani Air Force. Aircraft is unpainted and in a natural metal finish. Wings are white on the upper surfaces and light grey below.

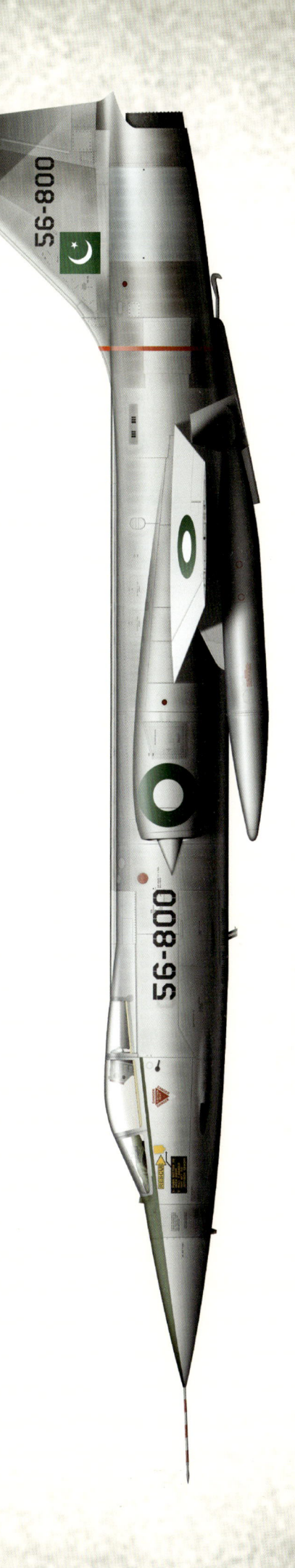

95

The F-104 in combat

Although the Starfighter was developed and operated at the peak of the Cold War and was one of the most significant aircraft of that era it did not see much combat, largely because there was no major East – West confrontation, for which it was envisaged. The most significant and effective combat use of the Starfighter took place in regional conflicts away from the Cold War – wars between Pakistan and India in 1965 and 1971. They were used in their original role of air superiority fighters. The F-104C variant saw combat in both air superiority and ground-attack roles during the Vietnam war.

The Quemoy crisis

On 23 August 1958, artillery of the People's Republic of China began massive shelling of Quemoy Islands off the Mainland China coast, held by the Nationalist China Government in Taiwan. The US government did not want to get into conflict with the PRC but was committed to defend Taiwan by the 1954 Mutual Defense Treaty. In response to the shelling of Quemoy US ordered the 7th Fleet into the Taiwan Straits and sent military aid to Taiwan. This included 12 F-104As (56-0791, 56-0795, 56-0817, 56-0823, 56-0828, 56-0837, 56-0838, 56-0842, 56-0844, 56-0849, 56-0850, 56-0860) from the 83rd Fighter Interceptor Squadron (FIS) USAF Air Defense Command, based at Hamilton AFB in California. These were deployed to Tao Yuan AB, Taiwan under Operation "Jonah Able" in September 1958 along with 2nd Missile Battalion of the US Army Air Defense Command, with Nike Hercules surface-to-air missile systems in October 1958, to help defend Taiwan from any PRC air attacks. The Starfighters were airlifted by C-124 "Globemaster" transport aircraft. The first cargo aircraft of the movement departed Hamilton AFB on 8 September 1958, less than 48 hours after the official notification. The first F-104A arrived in Taiwan on 11 September 1958. The next day at 4.00 pm the first F-104, flown by Squadron Commander Lt Col. John W. Bennett, took off for the first Combat Air Patrol. The deployment of US forces was effective, because the shelling of Quemoy was reduced on 13 September 1958 and was suspended on 6 October 1958. In December 1958 the control of these 12 F-104As was transferred to the 337th FIS from Westover AFB, Massachusetts, commanded by Lt Col. James Jabara. In March 1959 the Starfighters were transferred back to McClellan AFB in Sacramento, California for depot maintenance work. They were later assigned to other units within the Air Defense Command.

F-104A 56-0791 of the 83rd Fighter Interceptor Squadron USAF, Tao Yuan AB, Taiwan during the Quemoy crisis in September 1958. (USAF)

The Berlin crisis

In 1961 tension over Berlin between the USSR and the Allies rose. On 13 August 1961 construction of the Berlin Wall, separating three western sectors of Berlin, controlled by the USA, France and Great Britain from the eastern sector controlled by the USSR, began to stop the outflow of East Germans from East to West Berlin. On 30 August 1961, President Kennedy ordered the Air National Guard and Air Force Reserve to active duty in response to Soviet moves to cut off allied access to Berlin. He mobilized 28 ANG squadrons of which 11 were sent to Europe to reinforce USAFE.

In late October and early November, eight tactical fighter units with 216 aircraft were deployed to Europe under operation "Stair Step," the largest jet deployment in the Air Guard's history. Among them were three squadrons (60 aircraft) equipped with the F-104A/B: 197th Fighter Interceptor Squadron (FIS) Arizona ANG based at Skyharbor Airport, Phoenix, Arizona, 157th FIS South Carolina ANG based at McEntire ANGB, Eastover, South Carolina

And 151st FIS Tennessee ANG based at McGhee-Tyson ANGB, Knoxville, Tennessee.

The ANG F-104 squadrons were officially mobilized on 1 October 1961. Due to the F-104's short range and no in-flight refueling capability, they were airlifted to Europe by Military Air Transport Service Douglas C-124s in November 1961 under "Operation Brass Ring". Their task was to conduct air superiority and offensive air support operations if required to defend West Berlin.

In Europe, these squadrons were assigned to USAFE (US Air Force Europe). The 197th FIS and 151st FIS were assigned to Ramstein Air Base in West Germany under the 86th Air (Defense) Division of the 17th Air Force. The South Carolina ANG 157 FIS was assigned to Moron AFB, Spain under the 65th Air Defense Division.

For proficiency training while stationed in Europe each ANG squadron also sent two F-104Bs. Some F-104As and F-104Bs were

An F-104C Starfighter of 479th TFW refuels from a KC-135. (USAF)

lost in crashes during their deployment in Europe. The tension ended in the summer of 1962. These three F-104 squadrons were officially demobilized on 15 August 1962. Shortly after, they were redeployed back to their home bases in the US.

1965 Pakistan-India War

During the war in 1965 War the F-104A Starfighters, using the radar of their AN/ASG-14T1 fire-control system in conjunction with Sidewinder air-to-air missiles, were the only Pakistani Air Force high altitude interceptors, capable also of night operations. The simple and already obsolete fire-control radar was designed to detect high-flying bombers but it could not illuminate smaller targets against ground clutter. The standard high speed intercept tactic employed by PAF's F-104 pilots was to approach the target from below, with a typical height difference of 600–900 meters (2,000–3,000 feet), at a range of 10–15 kilometers. Limitations of the F-104's radar were known to the IAF's Canberra bomber pilots attacking targets in Pakistan, therefore to minimize the threat of interception during most of their ingress and egress over Pakistani territory the IAF Canberras flew about 1,000 feet (300 meters) above ground level. This made the night interception very difficult for the PAF's F-104s, which in this situation had to adopt an unconventional low-altitude intercept profile that severely challenged the capabilities of its airborne radar and was extremely dangerous. To pick up the low-flying bombers on their scope the F-104 pilots had to get beneath the target, down to about 300–500 feet above the ground, to point their radars upward and clear of ground clutter at the enemy. The problem was aggravated by the Canberra's tail warning audio alarm alerting the bomber crew of an F-104 closing from astern and enabling them to take timely evasive action to shake off the pursuer. Of 246 missions flown by F-104s during the conflict, 42 were night missions of this type against the IAF Canberras.

Despite their limitations the F-104s were feared by the Indian Air Force pilots. On 3 September 1965, even before the hostilities began, an Indian Gnat was forced by an F-104 to land at the abandoned airfield at Pasrur in Pakistan. Its pilot, Squadron Leader Brijpal Singh Sikand, was taken prisoner.

On 6 September, two Starfighters took off for a dawn patrol from Sargodha. They were vectored by Sakesar Radar towards four IAF Mysteres attacking a passenger train at Gakkhar railway station with bombs and rockets. One of the F-104 pilots was forced to return to base due to radio failure but the other pilot, Flight Lieutenant Aftab Alam Khan, dove his F-104 with full afterburner going supersonically through the Mystere formation, which scattered and tried to escape at about 50 feet above the ground. Khan shot down one Mystere with a Sidewinder missile, achieving the first aerial victory in a Starfighter.

On 7 September the other F-104 pilot, Flight Lieutenant Amjad Hussain, who had missed his chance the previous day, was scrambled at about 05:15 hours and directed by Sakesar radar towards an incoming raid at Sargodha. He was flying F-104 number 56-877. He spotted IAF Mysteres about seven miles away from Sargodha, flying at 150-200 feet on a south-easterly heading towards India and headed towards them. Hussain positioned himself behind one of them and fired an AIM-9 missile, which missed. The Mystere then began to dogfight with the Starfighter, which used its superior climb and acceleration to lift the combat from ground level to about 7,000 feet to gain room for maneuver. Hussain hit the Mystere with cannon fire. His aircraft was severely damaged by debris from the exploding Mystere. Flight Lieutenant Hussain ejected safely and reached his base. This was the only Starfighter lost through enemy action in the 1965 war.

On 21 September, Squadron Leader Jamal Khan, intercepted an Indian Air Force Canberra at about 33,000 feet and shot it down with a Sidewinder near Fazilka in Pakistan. The bomber's pilot, Flight Lieutenant Manmohan Lowe, ejected and was taken prisoner, while the navigator, Flying Officer A. K. Kapor, could not bail out and was killed in action because the British-made Canberra, had no ejection seat for the navigator. This was the first night victory achieved by an F-104 after a number of near misses due to the reasons described above.

During the war in 1965 the F-104s were also used for low level daylight reconnaissance missions over the IAF air bases. The speed of the Starfighter gave the Indians no time to react. The F-104s also escorted the slow Lockheed RT-33 reconnaissance aircraft on photographic missions deep into Indian territory. The presence of Starfighters virtually guaranteed no air opposition. Six F-104 pilots received gallantry awards during the 1965 War. During this conflict the F-104s flew a total time of 246 hours and 45 minutes.

1971 Pakistan-India War

After the beginning of the 1965 war the US Government imposed an embargo on arms sales to both India and Pakistan. Since India, a long-time ally of the Soviet Union, did not use American military equipment the sanctions degraded the combat potential of only the Pakistani Armed Forces, notably the PAF F-104 fleet. The situation changed in March 1971 when the US delivered a batch of spare parts which allowed the PAF to bring the remaining seven F-104As and two F-104Bs to operational status again.

Air operations in the 1971 Pakistan-India War commenced with a preemptive strike by the PAF. In the 1971 War the F-104s were also used for deep penetration strikes against enemy airfields and radars. Two F-104s each attacked Indian Air Force radars at Amritsar and Faridkot. The attack on Faridkot Radar was led by Wing Commander Arif Iqbal, who not only damaged the radar but also shot down an IAF *Krishak* aircraft.

On 4 December, Squadron Leaders Amanullah and Rashid shot down two IAF aircraft, a Gnat and an Su-7, while attacking Amritsar radar. On 5 December the F-104A number 56-804 piloted by S/L Amjad Hussain was shot down by Indian anti-aircraft artillery near Amritsar. Hussain ejected and was taken prisoner. He was the only PAF Starfighter pilot shot down by AA fire in either the 1965 or 1971 wars. On 8 December, Flight Lieutenant Manzoor Bokhari shot down an IAF Canberra. On 10 December, Wing Commander Arif Iqbal shot down an Indian Navy Alize aircraft while attacking the Indian harbor at Okha. Its crew was killed in action. On December 13 F-104A 56-773 was shot down by an IAF MiG-21, piloted Flight Lieutenant Arun Datta. The Starfighter pilot, Wing Commander Mervyn Leslie Middlecoat, was killed.

On 13 December 1971 nine F-104As of the RJAF arrived at Masroor (Mauripur) Air Base. The Jordanian pilots flew many air defense missions on these fighters within Pakistani air space. The PAF did not allow them to fly cross-border offensive missions over Indian territory. The Royal Jordanian AF aircraft sported PAF roundels.

On 17 December 1971 RJAF F-104A 56-767 was shot down by F/Lt Arun K. Datta flying a MiG-21FL. The pilot, F/Lt Samad Changezi (a Pakistani), was killed.

During the 1971 War, the F-104s flew a total of 103 hours and 45 minutes.

Vietnam war

When Operation Rolling Thunder began in April 1965, North Vietnamese fighters were a major threat to US aircraft attacking targets in North Vietnam and a need for escort fighters emerged. Within Operation Two Buck (deployment of several USAF aircraft to South-East Asia) on 7 April TAC ordered the 479th TFW to deploy its aircraft to the theatre and the first F-104Cs of the 476th TFS landed at Ching Chuang Kang AB, Taiwan, on 11 April. CCK AB was to serve as the main operating base for the F-104s, with regular rotation of aircraft to the forward operating base at Da Nang in North Vietnam. Twenty-eight F-104s were deployed to CCK AB, but four aborted en route due to technical problems. Fourteen aircraft were sent to Da Nang on a ten day rotation basis. After a work-up period of seven days, 14 F-104s arrived at Da Nang on 19 April and flew their first escort mission the next day.

They were primarily used to perform combat air patrols (CAPs) over the Gulf of Tonkin to protect EC-121 Warning Star aircraft, codenamed "College Eye" or "Disco". The EC-121 was an airborne early warning and control version of the Lockheed Constellation four-engine airliner, equipped with powerful radar in a dorsal radome. During the CAP missions a SAC (Strategic Air Command) Boeing KC-135 tanker was always flying in the vicinity to refuel the F-104s in the air during their patrols. A patrol consisted of two pairs of Starfighters each time – two on patrol and two in refueling and standby mode. The effect of F-104 patrols upon North Vietnamese and Chinese MiG operations was as intended. NVAF MiGs soon learned to avoid contact with USAF strikes escorted by F-104s. During the entire deployment of the 476th TFS only two distant encounters between F-104s and enemy fighters occurred which frustrated combat-greedy Starfighter pilots. Toward the end of the 476th's deployment, the F-104s began to be tasked for weather reconnaissance and ground attack missions. Weather reconnaissance missions typically involved a pair of F-104s, which flew near a target area in North Vietnam, close enough to determine the pre-strike weather conditions but without revealing the target's identity. Twenty-one strike and AAA-suppression sorties were flown against targets in North Vietnam, but the great majority of the 476th's ground attack sorties were Close Air Support (CAS) missions in South Vietnam directed by airborne Forward Air Controllers (FAC). From these CAS missions, the F-104s quickly gained appreciation for the accuracy of their cannon and bombs, and were specifically requested by FACs on numerous occasions thanks to their quick reaction time. The CAS missions took their toll – the F-104 number 56-0937 was lost during a sortie on 29 June, but luckily the pilot, Capt. Richard Cole was rescued with minor injuries. On 12 July 1965 476th TFS was replaced by 436th TFS which operated from Da Nang AB to 12 October 1965. In all, 476th aircraft had flown 1,182 combat sorties. More than 50% were EC-121 escort, the rest were MiGCAP patrols, ground attack and weather reconnaissance missions. During this period, the 476th F-104s maintained 94.7% serviceability rate thanks to the high qualifications of 476th maintenance personnel and to the simplicity and maintainability of F-104C systems.

The duty tour of the 436th TFS was different. There were a few escort and MiGCAP missions in July, but most of the sorties were CAS missions in South Vietnam and Rescue Combat Air Patrols (ResCAP) over North Vietnam. By late September the escort missions took precedence again. Although thanks to its high speed and small size the F-104C was a difficult target for artillery, low level ground attack missions resulted in aircraft returning with severe damage. On 23 July Capt. Roy Blakely was killed when landing his damaged F-104 56-0908 at Chu Lai. The worst day was 20 September 1965 when Major Philip W. Smith got lost when flying EC-121 escort and was shot down in 56-0883 over Hainan island by Chinese Shenyang F-6 (license MiG-19) fighters and became the only F-104 pilot taken prisoner in the Southeast Asia theatre and one of two USAF pilots captured by the Chinese. During a RESCAP (Rescue Combat Air

An F-104C Starfighter at Da Nang airbase flight line in 1966. During the second deployment to south-east Asia the aircraft were painted with SEA camouflage. (D. Guisinger)

Another photo of the same aircraft. (D. Guisinger)

Patrol) mission after the loss of Smith two further F-104Cs – 56-0911 and 56-0921 – collided in the air but the pilots, Captains Harvey Quackenbush and Dayle Carlson, ejected and survived. Despite these losses the 436th TFS' deployment was a success, since no enemy fighters were encountered during the air-to-air missions and the ground attack missions were executed with accuracy and the reaction time for an emergency call was quick. The 436th F-104s flew 1,382 combat sorties, for a total of 3,116 hours.

The 436th TFS was subsequently relieved by 435th TFS on 14 October 1965.

This deployment lasted until 21 November 1965 when the Starfighters returned to CCK AB and then to the US. The squadron flew 419 sorties – 12 of the CAS type, the rest were MiGCAP and ResCAP. The primary mission of the 435th was the escort of EC-121D and C-130E-II Silver Dawn aircraft over the Gulf of Tonkin.

The second deployment was made in June 1966, when 435th TFS was sent to Udorn Royal Thai Air Force Base (RTAFB), Thailand. It was assigned to the F-4 Phantom equipped 8th TFW based at Ubon. In total 20 airplanes were deployed in two batches. The squadron again flew escort missions and low-level strike missions against North Vietnamese communication lines. They began to escort the EF-105F Wild Weasel enemy air defense suppression aircraft. On 1 August 1966 two F-104Cs, 56-0928 and 57-0925, were lost to S-75 (SA-2) surface-to-air missiles. Both pilots, Capt. John Kwortnik and Lt Col. Arthur Finney, were killed. After these losses the Starfighters were reassigned to low-level strafing missions in Laos and South Vietnam. On 1 September 1966 Maj. Norman Schmidt was shot down by AAA over Laos in 57-0913 and later died in captivity. On 2 October 1966 56-0904 was shot

An F-104C Starfighter taxis after a mission at Udorn. (USAF)

Two F-104C Starfighters armed with 340 kg (750 lb) M117 bombs during a strike mission over Vietnam. (USAF)

down by an S-75 missile. The pilot, Capt. Norman Lockard, ejected and was rescued. On 20 October Capt. Charles Tofferi in 56-0918 was shot down by AAA over Laos and killed. To prevent further losses the Starfighters were assigned to EC-121 and EC-130 escorts over the Gulf of Tonkin. To protect the F-104Cs against radar-guided Vietnamese air defenses they were like other USAF strike aircraft equipped with the Radar Homing and Warning (RHAW) system, comprising the AN/APR-25 radar warning receiver and AN/APR-26 launch warning receiver. After this addition the F-104Cs could fly over North Vietnam again. On 2 January 1967 the Starfighters took part in the famous Operation Bolo (a ruse to decoy NVAF MiG-21s into aerial ambush by air-to-air missile-armed F-4 Phantoms of the 8th TFW, simulating a formation of bomb-laden F-105 Thunderchiefs). The ruse was necessary to destroy the MiGs because the Rules of Engagement imposed by President Johnson's administration at that time did not allow USAF to attack NVAF airfields. The ruse was successful – seven MiGs were shot down without American losses. The Starfighters covered the egress of the F-4 formations.

Since the Starfighter's range was insufficient, even with in-flight refueling, the losses encountered were severe and the TAC was in the process of phasing out of the type. They were withdrawn from the theatre on 19 July 1967. During this second deployment the 435th TFS logged 5,306 combat sorties for a total of 14,393 combat hours. Five Starfighters were lost in combat – three to S-75 missiles and two to anti-aircraft artillery. A further four were lost in accidents.

After the return to the US the F-104Cs were retired from active USAF service. Some were stored at Davis-Monthan AFB, Arizona and some equipped two squadrons, the 156th TFS and 198th TFS of the Puerto Rican Air National Guard, where they served until 1975. Their final retirement marked the end of active service of the F-104 in the USAF, but some remained in Systems Command and NASA.

Taiwan 1967

On 13 January 1967, Major Shih-Lin Hu and Captain Bei-Puo Shih of the Republic of China Air Force each shot down one People's Liberation Army Air Force MiG-19. These were the first and only F-104G combat victories.

Gulf War 1991

During the Gulf War in 1991 Italian Air Force's Orpheus reconnaissance pod equipped RF-104Gs of 28° *Gruppo*/3° *Stormo* flew reconnaissance missions over northern Iraq from Erhac base in Turkey.

Operation Allied Force

During Operation Allied Force, the NATO air campaign against Serbia in 1999, the Italian F-104S ASA-M Starfighters of 4°, 5°, 9° and 37° *Stormo* were assigned to the international NATO forces. Aircraft of 4° *Stormo* from Grosseto and 9° *Stormo* from Grazzanisse were deployed to Amendola, and aircraft from disbanded 22° *Gruppo* 51° *Stormo* joined 23° *Gruppo* 5° *Stormo* at Cervia on the Adriatic coast. The Starfighters were used for combat air patrols, "filling the gaps" when regularly patrolling fighters refueled or were directed to visually identify a bogey. During the wars in the ex-Yugoslavia the Starfighters showed their age and were unable to fly alongside other NATO fighters, mostly because of short endurance due to low fuel capacity and lack of aerial refueling capability. They were relegated to air base protection. In 2001 during the G-8 summit at Genova and NATO summit at Pratica di Mare in 2002 the Starfighters guarded no-fly zones around the locations of the summits.

RF-104G "3-13" MM6576 of 132° Gruppo 3° Stormo "Carlo Emanuele Buscaglia" fitted with Orpheus reconnaissance pod taxis at Villafranca. (Aldo Bidini)

Special versions

Apart from being a combat aircraft the Starfighter also served as a platform for several modifications, used for special training or testing of new concepts.

JF-104

In the late 1950s the YF-104A s/n 55-2691 was modified by NASA to continue the reaction control system (RCS) testing that had been started on the Bell X-1B, which was permanently grounded due to cracks in its fuel tank. The F-104 was selected as a substitute aircraft thanks to its similar performance to the X-1B. The data and experience from RCS tests were needed for the X-15 rocket aircraft program.

The reaction control system from the X-1B was installed in the YF-104A, redesignated JF-104A. The system comprised small thrusters powered by hydrogen peroxide which provided control in near-vacuum conditions of the stratosphere, where aerodynamic control surfaces are ineffective. Four were mounted in a cruciform layout in the nose to control pitch and yaw and two were mounted in wingtip pods to control roll. They were operated by a handle mounted in the cockpit. Hydrogen peroxide tanks were mounted behind the thrusters in the nose and wingtip pods and a compressed nitrogen tank, which forced the hydrogen peroxide out of the tanks, was mounted behind the cockpit. Twenty-eight test flights with the RCS were flown between 1959 and 1961. They were vital for the development of the RCS subsequently used in the NF-104A aerospace trainer, X-15 rocket-powered aircraft and in spacecraft.

JF-104, used by NASA for tests of the Reaction Control System (RCS). (NASA)

NF-104A

Another of these modifications, the NF-104A "Rocket Starfighter", was particularly spectacular. In 1963, three ex-USAF F-104As (56-0756, -0760, and -0762) were taken out of storage at Davis Monthan AFB and modified as NF-104A aerospace training aircraft to train future astronauts in the areas of boost to sub-orbit, zero-gravity operations, reaction control system use and re-entry manoeuvers. They were stripped of their military equipment and the original F-104A vertical fin was replaced by a larger one as used on the F-104G. The wingspan was increased to 7.9 m (25.94 ft) and the reaction control system was installed. It comprised 12 hydrogen peroxide control thrusters mounted at the nose and wingtips. Two were mounted in each wingtip, one on the top and one on the bottom for roll control. In the nose two were mounted on the top

Chuck Yeager before a flight in an NF-104A. (USAF)

Chuck Yeager in the cockpit of the NF-104A 56-0762 before the flight which ended with the near fatal crash on 4 December 1963. (USAF)

and two on the bottom to control pitch and two each were mounted on the left and right side of the nose for yaw control. They were operated by an additional handle in the cockpit, which fired the thrusters in appropriate axis – pitch, roll or yaw. The radar was removed from the nose to make room for the RCS thrusters and hydrogen peroxide tank. The tail unit was exchanged for a larger one from a two-seater. A Rocketdyne LR121/AR-2-NA-1 auxiliary rocket motor was mounted on the tail above the jet exhaust nozzle. This rocket engine could be throttled from 13.34 to 26.68 kN (3,000 to 6,000 lbf) of thrust, and the burn time was about 105 seconds. This engine used the same JP-4 fuel as the J79 and hydrogen peroxide as oxidizer, carried in two tanks replacing the F-104's auxiliary fuel tank aft of the cockpit. The air inlet cones were lengthened by 50 cm (20 inches) to enable the aircraft to fly at speeds of Mach 2.2.

The first NF-104A was delivered on 1 October 1963 and the other two in November to the Aerospace Research Pilot School at Edwards AFB, which was commanded at that time by Colonel Charles E. "Chuck" Yeager.

On 6 December 1963, the first NF-104A set an unofficial world altitude record of 35,966 m (118,860 ft) for aircraft taking off under their own power. Later, the same NF-104A flown by Major R. W. Smith reached an altitude of 36,819 m (120,800 feet).

To reach altitudes above 33,000 m (100,000 ft) a zoom maneuver, in which speed was traded for altitude, was used. At 11,480 m (35,000 ft) the aircraft started accelerating to Mach 1.9 when the rocket motor was ignited and at Mach 2.15 went into a 3.5 G pull-up. The J79 engine was shut down when going through 23,000 m to 26,200 m (70,000 to 80,000 ft), when it reached its temperature limit. The pilot controlled the pitch with the RCS. After the rocket motor shut down the aircraft reached the top of the trajectory and began the descent with speed brakes deployed. The jet engine was usually restarted below 24,600 m (75,000 ft).

On 10 December 1963, the second NF-104A (56-0762), with Chuck Yeager at the controls, went out of control at an altitude of 31,700 m (104,000 ft) and fell in flat spin to 3,350 m (11,000 ft). Yeager managed to eject successfully at that altitude, suffering burns on his face from the rocket motor of his ejection seat. This event is featured in the 1983 "The Right Stuff" movie. An investigation later showed that the crash had been caused by a spin resulting from excessive angle of attack and lack of aircraft response. The excessive angle of attack was not caused by pilot input but by a gyroscopic condition set up by the J79 engine spooling after shut down for the rocket-powered zoom climb phase.

In June 1971 the third NF-104A, flown by Capt. Howard C. Thompson, experienced an in-flight explosion of its rocket motor. Thompson managed to land safely but the aircraft was severely damaged and, since the program was about to end in any case, this aircraft was retired.

NF-104A 56-0756 during the zoom climb phase, with rocket motor ignited. (USAF)

The first NF-104A is currently on display on top of a pylon in front of the USAF Test Pilot School.

F-104G ZELL

At the height of the Cold War one of the main concerns of the USAF command was that if the real war broke out, NATO aircraft in permanent air bases with long concrete runways would be destroyed by Soviet nuclear strikes before they could go into action, making a retaliatory strike impossible. In order to avoid it the ZELL (Zero Length Launch) system was developed. It comprised a special launcher inclined at 20° and jettisonable rocket booster, mounted under the aircraft's lower aft fuselage. These aircraft were to be deployed to shelters remote from permanent bases. Successful trials of the ZELL system were conducted with USAF F-84G and F-100D Super Sabre fighter-bombers in the 1950s.

In 1963 similar trials were conducted at Edwards AFB with German F-104G number DA+102. The aircraft was fitted with a jettisonable Rocketdyne solid fuel rocket booster, originally intended for the Martin TM-61 Matador nuclear cruise missile. The booster was 74 cm in diameter, 4 m long, weighed 1,894 kg and produced 274.4 kN (65,000 lbf) of thrust for 8 seconds. Before launching actual aircraft tests with mockups, called Iron Crosses, made of concrete and steel beams with weight, center of gravity and moment of inertia matched to several external store duplications. After initial tests with the mockups, eight manned launches were made at Edwards with test pilot Ed Brown at the controls. Before the launch the J79 was started and advanced to full afterburner thrust. Hold-back fittings kept the aircraft in position on the launcher until the booster was ignited, causing them to shear and release the aircraft. Once airborne, the landing gear retracted. At booster burnout the aircraft was about 600 m down-range at 120 – 210 meters AGL flying at 250 – 350 knots (463 – 648

The second F-104G ZELL, DB+127 preserved at Luftwaffenmuseum der Bundeswehr Berlin – Gatow. *(Jarosław Dobrzyński)*

Details of the F-104G ZELL rocket booster mount. (Jerzy Dziedziniewicz)

105

km/h) IAS, depending on the weight. The booster and its cradle were then jettisoned and the Starfighter proceeded with its scheduled mission.

In May 1966 the ZELL tests were resumed at Lechfeld air base in Germany with the F-104G number DB+127. Initially the test pilot was again Ed Brown. The first flight took place on 4 May 1966 and lasted 51 minutes. On 5 July 1966 Horst Philipp of *Eprobungsstelle* 61 was the first German pilot to perform a ZELL launch. The system's maintenance and operation was quite a challenge. Most problems were related to ground support equipment to handle the booster/cradle installation, loading and unloading of the aircraft on the launcher and boresighting the booster. Athough the ZELL system proved to be feasible, it did not enter service.

F-104CCV

In the second half of the 1970s studies on active control systems of aerodynamically unstable aircraft (fly-by-wire systems), already implemented in US designs like the F-16 and F-117, began in Germany. The ability to artificially stabilize unstable aircraft configurations was a prerequisite for the design of a new generation of military and commercial aircraft and is still considered to be a key technology area. The technology used for the CCV program was the starting point for the design and development of the flight control system for the Eurofighter.

In order to conduct research it was decided to convert a Starfighter to give the aircraft negative stability characteristics. The F-104G (23+91, later renumbered 98+36) construction number 683D-8100, built by Fokker (ARGE-Nord) in 1963, previously operated by WTD 61 was leased to MBB and modified to become the CCV (Control Configured Vehicle) in 1977. In the first stage of trials ballast was added to the tail section to relocate the centre of gravity. In the second stage in 1980, a complete F-104 tailplane section was then grafted onto the spine on the upper fuselage forward of the wing to increase aircraft's instability. Over the wing fairings were added. Natural stability was replaced by a computer-controlled triple-redundant fly-by-wire system that allowed the aircraft to be made unstable. Twenty percent negative stability was finally achieved within the specified limits of Mach 1.3 and 650 knots (1203 km/h) by the time the trials were successfully concluded. This instability could then be controlled to provide extra agility. The data gathered was vital to the design of the Eurofighter and was also used during the development of the Rockwell/MBB X-31 testbed.

The test program ended on 17 April 1984. The F-104CCV was then struck off charge and transferred to the *Wehrtechnisches* Museum at Koblenz on 6 October 1984.

Front view of the F-104CCV preserved at Wehrtechnisches Museum at Koblenz. (Nikos Livados)

Additional F-104 tailplane installed in the F-104CCV. (Nikos Livados)

F-104G and F-104S technical description

Fuselage

The Starfighter's airframe was of all-metal construction. The main material was duralumin, but the rear fuselage section had stainless steel longerons and was covered with stainless steel and titanium skinning for better heat protection. The fuselage was about 2.5 times longer than the wingspan and housed all the most important aircraft systems and devices. The most forward section of the fuselage was the nose cone made of dielectric material, under which the radar was mounted. On the nose cone the pitot tube was located. Behind the radar was the cockpit. Aft of the cockpit avionics, electric, oxygen systems and the nosewheel well were located and, in the F-104C, F-104G, F-104S CB and some modified F-1014A variants, the M61 Vulcan cannon with ammunition. Further aft the fuel tanks, engine, hydraulic system and main wheel wells were located. Landing gear struts were hydraulically actuated and retracted forward. On the lower aft fuselage behind the main landing gear wells, there was a ventral stabilizing fin (and two smaller trapezium-shaped strakes with leading edge angled by 45° to increase directional stability at speeds above Mach 2.0 in the F-104S). Aft of the fin an arrestor hook was mounted and behind the hook, under the engine, the brake chute container was located. Two hydraulically-actuated airbrakes were mounted on the fuselage sides aft of the wing.

The vertical fin had nearly the same length and area as the wing. A one piece stabilator was mounted atop the fin. That position was necessary for optimum stability around the pitch axis throughout the F-104's wide Mach range.

The F-104 had quite a broad center of gravity range. At lightly loaded landing weight the CG was situated some 50 cm (20 in) aft of the wing leading edge and at heavy take-off weight the CG was located about 15 cm (6 in) forward of the wing leading edge.

Wing

The Starfighter's wings were short, straight, thin, had broad chord, extremely sharp leading edges and pronounced anhedral. Data from supersonic rocket tests revealed that short and thin trapezoidal wings had better aerodynamic features for supersonic flight than swept-back wings with thick chord and long span, which generates higher drag. The effective wing area includes the part of the wing buried in the fuselage, so the wing is more effective than it appears. Location of the stabilator high atop the vertical fin raised the center of pressure on the tail, increasing induced roll effect during side slip. To compensate for this the wings had 10° anhedral. The leading edge had 26° sweepback and the trailing edge had smaller sweep forward. The wing's maximum thickness was 10.66 cm (4.2 in) at the root, the minimum was 4.97 cm (1.96 in) at the tips. In order to improve low speed performance the Starfighter's wing featured leading and trailing edge flaps, converting the thin airfoil into a cambered high lift airfoil for take-off and landing. To delay flow separation at full flap travel and to increase lift, thus reducing the landing speed, the Boundary Layer Control (BLC) was added to the trailing edge flaps. The BLC system used high-pressure bleed air from the engine's compressor blowing through orifices along the flap hinge line. The high-velocity boundary layer air reduced pressure adjacent to the flaps and carried along the outer level of air, causing it to bend through the flap deflection angle.

The wings were attached to the fuselage with five forged fittings. Upper and lower skins were formed from single machined tapered plates. Root and tip forgings formed a torsion box comprising 12 intermediate channels that supported the airfoil contour

Flight controls

The primary flight control system comprised hydraulically actuated ailerons, rudder and stabilator, mounted on the top of the vertical fin. The secondary flight control system comprised electrically actuated leading and trailing edge flaps and hydraulically actuated speed brakes. The primary flight control surfaces were actuated by servos powered by two independent hydraulic systems. The control system continued functioning in case of failure of either of the hydraulic systems. Conventional control cables, torque tubes, quadrants and pushrods transmitted stick and rudder pedal movements to servo input linkages. The input signals were sent to the servos from pilot's control stick and rudder pedals, trim and autopilot systems and stability augmentation system.

Cockpit

The central instrument panel of the F-104G included main flight and navigation instruments, gauges for exhaust temperature, engine air inlet temperature, pitch rate fuel quantity and jet nozzle position.

On the lower panel the radar indicator, hydraulic and engine oil pressure gauges, fuel flow and cabin altitude indicators were located. Left of the radar indicator the armament control panel was situated.

A small panel located forward of the throttle lever contained the engine starter, landing and taxi light and external stores jettison switches. Behind the throttle lever, along the left cockpit wall, radar, autopilot and stability control panels were located. The right front panel contained multiple warning lights, generator switches and fuel quantity indicator test switch. Along the right cockpit wall oxygen control, navigation, bombing control and circuit breakers panel were located. Above, on the right wall, the cockpit opening lever and fresh air scoop were situated.

The canopy was manually opened to the left side. It was locked and unlocked by rotation of a lever mounted in the right fuselage side.

For ejection the hold-down hooks were automatically released simultaneously and two canopy ejection thrusters mounted on the forward bottom of the canopy frame fired. The canopy jettison could be initiated three ways: by pulling the jettison handle on the left side of the cockpit, automatically when the ejection seat was fired or from the exterior by pulling a cable stowed on the port side beneath the windscreen.

Ejection seats

The prototypes, pre-production aircraft and early production F-104As were equipped with downward-firing ejection seats of the Stanley B, Stanley C and Stanley C-1 type due to the limitations of available ejection seat catapults. This allowed for the best ability to clear the aircraft structure, including the vertical fin, at higher speeds and also affected the wind-blast on the pilot. This method of ejection was used successfully at altitude, but was

107

not suitable at low-level, especially in case of take-off and landing emergencies. To increase the pilot's chances of survival during a low-level bail-out the Lockheed C-2 upward-firing seat was introduced in later models and retrofitted to earlier aircraft. As a reminder of the downward-firing seat the ventral cockpit access panel was retained in later versions.

The C-2 could be safely fired at zero altitude and 90 knots indicated airspeed, which proved to be insufficient at extremely low altitudes. Problems with stability and separation of the pilot from the seat often occurred during high-speed ejections. In 1967 in Germany in order to improve the Starfighter's safety record the newly-appointed commander of Luftwaffe, Gen. Johannes Steinhoff, ordered retrofitting of the German Starfighters with British Martin-Baker Mk Q7(A) zero-zero seats. This seat greatly improved pilot's safety in low-level ejections. Italy and Denmark followed suit.

Powerplant
The single-spool axial flow General Electric J79 turbojet engine was designed by General Electric in the USA in the mid-1950s for combat aircraft exceeding twice the speed of sound. The chief designer was Gerhard Neumann, a German propulsion engineer working in the USA. J79 engines were built in several versions and powered such aircraft as Lockheed F-104 Starfighter, Convair B-58 Hustler, North American RA-5 Vigilante, McDonnell F-4 Phantom II and Israeli IAI Kfir.

The J79-GE-11A variant was developed for the export fighter-bomber version of the Starfighter, the F-104G. The engine comprised a 17-stage compressor, accessory drive section, annular combustion chamber, three-stage turbine and afterburner. The exhaust nozzle had variable geometry throughout the operating range of the engine. At idle RPM the nozzle was fully open, at cruise power the nozzle opening was reduced to the smallest diameter and in the afterburner range the nozzle gradually opened. A characteristic feature of the J79 engine was variable geometry of the stator vanes, enabling flight at supersonic speed with minimum risk of compressor stall and flameout. Thanks to these features the J79 operated a bit like a ramjet, with the thrust developed by the engine increasing with approximately the same rate as the aircraft's speed. The engine was rated at 10,000 lbf (45 kN) of static thrust and 70.28kN/7,165 kG/15,800 lbf of thrust with afterburner. The F-104S was powered by an uprated J79-GE-19, developing 11,870 lbf (53 kN) of static thrust and 17,900 lbf (80 kN) with afterburner.

The engine was started by an air starter mounted ahead of the compressor. The starter was driven by compressed air supplied through a hose from a special power cart. The hose connection socket was located in the starboard main wheel bay. Very important for the powerplant installation and aircraft performance was the air inlet arrangement. The F-104 featured fixed geometry inlet scoops with conical ramps protruding ahead of the scoop designed to give the best ram effect at speeds exceeding Mach 1.5. It created a shock wave pattern at supersonic speeds, which slowed the inlet air to lower supersonic speed while increasing the ram pressure at the inlet opening. The normal shock wave inside the duct reduced the flow to subsonic speed at high ram pressure.

During supersonic flight as speed increases the inlet airflow volume increases more rapidly than the engine's air requirements. The Starfighter's inlet area provided adequate flow for subsonic flight, but was oversized for speeds around Mach 2. To prevent the excess air from spilling out of the duct and increasing drag the Starfighter featured secondary airflow system which cooled the engine and improved the exit nozzle efficiency, passing the excess air around the engine. The excess air entered the secondary airflow opening aft of the shock cone and exited via the secondary exit nozzle. This solution made the complicated variable-geometry inlet system, used in other aircraft, unnecessary, eliminating maintenance and reliability problems related to such an arrangement.

When the engine was running on the ground, a low pressure condition existed at the front of the engine and behind the secondary exhaust nozzle. To avoid reverse airflow around the engine, spring-loaded suck-in doors, through which air was drawn into the engine compartment, were installed. The airflow entering through these doors divided – some air moved forward to the front of the engine and some moved aft to exit through the secondary nozzle.

Bleed air from the compressor's 17th stage was used in the Boundary Layer Control System, fuel transfer system, air conditioning and pressurization system, hot air jet rain removal system, for canopy and windshield defogging and defrosting, providing pressure for pilot's anti-G suit and for gun gas purging.

The accessory drive powered two hydraulic pumps, two variable-frequency generators, tachometer generator, engine fuel and oil system pumps.

To remove the engine the aft fuselage section had to be removed and the engine could be easily withdrawn on a rail.

Fuel system
The fuel system consisted of five self-sealing bladder-type internal fuel tanks with total usable capacity of 896 US gallons. These were the forward main tank, forward auxiliary tank, aft center tank and left and right aft tanks. The four fuel boost pumps were located in the main forward tank and fuel was supplied to the engine from that tank. As fuel was burned off, the aft center tank, as well as the auxiliary tank, kept the forward main tank full. The aft center tank transferred its fuel to the forward main tank and was kept full first by the pylon tanks, then by the tip tanks until they were empty. This transfer was automatic, and would continue in the event of electrical failure.

The left and right aft tanks transferred their fuel to the aft center tank through bottom tubes. The top tubes served as vents.

External tanks were mounted on inner underwing pylons and wingtips. Fuel was transferred to the aft center tank from the pylon tanks first and then from the tip tanks. The external tanks could be jettisoned when necessary. For extended range additional fuel tanks could be mounted in the gun compartment, case stowage compartment, and forward of the main fuel tank. The tanks could be refueled either individually, through gravity-flow fillers or from a single point pressure filler, located on the port side of the fuselage aft of the cockpit.

Hydraulic installation
The hydraulic installation comprised two independent systems, powered by two separate engine-driven constant pressure piston-type hydraulic pumps. No. 1 system powered the flight controls and autopilot actuators. No 2 system powered the flight controls, landing gear, nosewheel steering, airbrakes and hydraulic motors of the AC generators. There was also an emergency hydraulic pump driven by a Ram Air Turbine.

The electrical system
The electric system consisted of two batteries, two main engine-driven variable frequency 20 kVA AC generators, a constant frequency 400 Hz AC generator, driven by No 2 hydraulic system, and a ram

air driven constant frequency generator for emergency use. The main generators produced 115 to 200 volt AC power, the voltage and frequency depended on engine RPM. DC power was produced by two 28 V transformer rectifiers.

The Ram Air Turbine driven generator was located on the starboard side of the fuselage, aft of the air intake. When deployed, it drove a 4.5 kW 115 V 400 Hz generator and the emergency hydraulic pump.

Avionics

The avionics equipment was of decisive importance for the Starfighter's value as a combat aircraft. Its lightweight, integrated multipurpose electronic system comprised 7% of the aircraft's empty weight and around 30% of its cost.

The integration of the electronic systems was necessary to meet weight and size limitations, as well as the need for precise basic data in navigation, automatic flight control and fire control computations. The system integration precluded redundant installations. Several sub-systems supplied data to other sub-systems and nearly all of them were interconnected into at least one other sub-system.

There were four main sub-systems:

Communication and Identification sub-system, comprising the UHF Communication Radio, Emergency UHF Radio and IFF (Identification Friend or Foe) transponder.

Navigation and Basic Flight Reference subsystem, comprising Litton LN-3 inertial navigation system, air data computer, Position and Homing Indicator (PHI), Tactical Air Navigation (TACAN), gyro compass and emergency attitude indicator.

Automatic Flight Control System (AFCS) comprised the autopilot, three-axis stability augmentation system and automatic pitch control system.

Fire Control sub-system comprised the North American Search and Ranging Radar with air-to-air and air-to-ground modes, optical director, computing-type sight, infrared tracking sight, missile in-range computer and bombing computer.

Most of the electronic devices were located in a compartment just aft of the cockpit. The systems were individually packed in special containers, called "Jeep Cans" (because they were similar in shape and size to fuel cans carried on military Jeeps). They were installed on a shock-mounted rack with electrical connectors and central cooling air distribution hookups. Each contained a built-in test circuit which permitted rapid determination before flight if the equipment was operating correctly. The whole can could be replaced in case of a malfunction.

Air Data Computer

The air data computer installed in the electronics compartment gathered input of temperature, angle of attack, pitot pressure and static pressure and processed them into electrical signal outputs proportional to air density ratio, altitude, true airspeed, angle of attack, impact and total pressure and supplied this information in the form of analog electrical signals to other systems.

INS

The Litton LN-3 inertial navigation system (INS) provided precision navigation information for all weather strike/bombing missions. It served as a primary vertical reference for attitude information and principal directional reference for heading information. It was a completely independent system, functioning without receiving or emitting any electromagnetic signals that could be detected or jammed by an enemy. The INS supplied position, heading, bearing and attitude signals to the PHI, attitude indicator, autopilot and fire control system.

For flights requiring accurate navigation the system required 10–15 minutes for warm-up and fine alignment, but for alert intercept missions the system could provide necessary attitude and heading information in about 60 seconds. The Litton LN-3 INS was able to guide the aircraft to a target with an accuracy of around 1.8 km over a distance of 800 km.

Canadian CF-104s were initially equipped with the simpler LN-2 INS, which was replaced during service by a more modern one, designated LW-33.

PHI System

The Position and Homing Indicator (PHI) system continuously computed and displayed navigation information. It received data from various sources within the aircraft and translated it into range and

UTILITY HYDRAULIC SYSTEM

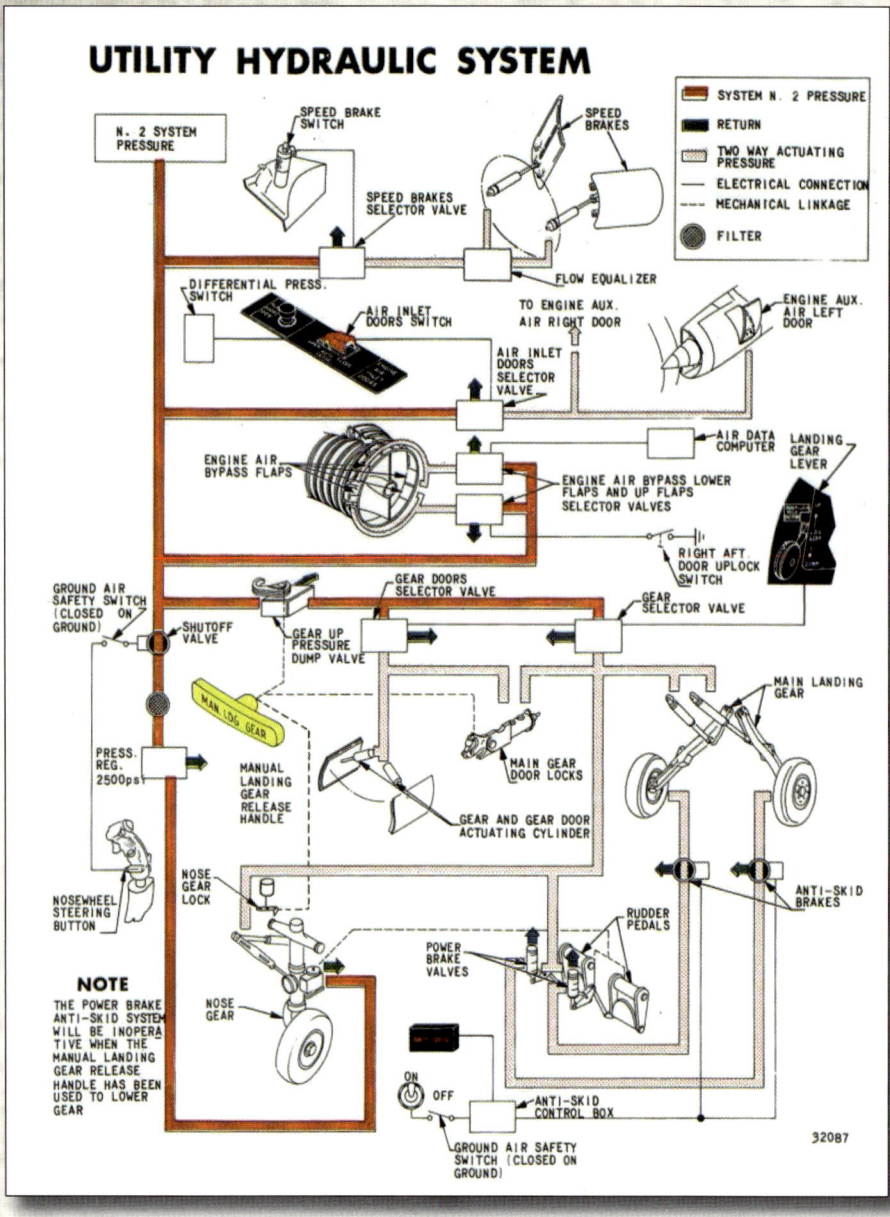

bearing information displayed on the PHI instrument. The system operated in three navigation modes: inertial, dead reckoning and TACAN.

The PHI system facilitated flying the Starfighter, performing most of the navigation work for the pilot. It displayed the aircraft's magnetic and grid heading, station bearing and range to any of 12 selected points within a 1,000 NM radius. The station selector could be pre-set with geographic positions of up to 12 points – targets, destinations, alternate bases, en-route checkpoints etc.

Automatic Flight Control System

The Automatic Flight Control System (AFCS) comprised the stability augmentation, autopilot and automatic pitch control equipment. The AFCS provided the F-104 with automatic stability augmentation about all three axes, autopilot control through ailerons and stabilizer and automatic pitch-up control of the pitch axis. All automatic functions of the flight control system could be overridden by the pilot.

The stability augmentation system provided maximum stability in any flight attitude and maneuver. Rate-sensing gyros detected any sudden change of attitude about the aircraft's three axis and produced electrical signals proportional to the deviation detected, and sent them to proper control surface servo valves which produced the proportional surface adjustment, correcting the attitude.

The autopilot controlled attitude in pitch and roll through aileron and horizontal stabilizer actuator. Various signals sensed or initiated by the autopilot and other electronic equipment were processed by the autopilot part of the AFCS computer to produce pitch and roll command output signals. The system provided heading hold in conjunction with altitude or Mach number hold. The pilot could over-ride the autopilot manually without disengaging it.

The automatic pitch control (APC) was a stall prevention device. Inputs from AOA vanes and pitch rate gyro were processed by computer which, when the aircraft was approaching the stall caused the control stick to shake as a warning for the pilot. If the nose-up attitude was continued until the stall was imminent the computer sent a signal to the stabilator hydraulic servo, which pushed the stick forward and rotated the stabilator down for a nose down attitude. The pitch attitude was visually presented to the pilot on the instrument panel.

Fire control system

The F-104G was equipped with Autonetics NASARR (North American Search and Ranging Radar) F15A-41B. In the air-to-air mode the radar provided search, tracking, lock-on and range information. It was able to detect aerial targets at distances of 45 to 65 km and track them at distances of 20 – 30 km. Lead angles for firing the gun or unguided rockets with breakaway distances were calculated by the armament control computer and displayed on the radar scope. In the air-to-ground mode it could perform ground mapping, contour mapping and terrain avoidance to allow low-level blind penetration, en-route navigation and target identification. The radar was able to detect ground targets at distances of 15 – 25 km, and supplied range, range rate, relative bearing and elevation analog signals to the computer. Using this data along with roll and pitch data from the INS and information from the air data computer, the computer automatically calculated release and firing times and produced visual steering signals enabling the pilot to place the aircraft in firing position.

The F-104S/CI was equipped with FIAR (Italian license production) NASARR F-15G radar, capable of guiding AIM-7 Sparrow semi-active radar homing air-to-air missiles. The Sparrow's guidance equipment occupied the space of the M61A1 cannon. The F-104S/CB had the NASARR R-21G radar and radar altimeter for low-level strike missions.

The F-104S/ASA featured a new radar system, the FIAR R-21G/M1 Setter, with look-down/shoot-down capability, Doppler system of selection of moving targets against the ground and higher jamming resistance. The radar's antenna, transmitter and receiver were mounted under the nose cone while the computer, power supply and electronic control amplifier were installed in the electronics compartment. The radar's control panel was on the pilot's left console and the indicator was in the lower centre of the forward instrument panel.

The integrated sighting system comprised the optical director (computing type) sight and an infrared tracking sight. The optical and infrared sight, servo amplifier and gun sight camera were mounted forward of the main instrument panel. The sight combining glass was installed in front of the centre windshield panel. When attacking an aerial target with the cannon the NASARR armament control computer provided lead-angle information to the director sight for positioning the reticle on the combining glass. The pilot positioned the airplane to have the target centered in the reticle and opened fire when the target was in range, which was indicated by the range cursor. The infrared tracking sight projected a symbol of the target on the combining glass so that visual contact with the airborne target was not necessary.

The missile in-range computer supplied data for the radar and sight for attack with the Sidewinder missiles, basing on range and range rate inputs from NASARR. The computer automatically determined launch range and G limits within which the missile could be effectively fired.

When attacking ground targets the pilot could cage the reticle in fixed position and set it manually to various lowered positions, depending on the weapon and mode of attack, to compensate for the vertical speed component imparted to the weapon at its release.

Some F-104Gs were equipped with a bomb computer, integrated with the rest of the armament system, which provided capability for high-level, low-level and blind bombing and using the bomb tossing technique as well. The computer was installed in the electronics compartment and its control panel was situated on the pilot's right console. Some airplanes could be also equipped with LABS (Low Altitude Bombing System) dual timer supplying information for pre-planned launch-and-escape nuclear bomb delivery maneuvers.

Armament
M61 Vulcan cannon

The only fixed armament of the F-104 was a single M61A1 Vulcan cannon. It was mounted in the following versions: F-104C, F-104G, F-104S/CB and some modified F-104As. The F-104C was the first aircraft to be equipped with this weapon. The M61A1 is a six-barrel, 20-mm caliber Gatling-type cannon. The rate of fire was up to 6,000 rounds per minute.

The gun was located in the forward left side of the aircraft's lower fuselage. The ammunition magazine, containing 725 rounds, was located above the cannon, behind the electronics compartment. The cannon was driven electrically by 208 volt AC power and the rounds were fired electrically. Rounds were electronically counted and the number of remaining rounds was displayed on the cockpit armament control panel. Empty cases were stowed in a compartment below the cannon and links were jettisoned. For strike missions the cannon could be replaced by a 462 liter fuel tank and its port faired over.

The F-104G could carry up to 1,814 kg of external stores on seven weapons pylons. On the wingtips, launch rails for the AIM-9B Sidewinder (from early 1980s also the AIM-9L) air-to-air infra-red homing missiles or fuel tanks could be carried. A twin-rail launcher for two Sidewinder missiles could be carried on the fuselage centerline station. On four underwing pylons fuel tanks (on inboard pylons) or various types of armament could be carried – Mk 81, Mk 82 or Mk 83 or Mk 117 bombs, BLU1/B napalm canisters, MLU-10/A or Hunting BL755 cluster bombs or LAU-51 rocket launchers, each containing nineteen 70 mm unguided rockets. The F-104Gs operated by the German Marineflieger also carried AS.30 and later AS.34 Kormoran 1 anti-shipping missiles.

On the centerline fuselage station the F-104G could carry the 907-kg Mk 43 nuclear bomb, designed specially for it. This weapon was quickly replaced by the Mk 57 bomb and finally the B61 thermonuclear bomb. Canadian BDU-8 or American SUU-21 practice bombs dispensers were also carried.

The F-104S/CB had nine weapon pylons – two more were added under the fuselage on so-called BL22 stations, although they were rather rarely used. Theoretically the F-104S/CB could carry up to 3,400 kg of external stores. The F-104S/CI could in theory carry two AIM-7 Sparrow and four AIM-9 Sidewinder missiles, but in practice due to the necessity to carry fuel tanks on inboard wing pylons the weapons load was reduced to two Sidewinders and two Sparrows. During QRA duty the aircraft usually flew with only one Sidewinder and one Sparrow missile, two inboard and two wingtip fuel tanks.

Italian F-104S armed with four AIM-9 and two AIM-7 Sparrow missiles. (Aldo Bidini)

Specifications

XF-104

Wingspan	6.69 m (21.9 ft)
Length	14.99 m (49.17 ft)
Height	4.11 m (13.49 ft)
Empty weight	5,216 kg (11,500 lb)
Maximum take-off weight	7,575 kg (16,700 lb)
Service ceiling	15,400 m (50,500 ft)
Maximum speed	Mach 1.74
Maximum range with external tanks	1,480 km (799 NM)
Powerplant	Initially Wright XJ65-W-6 rated at 34.7 kN (7,800 lbf) dry thrust, later Wright J65-W-7 rated at 45.8 kN (10,300 lbf) with afterburner
Armament	One 20-mm M61 Vulcan cannon (only the second prototype)

F-104A

Wingspan	6.69 m (21.9 ft)
Length	16.69 m (54.77 ft)
Wing area	18.21 m² (196.1 sq.ft)
Height	4.11 m (13.49 ft)
Empty weight	6,071 kg (13,384 lb)
Combat weight	8,159 kg (17,988 lb)
Maximum take-off weight	11,721 kg (25,840 kb)
Service ceiling	19,750 m (64,795 ft)
Rate of climb	60,395 ft/min
Maximum speed	1,669 km/h (901 kt) at 15,240 m (50,000 ft)
Fuel	Normal 3,395 l (897 USgal) Maximum 6,158 l (1,627 USgal)
Range	1,175 km (730 mi)
Maximum range with external tanks	2,253 km (1,400 mi)
Powerplant	GE J79-GE-3B rated at 42.7 kN (9,600 lbf) dry thrust and 65.8 kN (14,800 lbf) with afterburner
Armament	two AIM-9B Sidewinder air-to-air missiles

F-104B

Wingspan	6.69 m (21.9 ft)
Length	16.69 m (54.77 ft)
Wing area	18.21 m² (196.1 sq.ft)
Height	4.11 m (13.49 ft)
Empty weight	6,727 kg (13,727 lb)
Maximum take-off weight	11,300 kg (8,080 kg)
Service ceiling	19,750 m (64,500 ft)
Maximum speed	1,843 km/h at 19,812 m (65,000 ft)
Fuel	Normal 2,846 l (897 USgal) Maximum 5,609 l (1,482 USgal)
Range	740 km (460 mi)
Maximum range with external tanks	1,971 km (1,224 mi)
Powerplant	GE J79-GE-3B rated at 42.7 kN (9,600 lbf) dry thrust and 65.8 kN (14,800 lbf) with afterburner
Armament	two AIM-9B Sidewinder air-to-air missiles

F-104C

Wingspan	6.69 m (21.9 ft)
Length	16.69 m (54.77 ft)
Wing area	18.21 m² (196.1 sq.ft)
Height	4.11 m (13.49 ft)
Empty weight	5,788 kg (12,760 lb)
Maximum take-off weight	12,634 kg (12,634 lb)
Service ceiling	17,678 m (58,000 ft)
Maximum speed	1,851 km/h (1,000 kt) at 15,240 m (50,000 ft)
Fuel	Normal 3,395 l (897 USgal) Maximum 6,158 l (1,627 USgal)
Range	1,368 km (850 mi)
Maximum range with external tanks	2,414 km (1,500 mi)
Powerplant	GE J79-GE-7 rated at 44.48 kN (10,000 lbf) dry thrust and 70.3 kN (15,800 lbf) with afterburner
Armament	M61A1 Vulcan 20-mm cannon, four AIM-9B Sidewinder air-to-air missiles or 907 kg (2,000 lb) of other ordnance

F-104G

Wingspan	6.69 m (21.9 ft)
Length	16.69 m (54.77 ft)
Wing area	18.21 m² (196.1 sq.ft)
Height	4.11 m (13.49 ft)
Empty weight	6,348 kg (13,996 lb)
Combat weight	9,362 kg (20,640 lb)
Maximum take-off weight	13,172 kg (9,362 kg)
Wing loading	105 lb/ft² (514 kg/m²)
Service ceiling	15,240 m (50,000 ft)
Maximum speed	2,137 km/h (1,154 kt) at 10,668 m (35,000 ft)
Rate of climb	244 m/s (48,000 ft/min)
Fuel	Normal 3,395 l (897 USgal) Maximum 6,158 l (1,627 USgal)
Range	1,738 km (1,080 mi)
Maximum range with external tanks	2,623 km (1,630 mi)
Powerplant	GE J79-GE-11A rated at 44.5 kN (10,000 lbf) dry thrust and 70.3 kN (15,800 lbf) with afterburner German aircraft after 1969: J79-MTU-J1K rated at 46.5 kN (10,453 lbf) dry thrust and 70.9 kN (15,938 lbf) with afterburner
Armament	M61A1 Vulcan 20-mm cannon with 725 rounds, four AIM-9B Sidewinder air-to-air missiles or 1,814 kg (4,000 lb) of other ordnance

F-104S

Wingspan	6.69 m (21.9 ft)
Length	16.69 m (54.77 ft)
Wing area	18.21 m² (196.1 sq.ft)
Height	4.11 m (13.49 ft)
Empty weight	6,760 kg (14,900 lb)
Maximum take-off weight	14,060 kg (31,000 lb)
Wing loading	680 kg/m²

Service ceiling	17,680 m (58,000 ft)
Rate of climb	277 m/s (54,850 ft/min)
Maximum speed	2,330 km/h at 11,000 m (36,000 ft)
Fuel	Normal 3,395 l (897 USgal) Maximum 6,158 l (1,627 USgal)
Range	1,250 km (776 mi)
Maximum range with external tanks	2,920 km (1,814 mi)
Powerplant	GE J79-GE-19 rated at 52.8 kN (11,870 lbf) dry thrust and 79.6 kN (17,900 lbf) with afterburner
Armament	F-104S/CB: M61A1 Vulcan 20 mm cannon with 725 rounds and up to 2380 kg of other ordnance F-104S CI: two AIM-7 Sparrow and up to four AIM-9B Sidewinder air-to-air missiles F-104S ASA/M: two AIM-7 Sparrow or Aspide and up to four AIM-9L Sidewinder air-to-air missiles

Flying the F-104

The F-104 Starfighter was a highly demanding aircraft. Due to the small wing area the wing loading was very high (and even higher when carrying external stores), which required sufficient airspeed to be maintained at all times. The lift-off speed was around 352 km/h and the pilot had to raise the landing gear within two seconds to avoid exceeding the limit speed of 481 km/h. Landing was also at high speed. When entering the circuit, the downwind leg was flown at around 389 km/h with "land" flap selected and then a long flat final approach was typically flown at speeds around 333 km/h, depending on the weight of fuel remaining. High engine power had to be maintained on the final approach to provide adequate airflow for the BLC system; consequently pilots were instructed not to cut the throttle until the aircraft was actually on the ground. The drag chute was almost always used to shorten the landing roll. The F-104 with its single engine lacked any safety margin in the case of an engine failure, and without thrust had a poor glide ratio. At extremely high angles of attack the F-104 had tendency to "pitch-up" (stall) and enter a spin, which in most cases was impossible to recover from. To reduce the risk the high angle of attack area of flight was protected by the Automatic Pitch Control system, warning the pilot of an approaching stall by shaking the control stick, and if this was ignored a stick pusher system would pitch the aircraft's nose down to a safer angle of attack. Despite flight manual warnings against this practice this was often overridden by the pilots and became the cause of several crashes.

The Starfighter was the first combat aircraft capable of sustained Mach 2 flight, and its speed and climb performance remain impressive even by modern standards. At around Mach 2 a "slow" light illuminated on the instrument panel to indicate that the engine compressor was nearing its limiting temperature and the pilot should throttle back. It had a great thrust margin, which enabled it to make combat maneuvers at Mach 2. Thanks to the "zoom climb", in which speed was traded for altitude, it could attain an altitude in excess of 30,500 m (100,000 ft). The zoom maneuver was initiated at about 12,000m (36,000 ft) and speed of Mach 2. Having attained that speed the pilot pulled up and the plane entered a 45-degree climb along a ballistic trajectory. About 15,000 m (45,000 ft) of additional altitude could be attained that way. When the Starfighter was going over the top at about 24,300 m (80,000 ft) the Mach number was about 0.4 and the G load was nearing zero. During the descent the speed and load factor built up as the initial altitude was approached.

The F-104 was designed for optimum performance at Mach 1.4. If used appropriately, with high-speed surprise attacks and good use of its exceptional thrust-to-weight ratio, it could be a formidable air superiority fighter and, being exceptionally stable at high speed (600+ kts) at very low level, was also a formidable tactical nuclear strike aircraft. Due to the high speeds required for maneuvering the Starfighter's turn radius was large, so it was not suitable for dogfighting with slower but more agile aircraft.

An F-104S ASA-M takes off at sunset. (AMI)

F-104 Production

USA

F-104
Prototype single seat interceptor fighter, produced 1954, Lockheed Burbank, California (LCC)
No arrestor hook, no stabilizing fin, nose wheel gear retracts rearwards, downward firing ejection seat
engine: Wright J65-B-3, no afterburner, later engine: Wright J65-W-7, 4750 kp / 45.4 kN / 10.200 lbs thrust with afterburner.

Serial numbers	Construction numbers	Prodution	
53-7786, 53-7787	083-1001, 1002	2	Total: 2

YF-104A
Similar to XF-104, lengthened fuselage, engine upgrade. Later upgraded to F-104A standard, produced 1955–1956, Lockheed Burbank, California (LCC).
Engine: J79-GE-3A, 6710 kp / 65.8 kN / 14.800 lb thrust with afterburner, diffuser engine inlet cone, BLC (Boundary Layer Control), later modified with stabilizing fin, downward firing ejection seat, no arrestor hook, nose wheel gear retracts forward.

Serial numbers	Construction numbers	Production	
55-2955 – 55-2971	183-1001 – 1017	17	Total: 17

F-104A (company designation Model 183-92-02).
Similar to YF-104A, engine upgrade, ventral fin, equipment upgrades, produced 1956–1958, Lockheed Burbank, Lockheed Burbank, California (LCC).

Serial numbers	Construction numbers	Prodution	
56-730 – 56-882	183-1018 – 1170	153	Total: 153

RF-104A – 1954, reconnaissance version of F-104A, 18 cancelled (Model 383-93-04).

TF-104A – Trainer version of F-104A, cancelled in favor of F-104B.

F-104B
Developed from F-104A, 2-seater trainer, larger tail, produced 1956–1958, Lockheed Burbank, California (LCC).

Serial numbers	Construction numbers	Production	
56-3719 – 56-3724	283-5000 – 5005		
57-1294 – 57-1313	283-5006 – 5025	26	Total: 26

F-104C
Follow-on version from F-104A, tactical strike version, engine upgrade, produced 1958–1959, Lockheed Burbank, California (LCC). 363 additional airframes cancelled.

Serial numbers	Construction numbers	Production	
56-883 – 56-938	383-1171 – 1226		
57-910 – 57-930	383-1227 – 1247	77	Total: 77

F-104D
Developed from F-104C, 2-seater trainer, produced 1958–1959, Lockheed Burbank, California (LCC).
83 additional airframes cancelled.

Serial numbers	Construction numbers	Production	
57-1314 – 57-1334	483-5026 – 5046	21	Total: 21

F-104DJ
Similar to F-104D, version for Japan, components built by Lockheed, assembled by Mitsubishi, produced 1962–1964, Lockheed Burbank, California (LCC).

Serial numbers	Construction numbers	Production	
JASDF 16-5001 – 46-5020	583B-5401 – 5420	20	Total: 20

F-104F
Similar to F-104D, version for West Germany, produced 1959–1960, Lockheed Burbank, California (LCC).

Serial numbers	Construction numbers	Production	
59-4994 – 59-5023	483-5047 – 5076	30	Total: 30

CF-104D
Similar to F-104D, RCAF designation, version for Canada, produced 1961, Lockheed Burbank, California (LCC).

Serial numbers	Construction numbers	Production	
RCAF 12631 – 12668	583A-5301 – 5338	38	Total: 38

F-104G
As F-104C, engine upgrade, various improvements, USAF serial number, all delivered to foreign users under MAP, produced 1960–1962, Lockheed Burbank, California (LCC).

Serial numbers	Construction numbers	Production	
61-2601 – 61-2623	683C-4001 – 4023	23	
62-12214 – 62-12231	683C-4067 – 4084	18	
63-13274 – Belgium, pattern aircraft, KH+101	683-9001, BAF	1	
MM6501 Italy – pattern airframe	683-6501 AMI	1	
Germany – DA+101-DA+121, KF+101-KF+126 – 30 operated with US with 63-13230 – 63-13259	683-2001 – 2050		
Germany – KF+127-KF+172 - 9 operated with US with 63-13260, 63-13262 – 63-13268, 67-14887	683-2052 – 2097	96	Total: 139

RF-104G
As F-104G, reconnaissance version, all delivered to foreign users under MAP, produced 1962 – 1963, Lockheed Burbank, California (LCC).

Lockheed built 40 RF-104G, intended to be unarmed recce-planes. Only 24 were delivered in the RF-104G modification. Some of these, including the 16 Norwegian planes, were deivered in F-104G configuration, fully armed.
ROCAF received 8 RF-104G from this lot.

Serial numbers	Construction numbers	Production	
61-2624 / 61-2633	683C-4024 to 4033		
62-12232 / 62-12261	mixed 683C-4034 to 4066	40	Total: 40

TF-104G
As F-104G, 2-seater trainer. USAF serial number, all delivered to foreign users under MAP, produced 1962–1966, Lockheed Burbank, California (LCC).

Serial numbers	Construction numbers	Production	
61-3025 – 61-3030	583C-5501 – 5506		
61-3031 – 61-3084	mixed 583D-5701 to 5755		
62-12262 – 62-12279	583C-5507 – 5524		
63-8452 – 63-8469	mixed 583D-5756 to 5779		
63-12681 – 63-12684	583C-5525 – 5528		
63-12685 – 63-12696	mixed 583D-5767 to 5785 (12 for Italy)		
64-15104 – 64-15106	583D-5786 – 5788		
65-9415	583C-5529		
66-13622 – 66-13631	583F-5933 – 5942	126	
N104L (civil reg.) to the Netherlands as D-5702	583D-5702	1	
Belgium FC04 – FC12	583G-5101 – 5109	9	
Italy MM54250 – MM54261	583H-5201 – 5212 – assembled by FIAT	12	
Netherlands D-5801 – 5817	583E-5801 – 5817	17	
Germany KF+201 – KF+232	583F-5901 / 5932	32	
Germany (KF233 – KF243)	583F-5933 / 5942	10	
Germany KE+201 – KE+223	583F-5943 – 5965 – assembled by Messerschmitt	23	Total: 220

RTF-104G1 – proposed reconnaissance version for Luftwaffe, cancelled.

F-104J
As F-104G, version for Japan, produced 1961 Lockheed Burbank, California (LCC).

Serial numbers	Construction numbers	Production	
JASDF 26-8501/26-8503; initially coded 16-8501/16-8503	683B-3001 / 3003	3	Total: 3

F-104N
As F-104G, version for NASA as chase aircraft, 8 other F-104's also converted for NASA duties, produced 1963 Lockheed Burbank, California (LCC).

Serial numbers	Construction numbers	Production	
NASA 811, 812, 813	683C-4045, 4053, 4058	3	Total: 3

Foreign built.

Belgium: F-104G
License built version of the F-104G, produced Societe Anonyme Belge de Constructions Aeronautiques (SABCA), Gosselies, Belgium.

Serial numbers	Construction numbers	Production	
Germany KH+102 – KH+188 - 4 operated by USAF with serial numbers: 63-13275 – 63-13278	mixed 9002 to 9189	87	
Belgium FX1 – FX100	mixed 9016 to 9176	100	
Belgium FX27, duplicated serial number due to loss	9082	1	Total: 188

Canada:

CF-104
License built version of the F-104A (mod G version) 56-0770, converted as prototype with RCAF s/n: 12700, later 104700. Reserialled as 104701 through 104900 from 2 June 1970. Produced 1961–1963 Canadair Ltd., Cartierville, Montreal, Quebec, Canada.

Serial numbers	Construction numbers	Production	
RCAF 12701 / 12900	1001 / 1200	200	

F-104G
License built version of the F-104G. All delivered to foreign users under MAP, production 1963–1964 Canadair Ltd., Cartierville, Montreal, Quebec, Canada.

Serial numbers	Construction numbers	Production	
62-12302 / 62-12349	6001 / 6048		
62-12697 / 62-12734	6049 / 6086		
63-13638 / 63-13647	6087 / 6096		
64-17752 / 64-17795	6097 / 6140	140	Total: 340

Italy:

F-104G
License built version of the F-104G. Fiat Aircraft Group became Aeritalia in 1969, then Alenia Aeronautica in 1990, production by FIAT, Turin, Italy.

Serial numbers	Construction numbers	Production	
For Italy: MM6502 to MM6660 with gaps	6502 to 6660	105	
For The Netherlands: D-6652 to D-6700 with gaps	6652 to 6700	25	
For Germany: KC+101 to KC+115 with gaps	6600 to 6620	15	

RF-104G
License built version of the RF-104G, production FIAT, Turin, Italy.

Serial numbers	Construction numbers	Production	
For Italy: MM6631 to MM6660 with gaps	6631 to 6660	20	
For Germany: KC+116-KC+150	mixed 6621 to 6693	35	

F-104S
More powerful version of the Starfighter with the new J79-GE-19 engine.

Serial numbers	Construction numbers	Production	
Italy: MM6701 – MM6850	783-1001 / 1150		
Italy: MM6869 – MM6881	783-1169 / 1181		
Italy: MM6886, MM6887	783-1186, 1187		
Italy: MM6890	783-1190		
Italy: MM6907 – MM6946	783-1207 / 1246	206	
Turkey: 6851 / 6868	783-1151 / 1168		
Turkey: 6882 / 6885	783-1182 / 1185		
Turkey: 6888, 6889	783-1188, 1189		
Turkey: 6891 / 6906	783-1191 / 1206	40	Total: 445

Japan:

F-104J
License built version of the F-104G, production 1962–1967, Mitsubishi Heavy Industries Ltd., Nagoya, Japan.

Serial numbers	Construction numbers	Production	
JASDF 26-8504 / 26-8507	683B-3004 / 3007		
JASDF 36-8508 / 36-8563	683B-3008 / 3063		
JASDF 46-8564 / 46-8658	683B-3064 / 3158		
JASDF 56-8659 / 56-8680	683B-3159 / 3180		
JASDF 76-8681 / 76-8710	683B-3181 / 3210	207	Total: 207

Netherlands:

F-104G
License built version of the F-104G, production by Fokker Aircraft Co., Amsterdam, The Netherlands.

Serial numbers	Construction numbers	Production	
For The Netherlands – D-8013 to D-8343 with gaps	8013 to 8343	77	
For Germany: KG+101 to KG+450 with gaps - 12 operated in US with serial number: 63-13229, 63-13261, 63-13269 – 63-13273, 63-13690, 63-13691, 65-12746, 65-12749 – 64-12754, 67-14893	8101 to 8350	154	

RF-104G
License built version of the RF-104G. Production by Fokker Aircraft Co., Amsterdam, The Netherlands.

Serial numbers	Construction numbers	Production	
The Netherlands: D-8101 to D-8119 with gaps	8101 to 8119	18	
Germany: KG+185 to KG+376 with gaps - 4 operated in US with serial number: 67-14890 – 67-14892, 67-22517	8085 to 8276	101	Total: 350

Germany:

F-104G
License built version of the F-104G. Production by Messerschmitt-Bölkow GmbH, Augsburg, West Germany. Manufacturer became MBB in 1969.

Serial numbers	Construction numbers	Production	
Germany: KE+301 – KE+510 - 10 operated in US with 65-12745, 65-12747, 65-12748, 66-13524 – 66-13526, 67-14885, 67-14886, 67-14888, 67-14889	7001 – 7210	210	

Messerschmitt-Bölkow-Blohm (MBB), Augsburg, West Germany.

Serial numbers	Construction numbers	Production	
Germany: 26+41 – 26+54	7301 – 7314		
Germany: 26+55 – 26+90	7401 / 7436	50	Total: 260

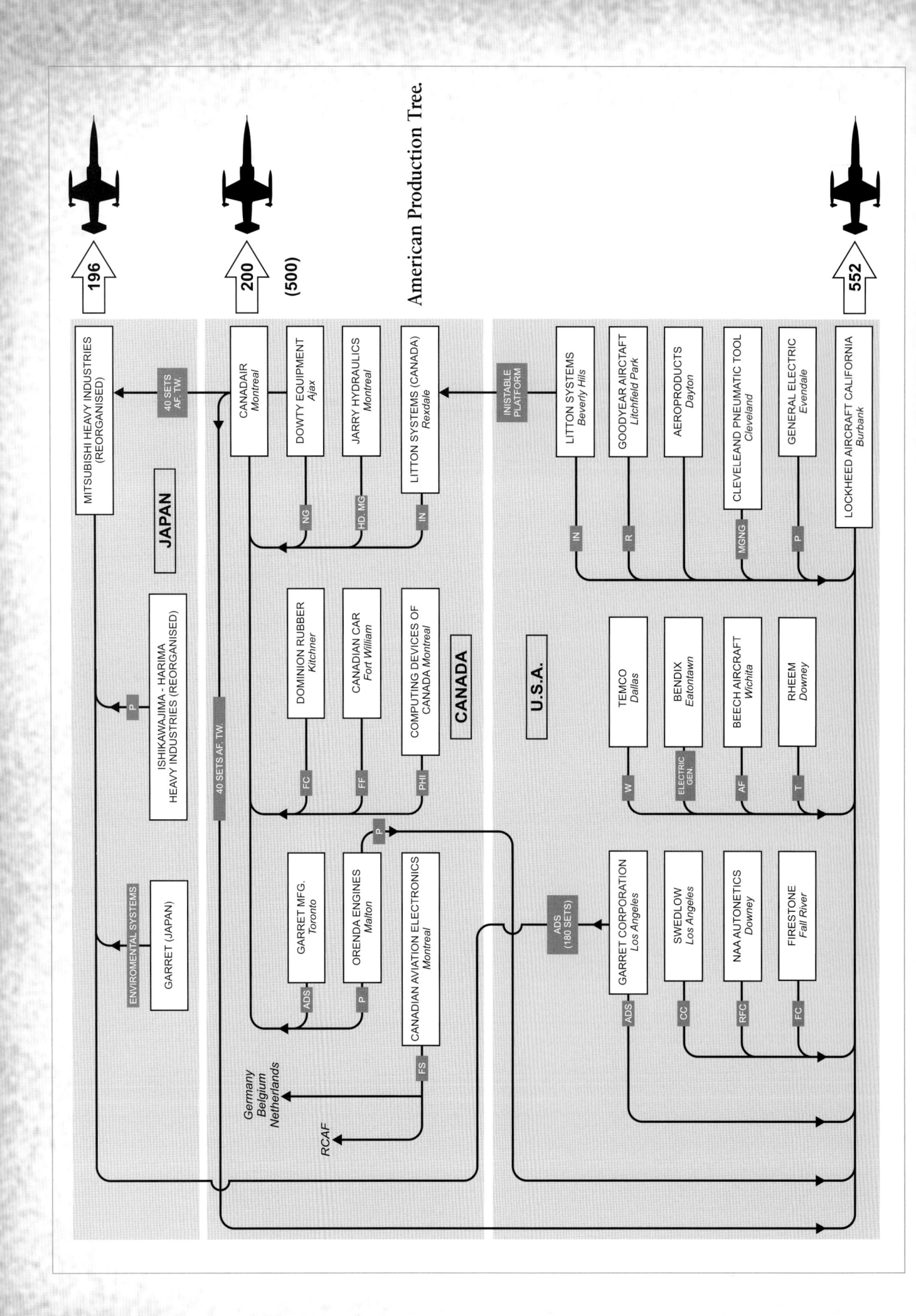

American Production Tree.

JAPAN

→ 196 MITSUBISHI HEAVY INDUSTRIES (REORGANISED) ← 40 SETS AF. TW.

ISHIKAWAJIMA - HARIMA HEAVY INDUSTRIES (REORGANISED) —P→

GARRET (JAPAN) ← ENVIRONMENTAL SYSTEMS

CANADA

→ 200 (500) CANADAIR Montreal
- DOWTY EQUIPMENT Ajax — NG
- JARRY HYDRAULICS Montreal — HD, MG
- LITTON SYSTEMS (CANADA) Rexdale — IN ← INSTABLE PLATFORM

40 SETS AF. TW.

- DOMINION RUBBER Kitchner — FC
- CANADIAN CAR Fort William — FF
- COMPUTING DEVICES OF CANADA Montreal — PHI

- GARRET MFG. Toronto — ADS
- ORENDA ENGINES Malton — P
- CANADIAN AVIATION ELECTRONICS Montreal — FS

→ Germany, Belgium, Netherlands
→ RCAF

U.S.A.

→ 552 LOCKHEED AIRCRAFT CALIFORNIA Burbank
- LITTON SYSTEMS Beverly Hls — IN
- GOODYEAR AIRCRAFT Litchfield Park — R
- AEROPRODUCTS Dayton
- CLEVELEAND PNEUMATIC TOOL Cleveland — MGNG
- GENERAL ELECTRIC Evendale — P

- TEMCO Dallas — W
- BENDIX Eatontawn — ELECTRIC GEN.
- BEECH AIRCRAFT Wichita — AF
- RHEEM Downey — T

ADS (180 SETS)

- GARRET CORPORATION Los Angeles — ADS
- SWEDLOW Los Angeles — CC
- NAA AUTONETICS Downey — RFC
- FIRESTONE Fall River — FC

120

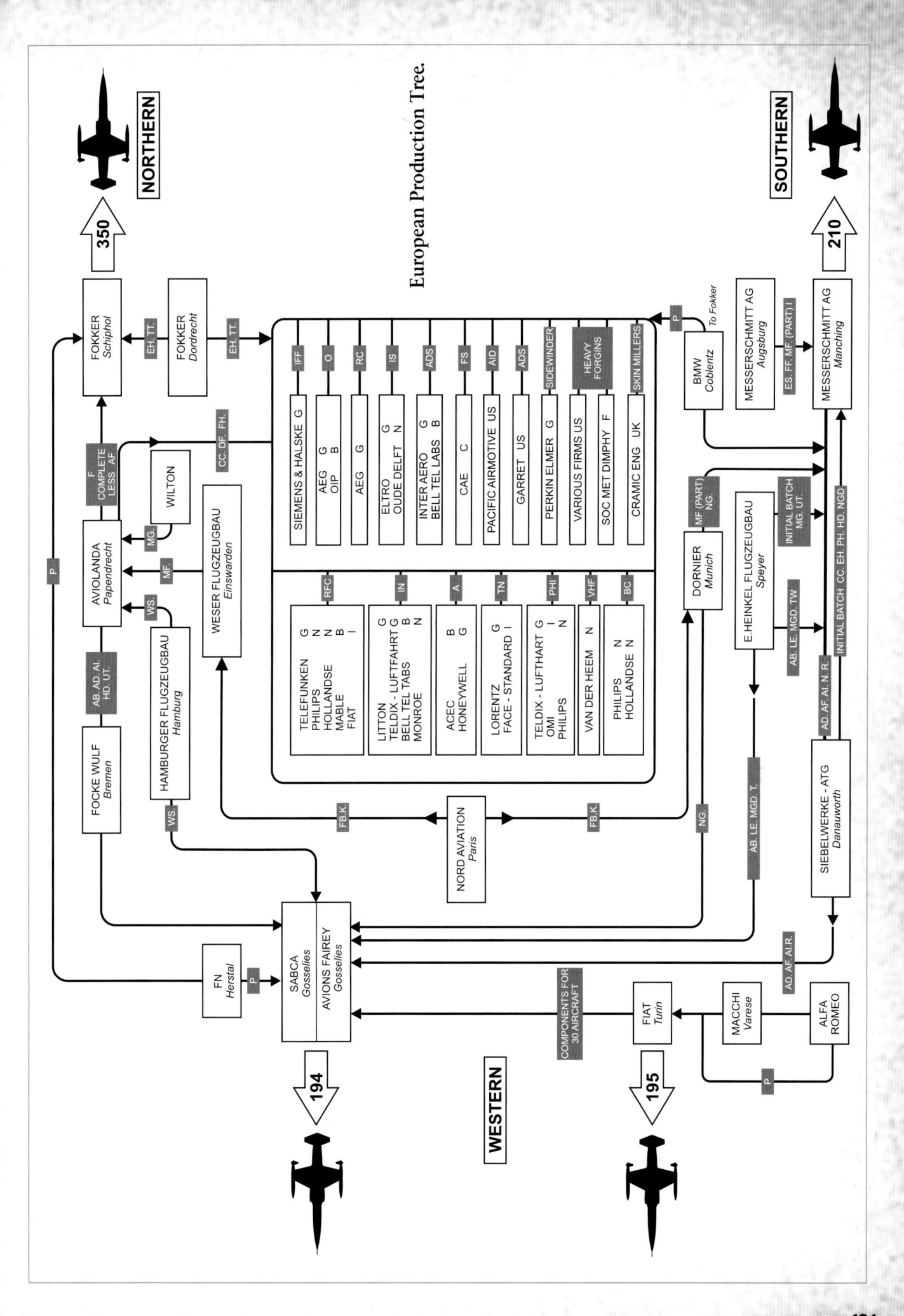

European Production Tree

NORTHERN → 350

SOUTHERN → 210

WESTERN → 194, 195

Northern group
- FOKKER *Schiphol*
- FOKKER *Dordrecht*
- AVIOLANDA *Papendrecht*
- WILTON
- FOCKE WULF *Bremen*
- HAMBURGER FLUGZEUGBAU *Hamburg*
- WESER FLUGZEUGBAU *Einswarden*

Central suppliers (upper block)
Code	Supplier	Country
IFF	SIEMENS & HALSKE	G
O	AEG / OIP	G / B
RC	AEG	G
IS	ELTRO / OUDE DELFT	G / N
ADS	INTER AERO / BELL TEL LABS	G / B
FS	PACIFIC AIRMOTIVE	US
AID	CAE	C
ADS	GARRET	US
SIDEWINDER	PERKIN ELMER	US
HEAVY FORGINS	VARIOUS FIRMS	
	SOC MET DIMPHY	F
SKIN MILLERS	CRAMIC ENG	UK

Central suppliers (lower block)
Code	Supplier	Country
RFC	TELEFUNKEN / PHILIPS / HOLLANDSE / MABLE / FIAT	G / N / B / I
IN	LITTON / TELDIX - LUFTFAHRT / BELL TEL TABS / MONROE	G / B / N
A	ACEC / HONEYWELL	B / G
TN	LORENTZ / FACE - STANDARD	I
PHI	TELDIX - LUFTHART / OMI / PHILIPS	G / I / N
VHF	VAN DER HEEM	N
BC	PHILIPS / HOLLANDSE	N

Southern group
- BMW *Coblentz* → *To Fokker*
- MESSERSCHMITT AG *Augsburg*
- MESSERSCHMITT AG *Manching*
- DORNIER *Munich*
- E. HEINKEL FLUGZEUGBAU *Speyer*
- SIEBELWERKE - ATG *Danauworth*

Western group
- NORD AVIATION *Paris*
- FN *Herstal*
- SABCA *Gosselies*
- AVIONS FAIREY *Gosselies*
- FIAT *Turin*
- MACCHI *Varese*
- ALFA ROMEO

Components for 30 aircraft

121

In Detail
General View

Above: F-104S Starfighter taxis at Pratica di Mare AB during air show.
Right: F-104S "Black Beauty" of 4° Stormo in special paint scheme.
Botom: The mighty F-104 Starfighter. In this case in a TF version. In December 2003 the 20th Gruppo of the Italian Air Force painted this TF-104G with the lion's head, symbol of the unit. The occasion was the 40 years of service of the "Spillone", "Hatpin" in Italian with the Italian Air Force.
(All photos Ludovic Mac Leod)

F-104S Starfighter (MM6930) c/n 783-1230) 10° Gruppo in special red and white colours with the Ferrari badge on the tail and '999' markings to promote the Ducati motorcycle. (Ludovic Mac Leod)

Right: F-104G ZELL, DB+127 preserved at Luftwaffenmuseum der Bundeswehr Berlin – Gatow. (Grzegorz Karnas)

Two photos of F-104S Starfighters in special paint scheme at Pratica di Mare AB. (Ludovic Mac Leod)

F-104S Starfighters at Pratica di Mare AB. (Both photos Ludovic Mac Leod)

Fuselage

Lockheed F-104G Starfighter on display at the Luftwaffenmuseum *in Berlin-Gatow.*

Lockheed F-104G 20+37 displayed inside the Luftwaffenmuseum der Bundeswehr *Berlin-Gatow. (Both Dariusz Karnas)*

Above & left: TF-104 and F-104G Starfighter on display at the Luftwaffenmuseum in Berlin-Gatow. (Dariusz Karnas)

F-104S Starfighter at Pratica di Mare AB. Port side of the fuselage is shown. (Ludovic Mac Leod)

127

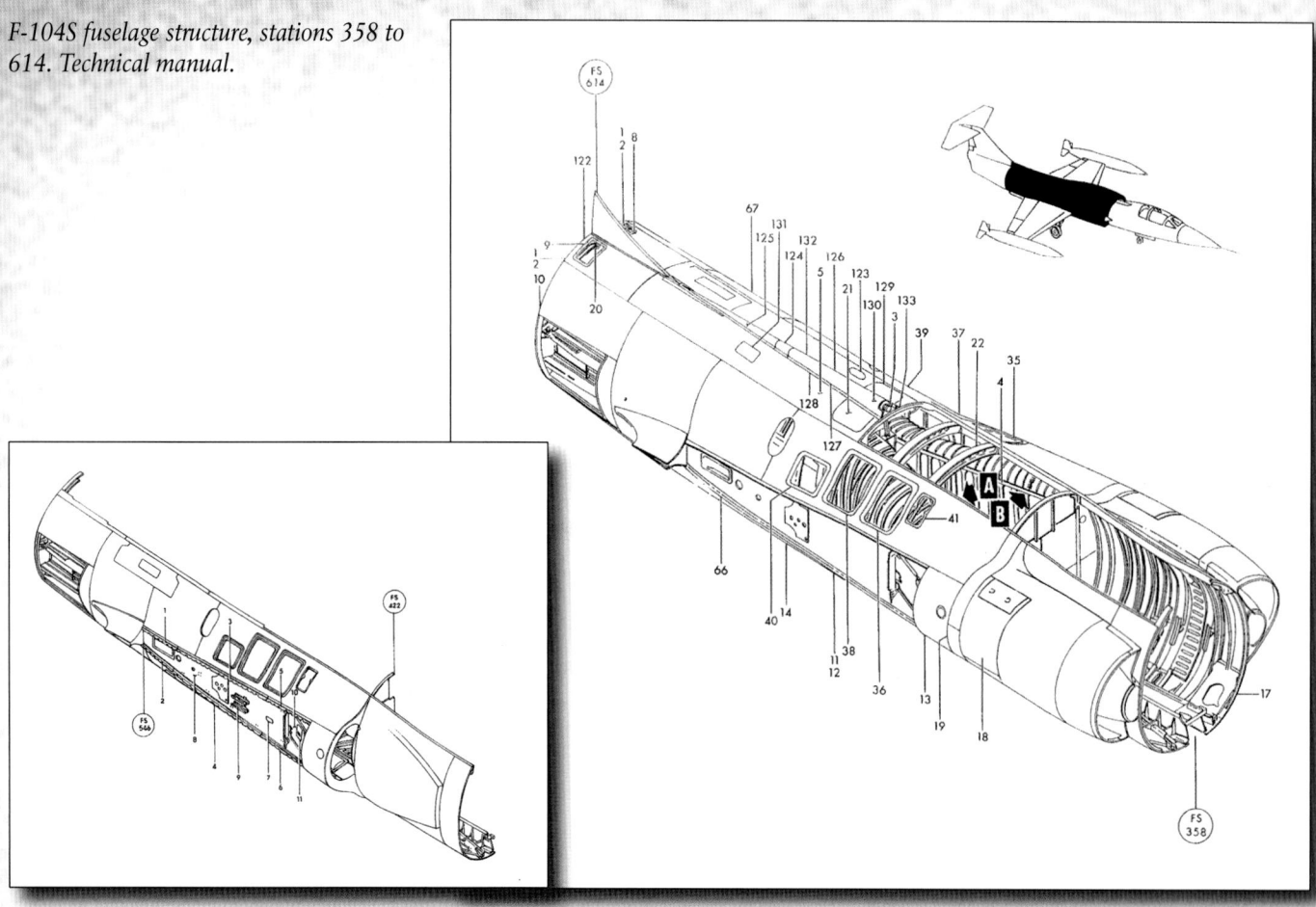

F-104S fuselage structure, stations 358 to 614. Technical manual.

F-104S Aft fuselage structure. Technical manual.

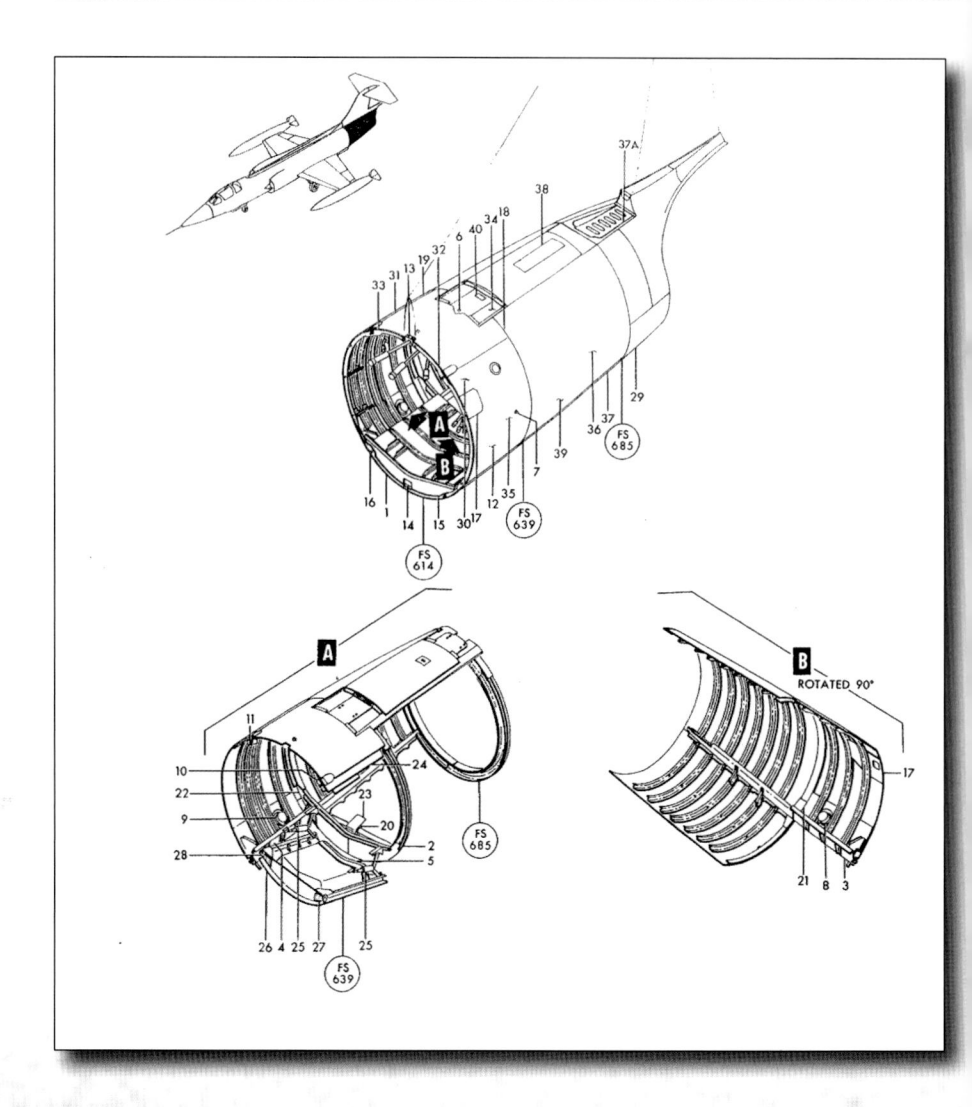

128

Fuselage access covers. Technical Manual.

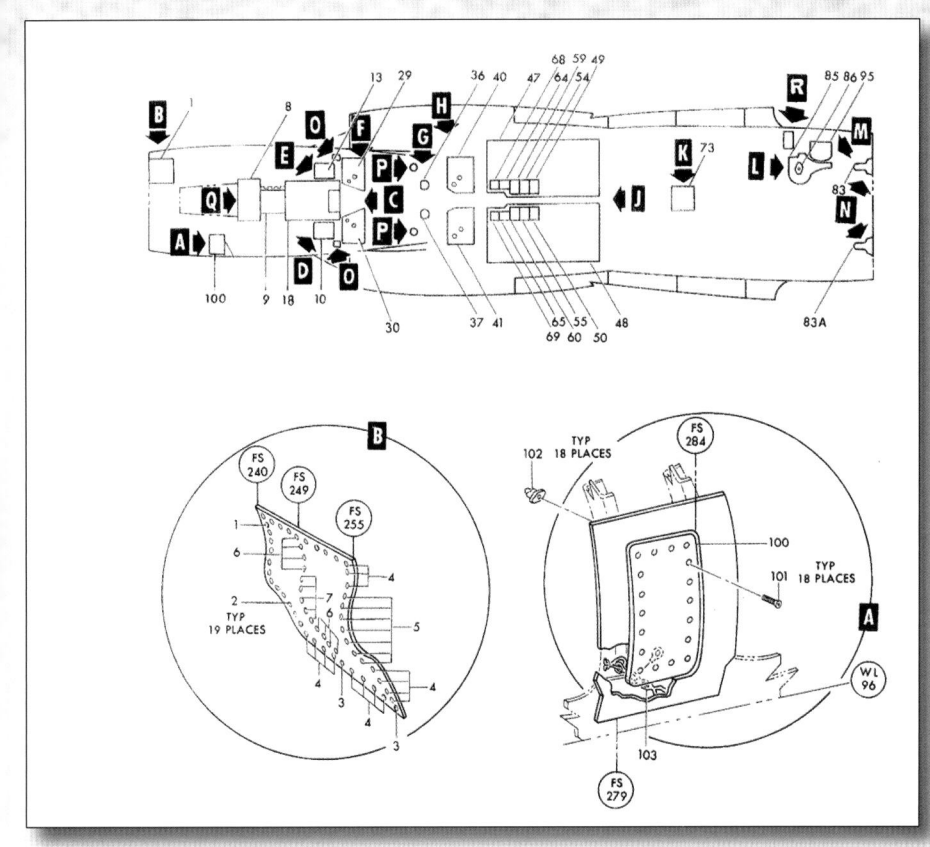

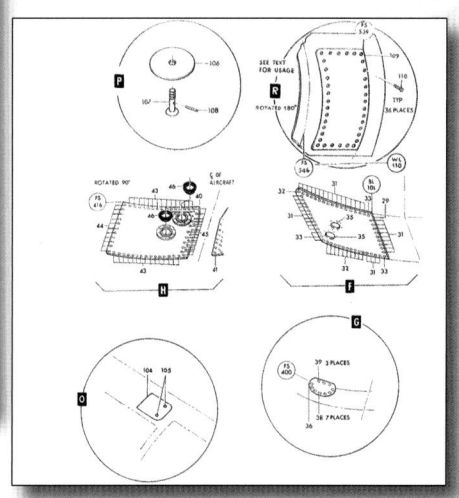

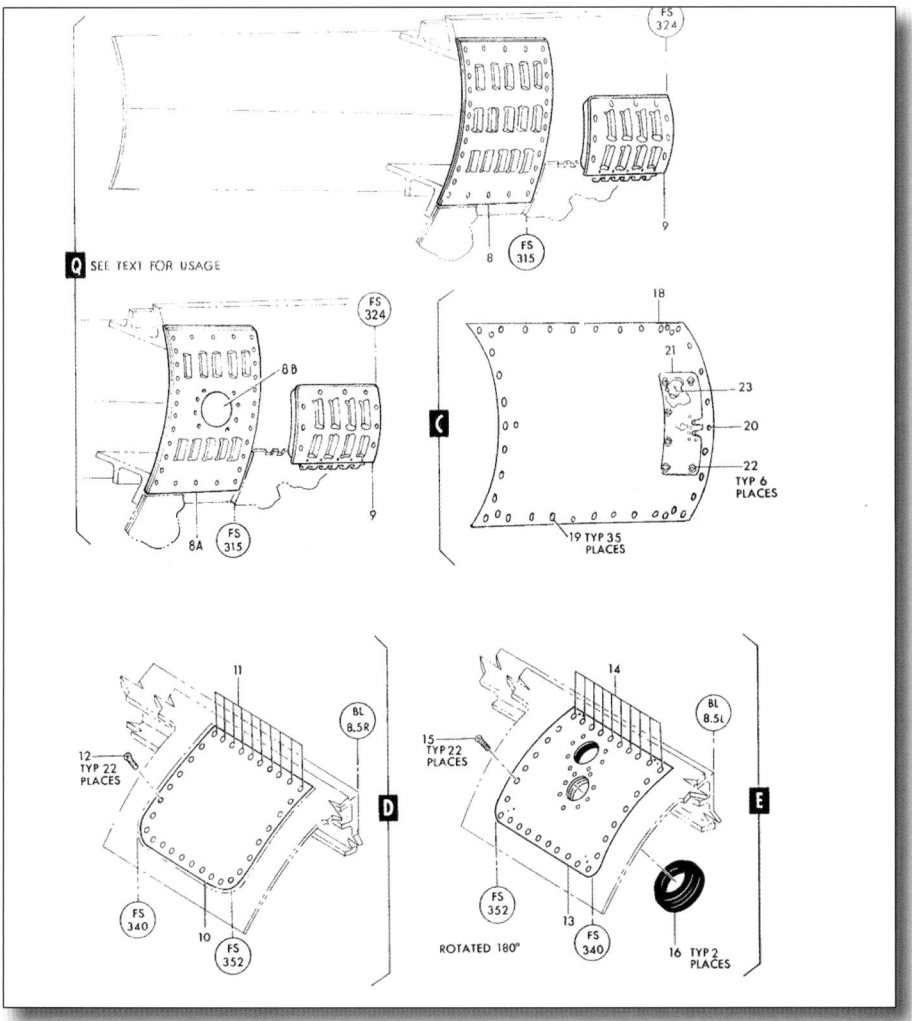

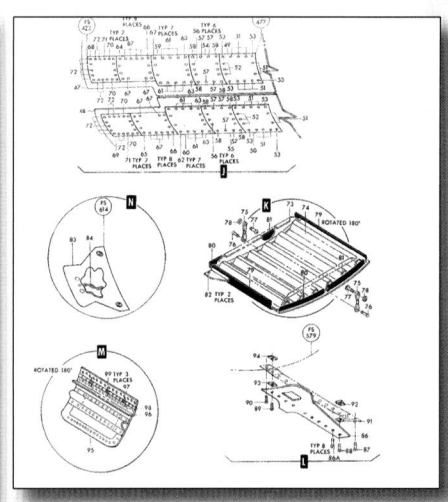

Above: Starboard side of the forward fuselage of F-104S ASA-M MM6876 with canopy opening lever. The golden plaque says that the aircraft was neutralized in accordance with the CFE treaty. (Jarosław Dobrzyński)

Right: Pilot's fresh air scoop.

Port side of the forward fuselage of F-104S ASA-M MM6876 with canopy jettison handle hatch and angle of attack control vane. (Jarosław Dobrzyński)

Infra-red sensor with the badge of the 9° Stormo. (Jarosław Dobrzyński)

Pitot head. (Jarosław Dobrzyński)

Aft fuselage section of F-104S ASA-M. (Jarosław Dobrzyński)

Arrestor hook and brake chute container. (Jarosław Dobrzyński)

Open engine access hatch of the F-104G. (George Papadimitriou)

Open brake chute compartment of the F-104G with stowed parachute. (George Papadimitriou)

Open airbrakes of the F-104F. (Przemysław Skulski)

Left: Open airbrakes of the F-104F. (Przemysław Skulski)

Above: Tail section of a TF-104G. The red line shows the location of the turbine. (George Papadimitriou)

Left: Tail section with closed airbrakes of the F-104G. (Przemysław Skulski)

Belgian TF-104G FC11 in flight. (BAF)

Wing

Boundary Layer Control orifices on the wing's trailing edge. (Jarosław Dobrzyński)

A section of the wing with the BLC orifices. (Przemysław Skulski)

TF-104G wing with five attachment forgings. (Jarosław Dobrzyński)

Above: F-104G portside wing with AIM-9 Sidewinder missile.

Right: Wing-fuselage intersection – trailing edge.
(Both Grzegorz Karnas).

Bottom: Front view of the F-104S showing characteristic Starfighter wing anhedral. (Ludovic Mac Leod)

TF-104G wing with five attachment forgings. (Jarosław Dobrzyński)

Fuselage/wing intersection of the TF-104G. (Jarosław Dobrzyński)

Right wingtip of the F-104S ASA-M. (Jarosław Dobrzyński)

Wing structure and attachment points.

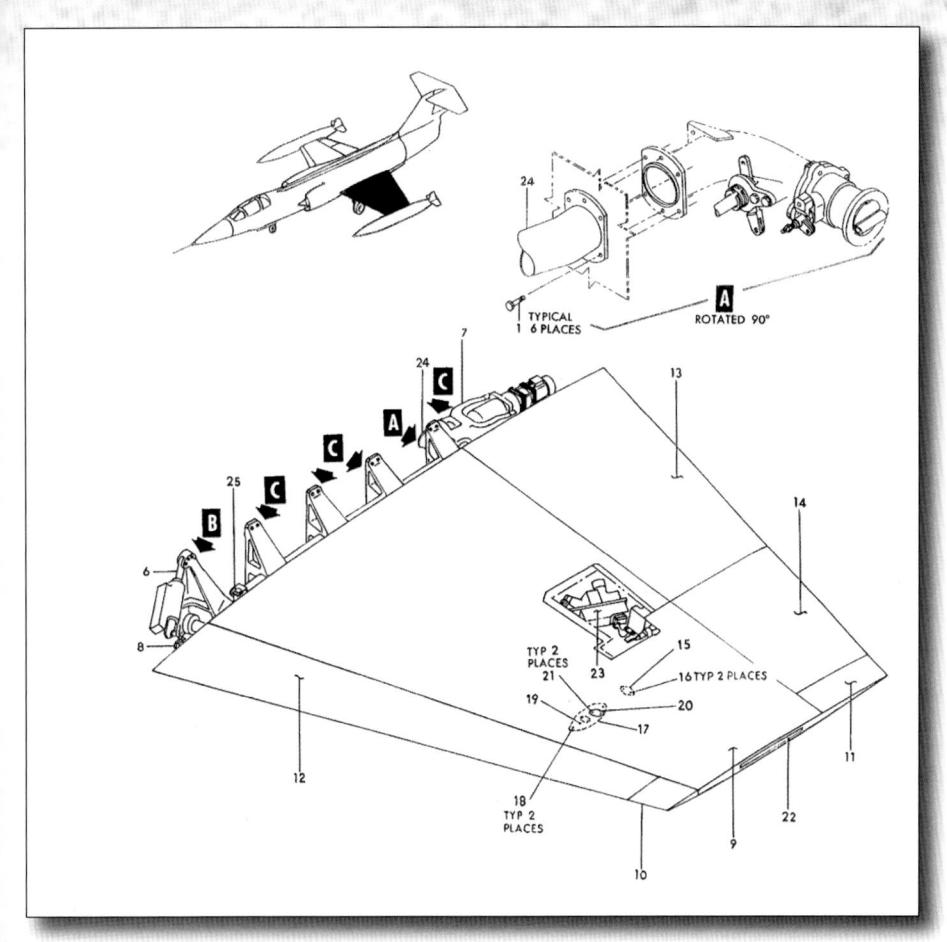

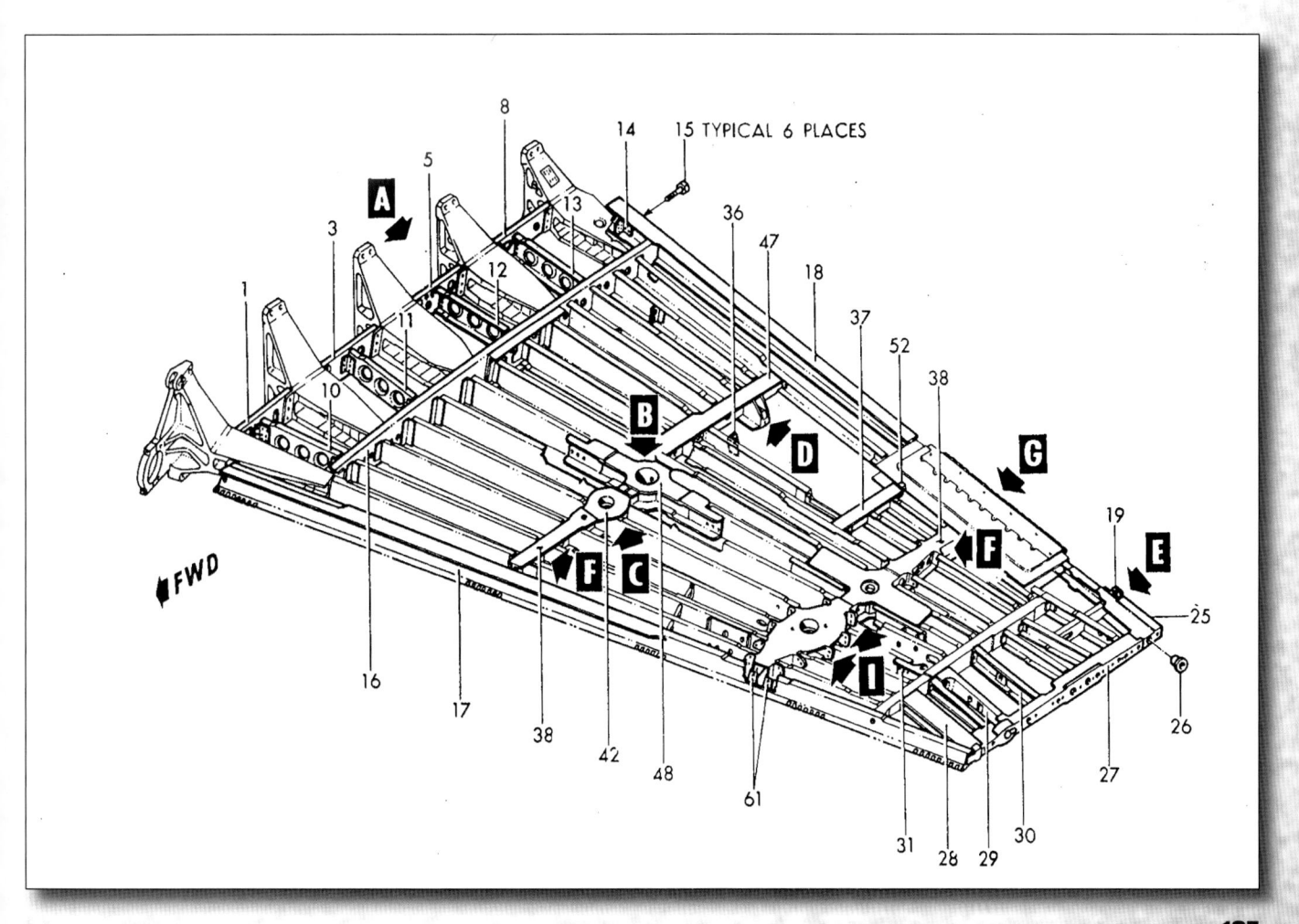

Electronic Systems

Above: Open avionics compartment of the F-104S ASA-M, with so-called Jeep cans containing avionics equipment and circuit breaker panel behind the ejection seat. (Jarosław Dobrzyński)

Right: Open avionics compartment in the F-104G with the cannon ammunition container to the left. (George Papadimitriou)

Open avionics compartment in the F-104G with the cannon ammunition container to the left. (George Papadimitriou)

Avionics equipment.

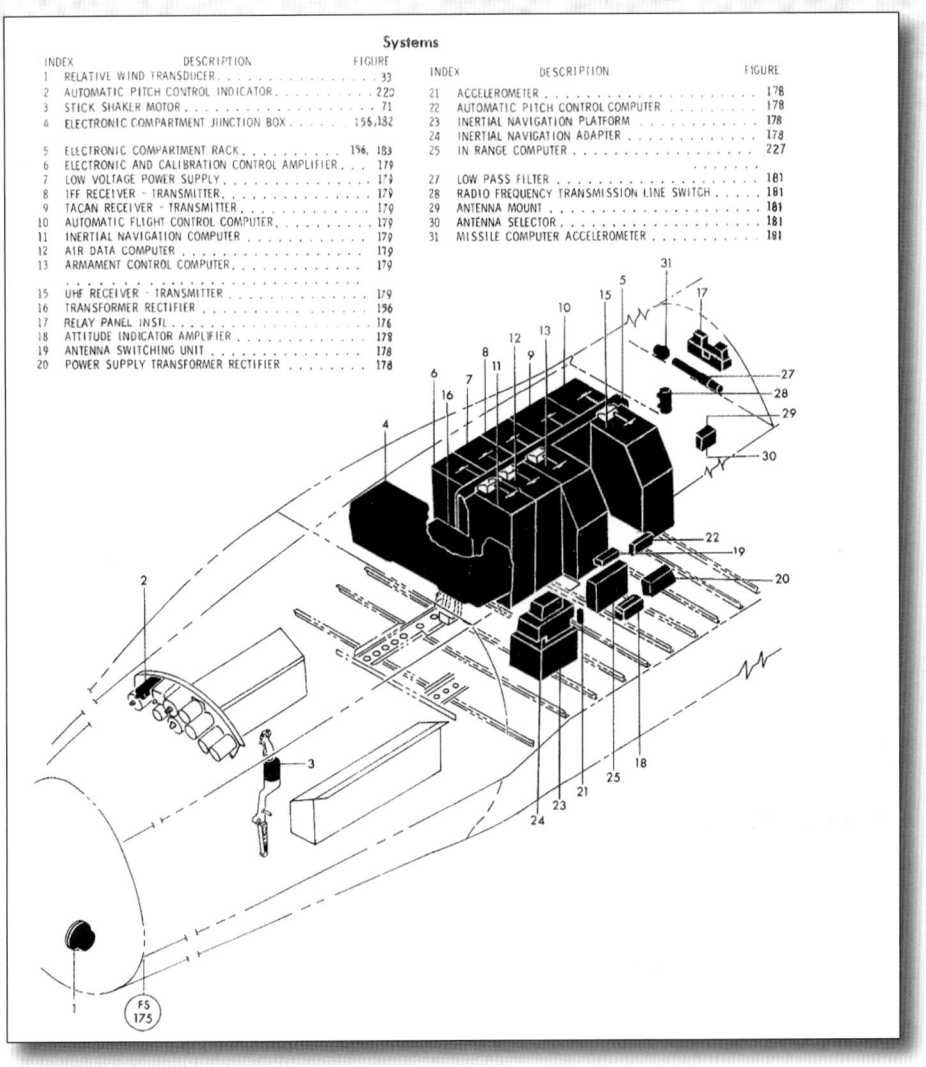

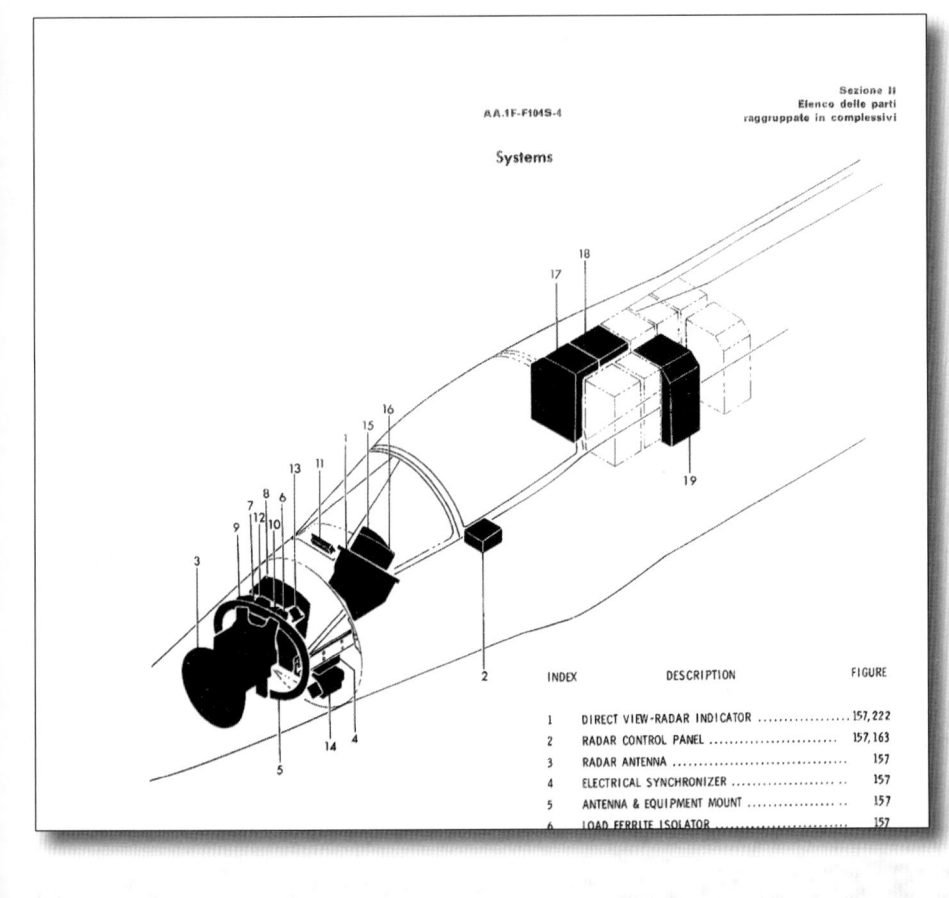

Systems:
1. Direct view-radar indicator
2. Radar control panel
3. Radar antenna
4. Electrical synchronizer
5. Antenna & equipment mount
6. Load ferrite isolator
7. Automatic frequency control
8. Radar transmitter
9. Waveguide coupler
10. Flexible waveguide
11. clearance plane and antenna tilt indicator
12. Waveguide switch
13. Dummy load
14. Intermediate frquency post amplifier
15. Radar visor-indicator
16. Radar filter-indicator
17. Electronic nad calibraton control amplifier
18. Low voltage power supply
19. Armament control computer

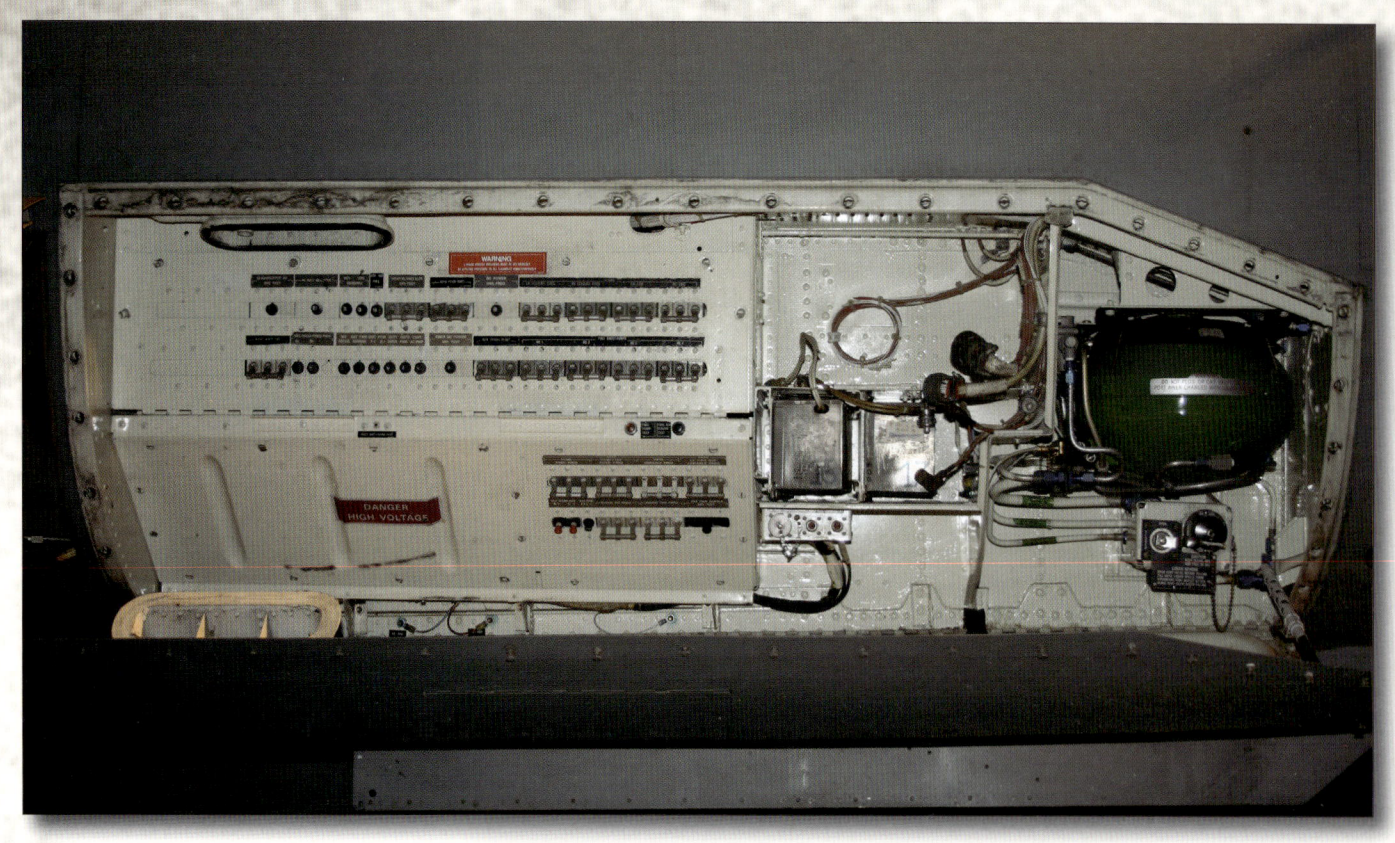

Open circuit breakers bay. Liquid oxygen filler valve is on the right. (Jarosław Dobrzyński)

Right: *Open missile guidance equipment bay. (Jarosław Dobrzyński)*

Missile type selector switch in missile guidance equipment bay. (Jarosław Dobrzyński)

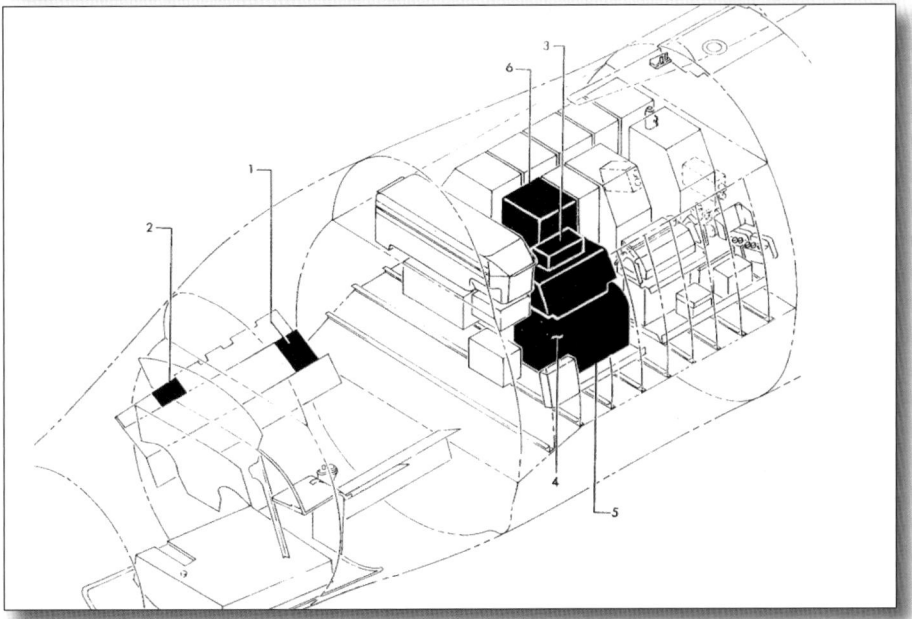

Inertial Navigation System:
1. Inertial navigation aligment control
2. Inertial navigation control
3. Inertial navigation adapter
4. Insulating blanket
5. Inertial navigation platform
6. Inertial navigation computer

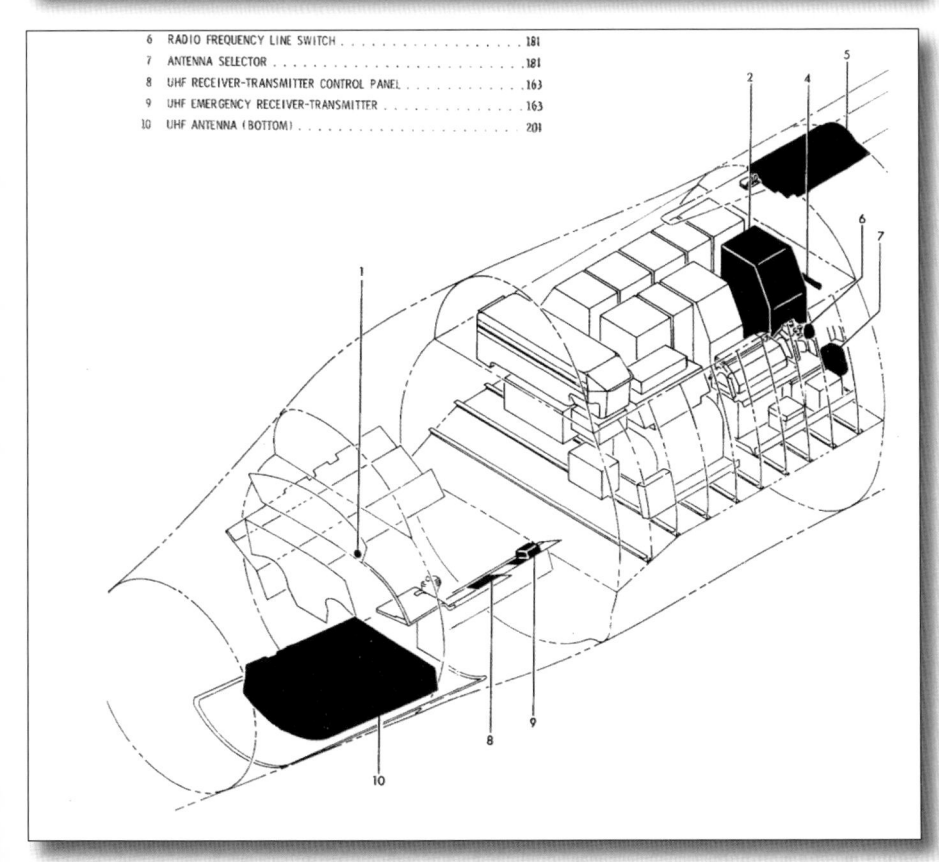

6 RADIO FREQUENCY LINE SWITCH 181
7 ANTENNA SELECTOR 181
8 UHF RECEIVER-TRANSMITTER CONTROL PANEL 163
9 UHF EMERGENCY RECEIVER-TRANSMITTER 163
10 UHF ANTENNA (BOTTOM) 201

UHF Communication System
1. Channel selector switch
2. UHF radio receiver-transmitter
3.
4. Low pass filter
5. Top UHF antenna
6. Radio frequency line switch
7. Antenna selector
8. UHF control panel
9. UHF emergency receiver-transmitter
10. UHF antenna (bottom)

141

Cockpit

F-104S ASA-M central instrument panel. (Jarosław Dobrzyński)
Left cockpit console of the F-104 ASA-M. The black handle behind the throttle lever is for radar control. (Jarosław Dobrzyński)

Right cockpit console of the F-104 ASA-M. (Jarosław Dobrzyński)

F-104G instrument panel drawing by Centennial02.

143

F-104G instrument panel. Technical Manual published in early 60s.

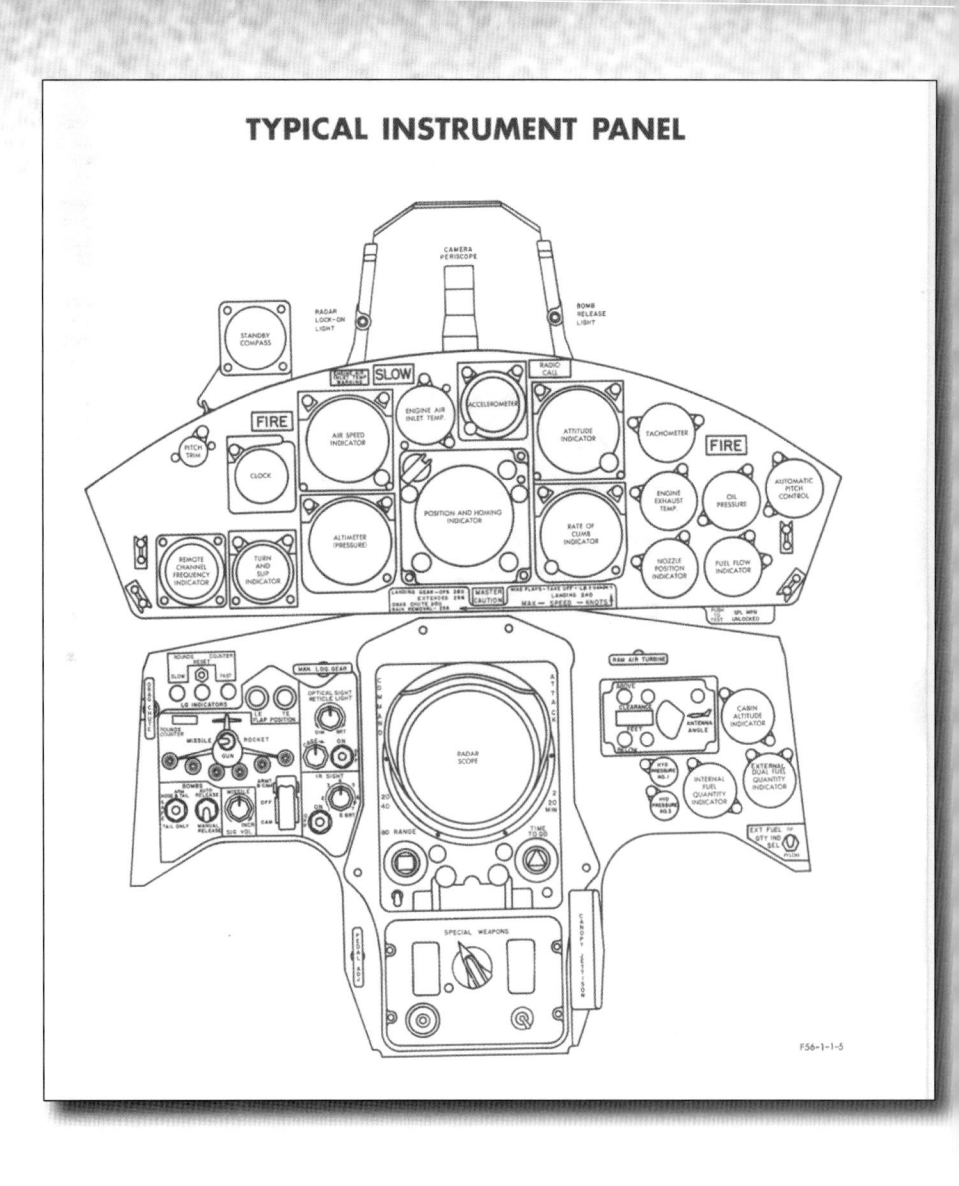

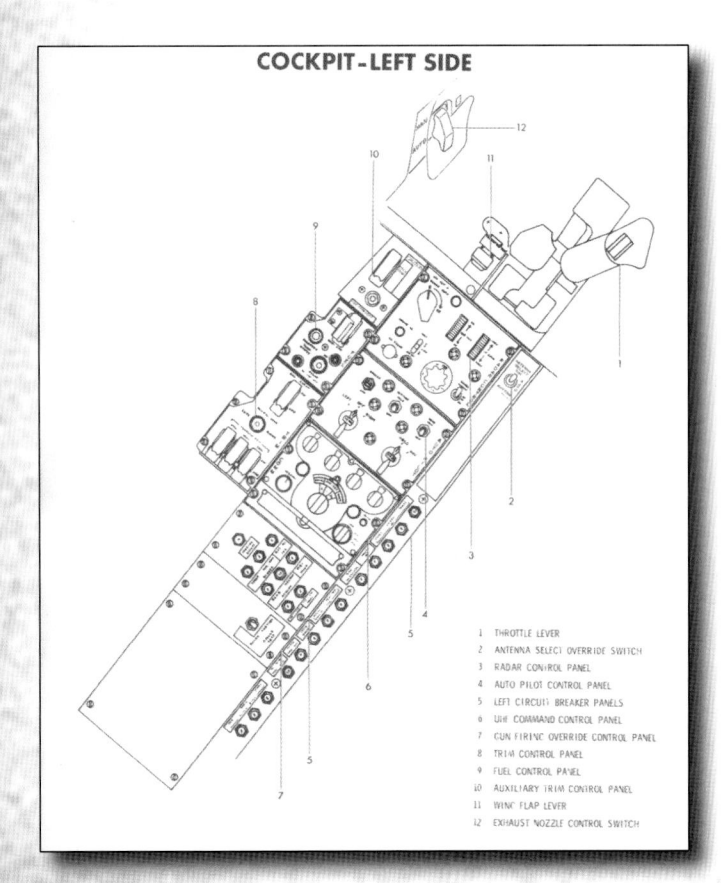

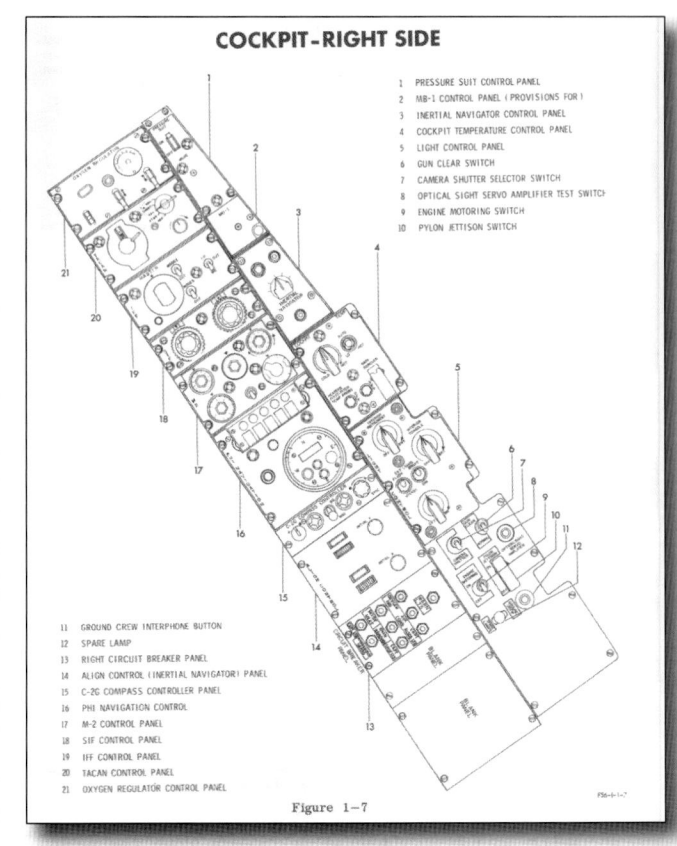

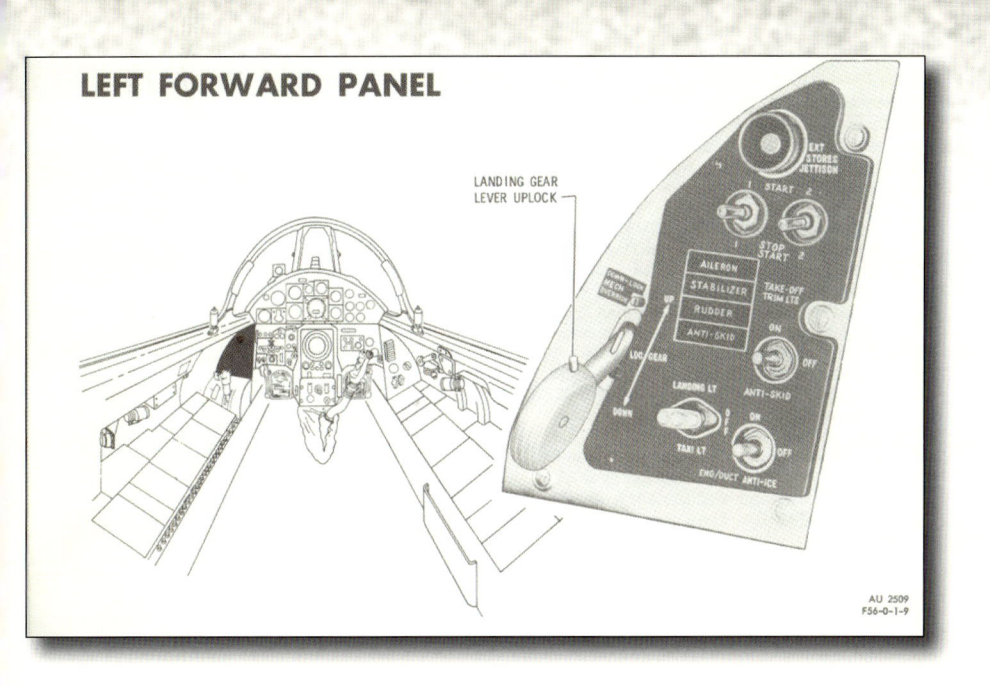

LEFT FORWARD PANEL

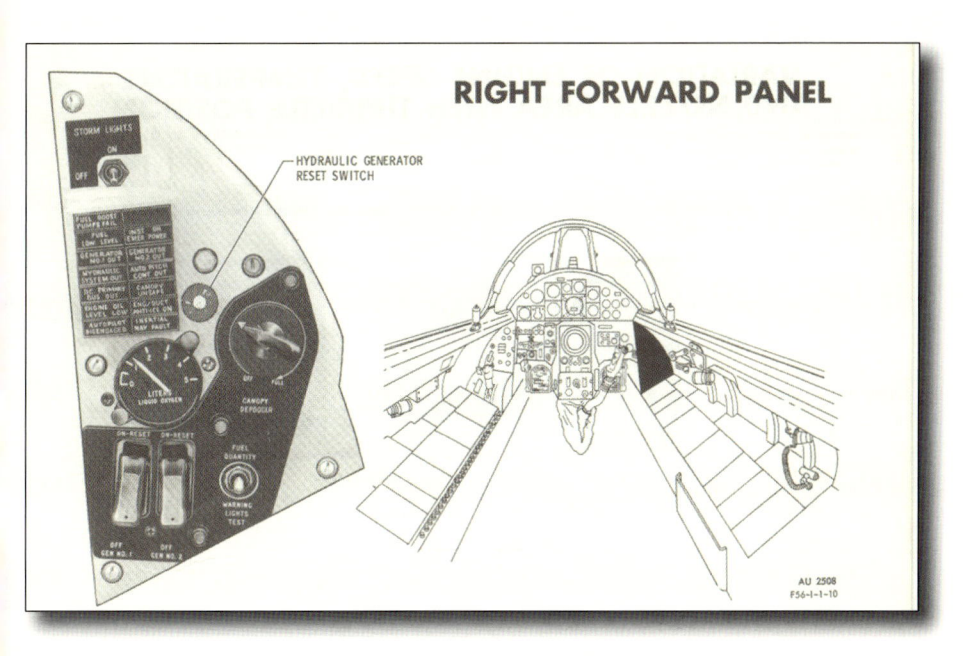

Figure callouts: LANDING GEAR LEVER UPLOCK

RIGHT FORWARD PANEL

Figure callout: HYDRAULIC GENERATOR RESET SWITCH

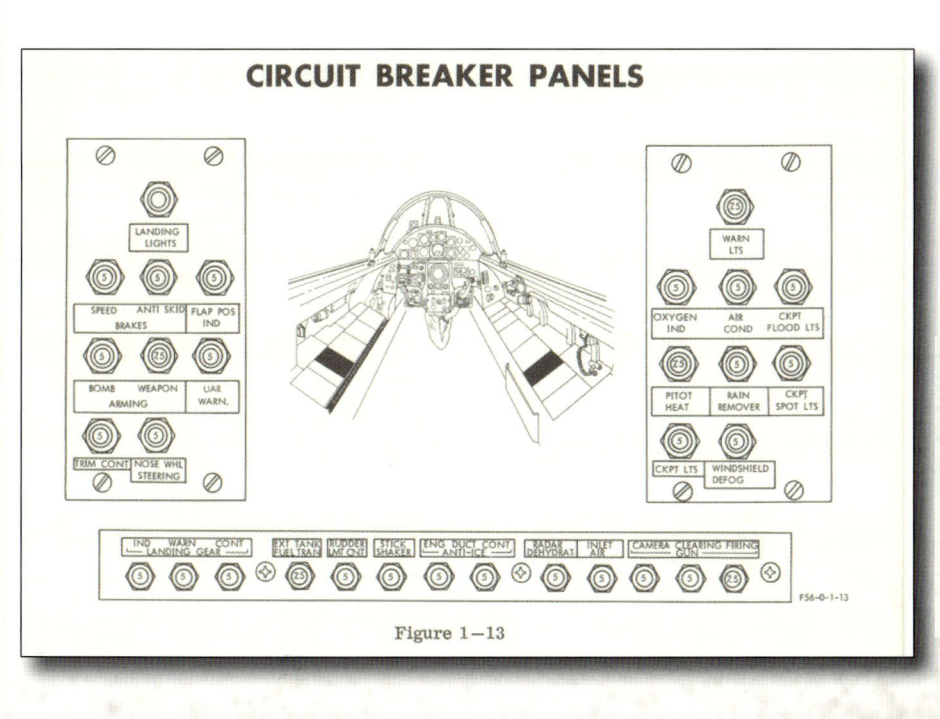

CIRCUIT BREAKER PANELS

Figure 1-13

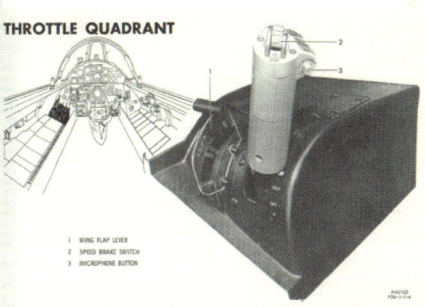

THROTTLE QUADRANT

1 WING FLAP LEVER
2 SPEED BRAKE SWITCH
3 MICROPHONE BUTTON

Central instrument panel of the F-104G. (George Papadimitriou)

Left cockpit console of the F-104G. (George Papadimitriou)

Right cockpit console of the F-104G. (George Papadimitriou)

Central instrument panel of the CF-104. Note different instrument layout than in the F-104G. (George Papadimitriou)

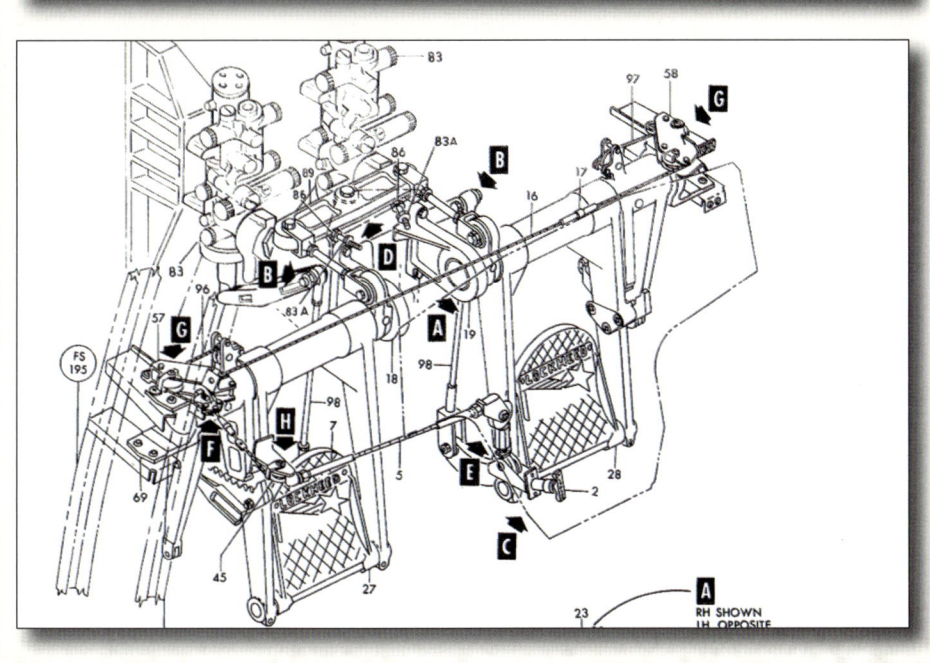

Above: Control grip.
1. Aileron and horizontal stabilizer trim switch
2. Droppable stores release button
3. Trigger switch
4. Radar action reject button
5. Nosewheel steering/microphone button
6. APC emergency disconnect switch
7. Stick shaker assembly

147

Lockheed C-1 downward-firing ejection seat. (George Papadimitriou)

Bottom, right: *Martin Baker Mk Q7(A) ejection seat. (George Papadimitriou)*
Bottom, left: *Martin Baker Mk Q7(A) ejection seat in the cockpit of an F-104 ASA-M. (Jarosław Dobrzyński)*

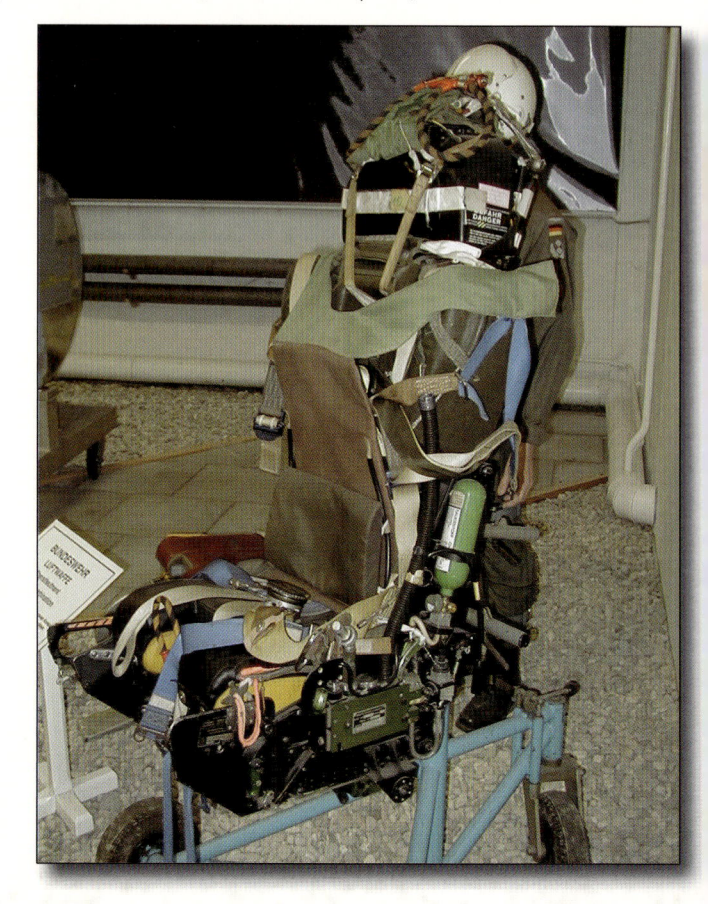

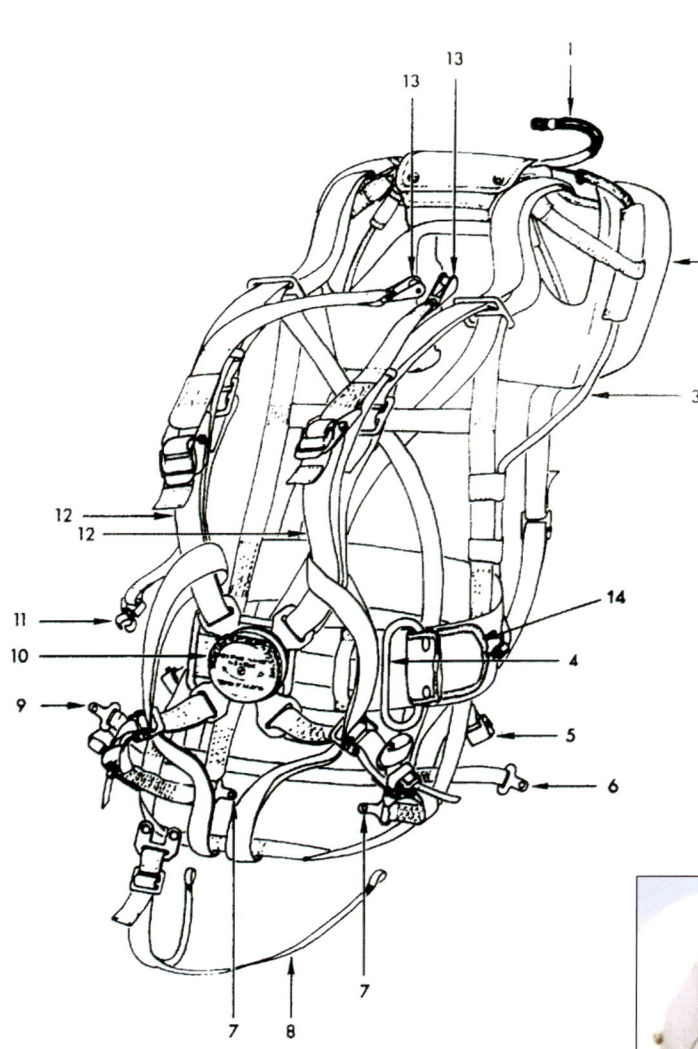

Main parachute and combined harness.
F-104S & ASA-M Filght Manual.
1. Parachute withdrawal line
2. Parachute pack
3. Ripcord cable
4. D-ring
5. Survival pack quick release fitting
6. Sticker strap lug
7. Lower harness lug
8. Negative G-strap
9. Sticker strap lug
10. Quick release box
11. Safety clip
12. Combined harness
13. Waist belt

A PULLING THE FIRING HANDLE (PRIMARY OR SECONDARY), THE EJECTION SEQUENCE BEGINS.
B WHILE THE CANOPY IS JETTISONED AND THE EJECTION GUN IS ACTUATED, THE HARNESS POWER RETRACTION UNIT OPERATES AND THE PILOT IS BROUGHT TO THE CORRECT EJECTION POSTURE
C AFTER FIRING OF EJECTION GUN, AS THE SEAT ASCENDS, THE DROGUE GUN, THE TIME RELEASE UNIT AND THE EMERGENCY OXYGEN SYSTEM ARE OPERATED, AND THE AIRCRAFT PORTION OF THE P.E.C. IS DISCONNECTED. AT THE SAME TIME, THE LEG RESTRAINT CORDS TIGHTEN TO DRAW BACK AND RESTRAIN THE PILOT'S LEGS TO THE FRONT OF THE SEAT PAN.
WHEN THE SEAT LEAVES THE AIRCRAFT, THE ROCKET PACK IS FIRED TO SUPPLEMENT THE UPWARD THRUST OF THE EJECTION GUN.
D 3/4 SEC. AFTER EJECTION, THE DELAY MECHANISM OPERATES AND THE DROGUE GUN IS FIRED DEPLOYING THE DROGUES.
E THE DROGUES, WHEN FULLY DEVELOPED, STABILIZE AND RETARD THE SEAT AS LONG AS THE CONDITIONS OF HEIGHT AND SPEED ARE SUCH THAT THE BAROSTAT DOES NOT ALLOW THE TIME-RELEASE UNIT TO OPERATE.
F THE TIME-RELEASE UNIT OPERATES, ALLOWING OPENING OF SCISSOR SHACKLE.
G THE HARNESS LOCKS, THE LEG CORDS AND THE MAIN PORTION OF THE P.E.C. ARE RELEASED. AT THE SAME TIME, THE DROGUES DEPLOY THE PARACHUTE AND THE PILOT IS LIFTED OUT OF THE SEAT PAN.

An Italian pilot in the cockpit of an F-104G. Note two canopy ejection thrusters mounted in front of the windshield. (AMI)

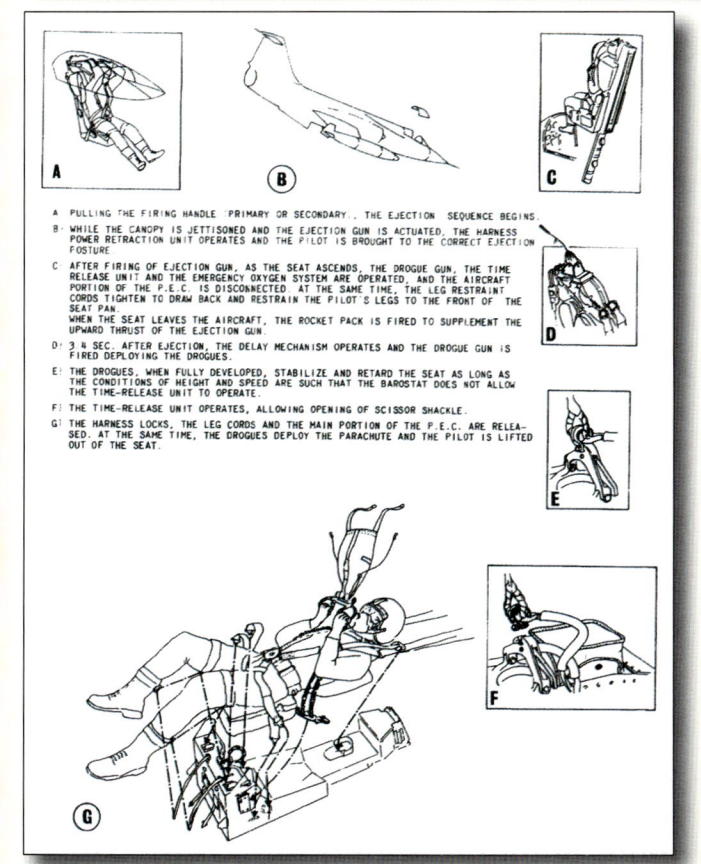

Seat Ejection Sequence.
F-104S & ASA-M Filght Manual.

Radar

Autonetics NASARR F15A-41B radar of the F-104G. (Luftwaffe)

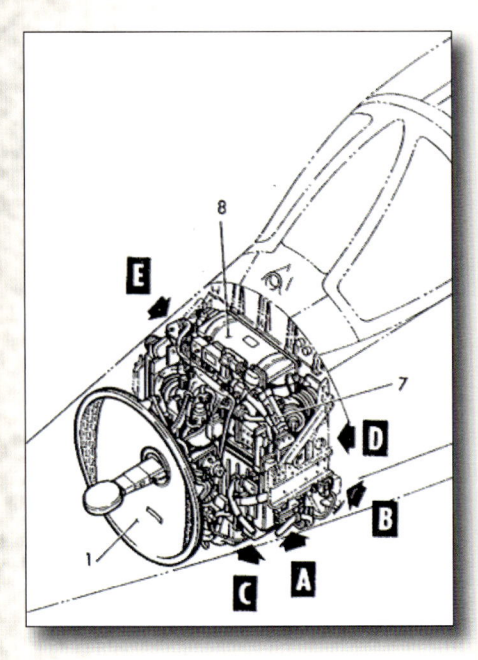

FIAR R-21G/M1 Setter radar of the F-104 ASA-M. (Jarosław Dobrzyński)

Cannon

Above: General Electric M61A1 20 mm rotary cannon. (Jarosław Dobrzyński)

Left: Expended ammunition belt links ejector. (Jarosław Dobrzyński)

Details of the General Electric M61A1 20 mm rotary cannon drive mechanism. (Przemysław Skulski)

Details of the General Electric M61A1 20 mm rotary cannon drive mechanism. (Przemysław Skulski)

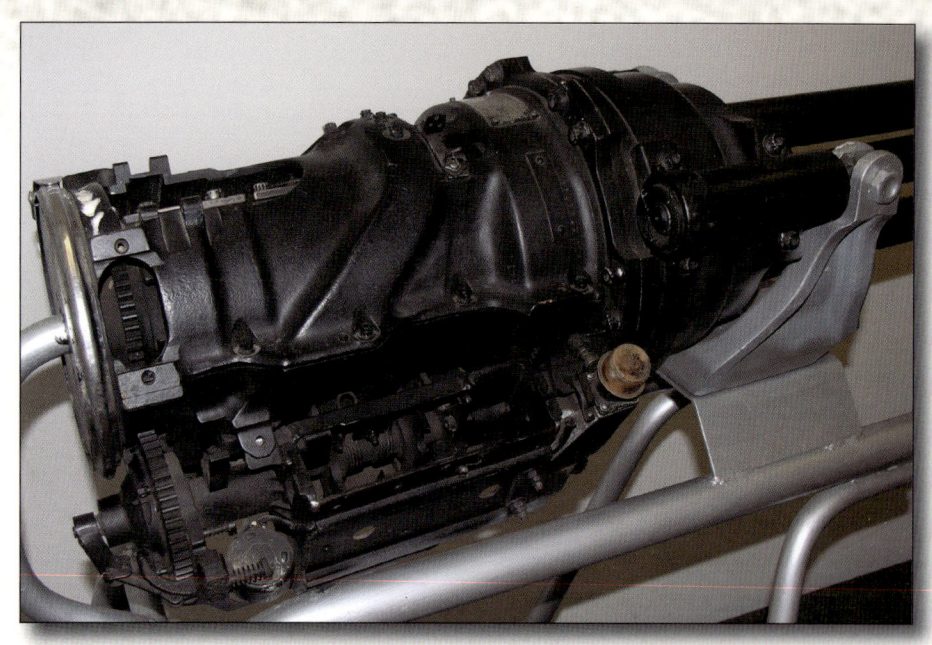

M61A1 Vulcan of a Norwegian CF-104 (F-104G). (George Papadimitriou)

Cannon ammunition container of the F-104G. (George Papadimitriou)

F-104G FX 30 of the Belgian Air Force with cannon ammunition loader. (BAF)

153

Stores

AIM-9B Sidewinder missile.
(Jarosław Dobrzyński)

Exhaust nozzle and stabilizer fins with rollerons of the AIM-9B Sidewinder missile.
(Przemysław Skulski)

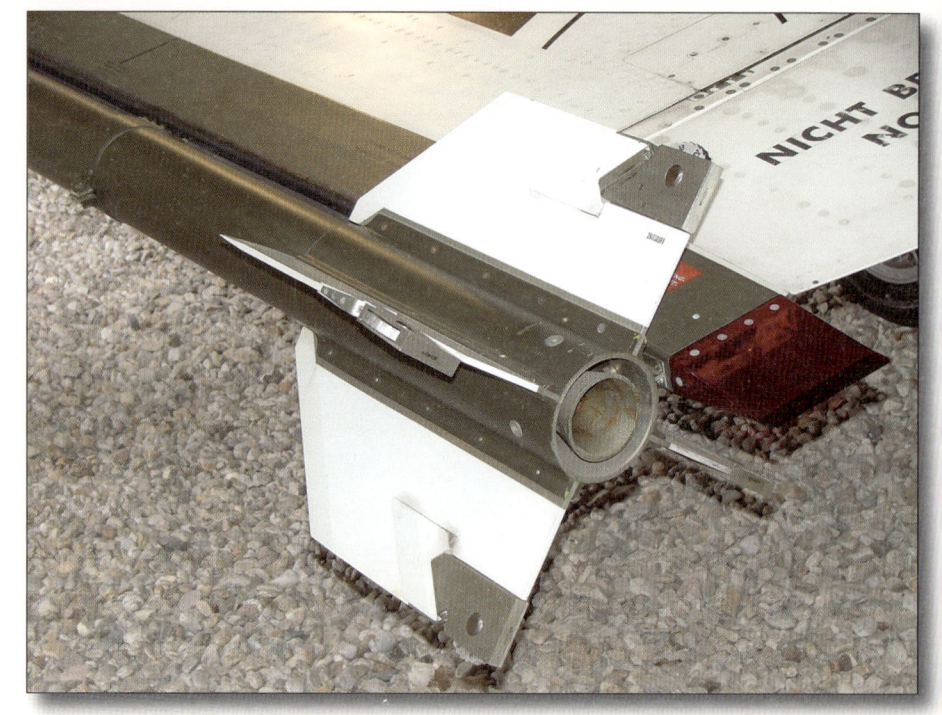

19-tube 2.75" (70 mm) LAU 3/A unguided rocket launcher under the wing of a Greek TF-104G. (George Papadimitriou)

Underwing weapon pylon of a F-104G. (George Papadimitriou)

Mk-82 Snakeye bomb under the wing of a Greek F-104G. (George Papadimitriou)

Other weapons carried by the F-104G: 4-tube 127 mm (5") LAU-10/A rocket launcher, LAU 68B/A 7-Tube 70 mm (2.75") rocket launcher and SUU-21 practice bomb dispenser. (George Papadimitriou)

Lockheed F-104G Starfighter 7151 of the 336th Olympos Squadron of the Hellenic Air Force preserved at the HAF Museum at Dekelia-Tatoi and various types of bombs carried by this type. (Jarosław Dobrzyński)

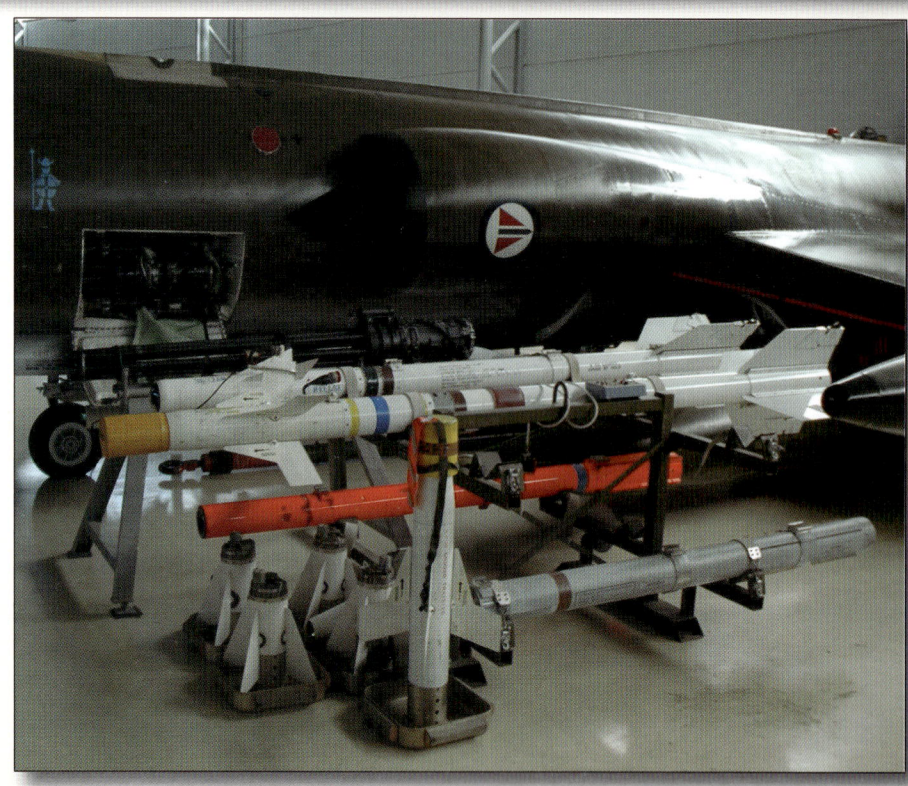

M61A1 Vulcan and AIM-9 Sidewinder missiles carried by Norwegian CF-104s (F-104G). (George Papadimitriou)

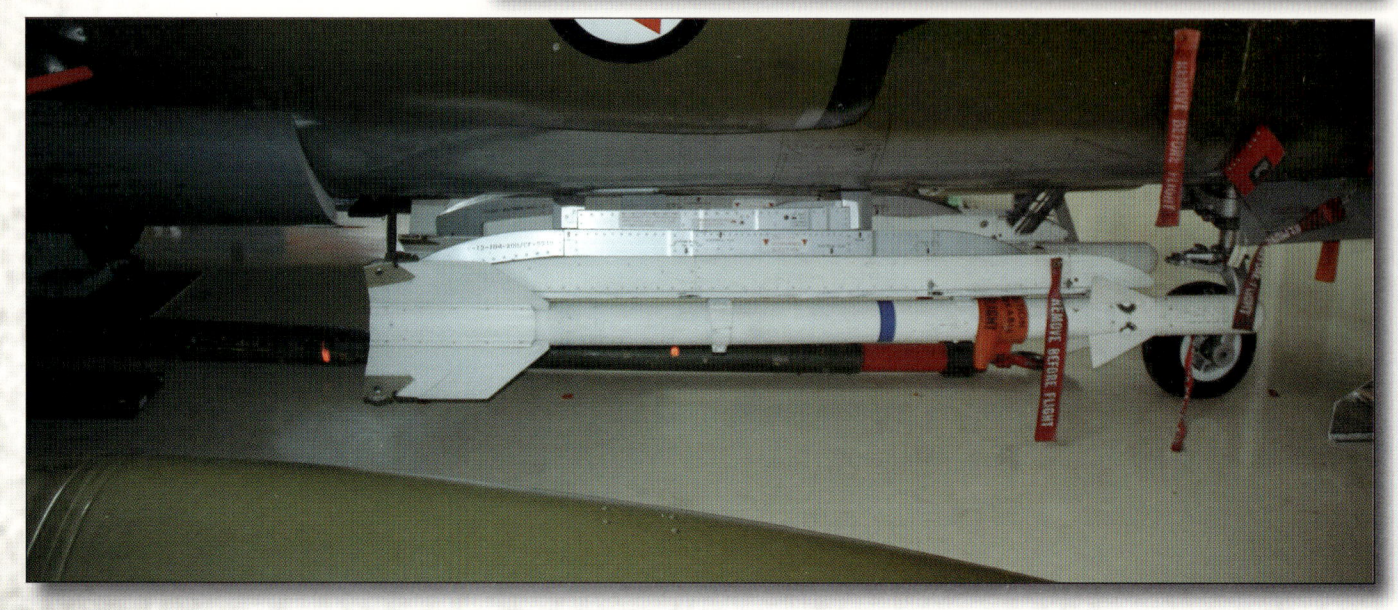

AIM-9 Sidewinder missiles carried on centerline launcher by a Norwegian CF-104 (F-104G). (George Papadimitriou)

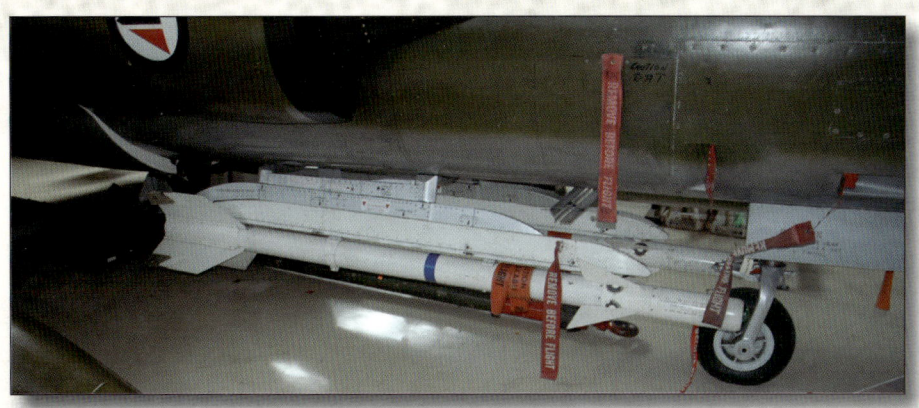

AIM-9 Sidewinder missiles carried on centerline station by a Norwegian CF-104 (F-104G). (George Papadimitriou)

AIM-9 Sidewinder missiles carried on centerline station by a Norwegian CF-104 (F-104G). (Przemysław Skulski)

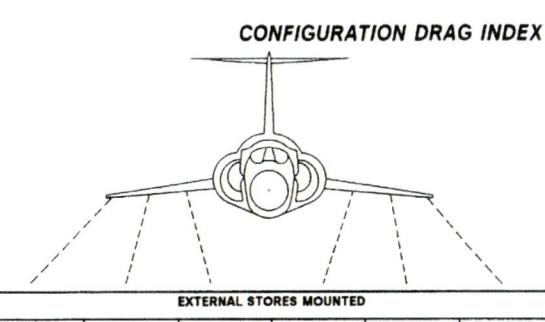

Configuration drag index. F-104S & ASAM-1 Flight Manual.

CONFIGURATION DRAG INDEX

_	EXTERNAL STORES MOUNTED				_	TAKEOFF WEIGHT (LBS)	CONFIGU-RATION DRAG INDEX
WING TIP	BL 104	BL 75	BL 75	BL 104	WING TIP		
AIM-9L (*)					AIM-9L (*)	22274	15
AIM-9L (*)		TANK	TANK		AIM-9L (*)	25504	67
	AIM-9L (*)			AIM-9L (*)		22406	36
	AIM-9L (*) (**)					21975	18
TANK	AIM-9L (*)			AIM-9L (*)	TANK	25137	52
AIM-9L (*)	AIM-9L (*)			AIM-9L (*)	AIM-9L (*)	23136	51
AIM-9L (*)	AIM-9L (*)	TANK	TANK	AIM-9L (*)	AIM-9L (*)	26366	103
AIM-9L (*)	MRAAM (***)			MRAAM (***)	AIM-9L (*)	23512	47
AIM-9L (*)	MRAAM (***)	TANK	TANK	MRAAM (***)	AIM-9L (*)	26742	99
	AIM-9L (*)			MRAAM (***)		22594	34
	AIM-9L (*)	TANK	TANK	MRAAM (***)		25824	86
TANK	AIM-9L (*)			MRAAM (***)	TANK	25325	50
TANK	AIM-9L (*)	TANK	TANK	MRAAM (***)	TANK	28555	102
	MRAAM (***)			MRAAM (***)		22782	32
				MRAAM (**)		22163	16
TANK	MRAAM (***)			MRAAM (***)	TANK	25513	48
	MRAAM (***)	TANK	TANK	MRAAM (***)		26012	84
TANK	MRAAM (***)	TANK	TANK	MRAAM (***)	TANK	28743	100
TANK					TANK	24275	16
	AIM-9L (*)	TANK	TANK	AIM-9L (*)		25638	88
TANK	AIM-9L (*)	TANK	TANK	AIM-9L (*)	TANK	28370	104

(*) Or AIM-9L/I or AIM-9L/I-1
(**) The "real external store" asymmetric configuration drag indeces do not take into account any suspension devices on the unloaded wing
(***) AIM-7E OR ASPIDE MISSILE

Notes:
1) Operating mass empty: 15044 lbs
2) Take-off weights computed considering full internal and external fuel tanks (when applicable)
3) Usable fuel:
   Internal fuel   6500 lbs
   External fuel   4876 lbs
   Total usable fuel 11376 lbs
4) 170 gall. external tank (P/N 851717) on wing tip
5) 195 gall. external tank (P/N 791210) on BL 75
6) Takeoff weights, for the configurations fitted with BL 104 MRAAM, are referred to the AIM-7E Sparrow Missile, which has a mass of 619 lbs, launcher included. If ASPIDE missile(s) is/are fitted, add 56 lbs, for each ASPIDE missile installed, to the above takeoff weight datum

Engine

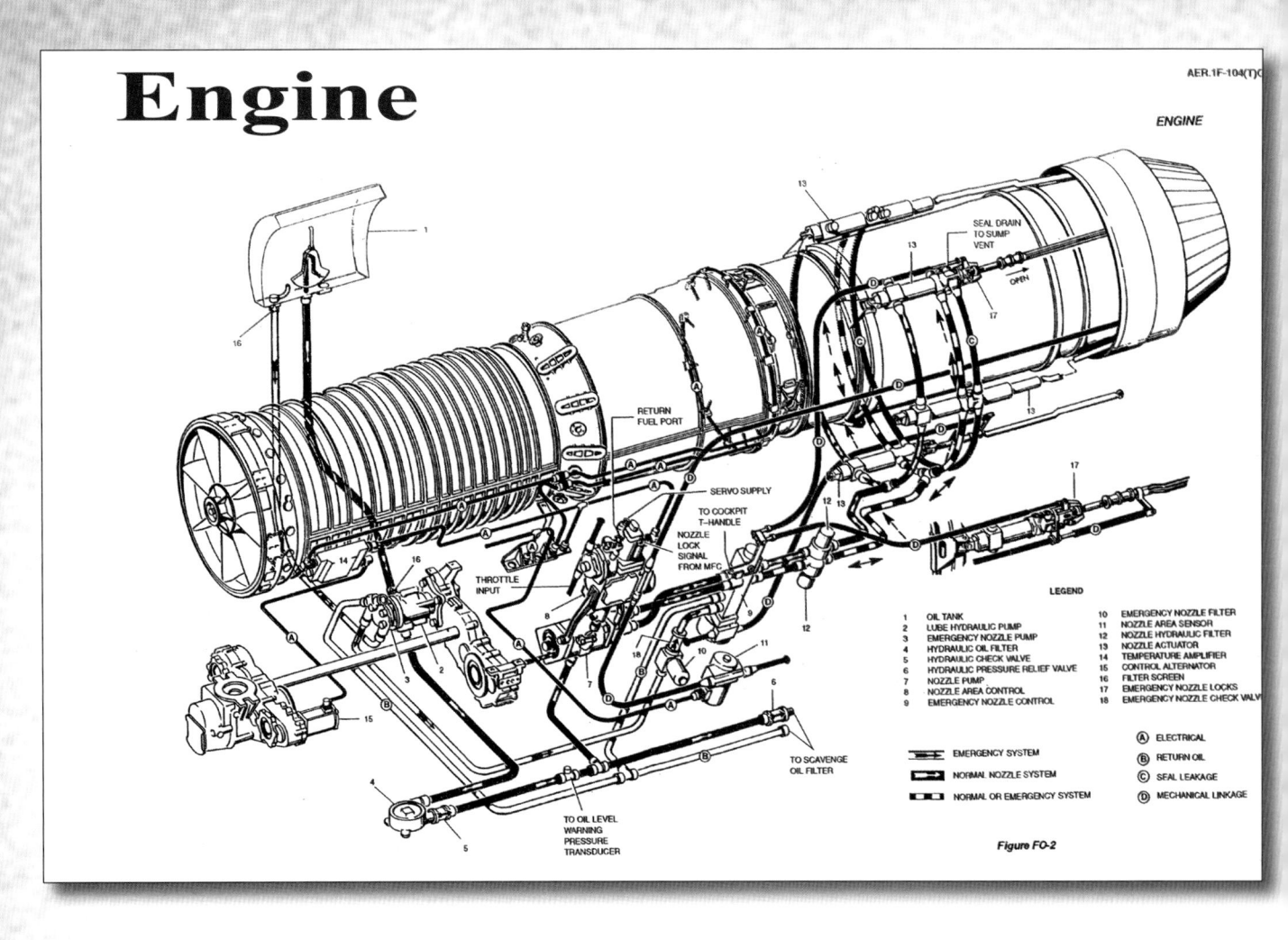

YF-104A and General Electric J79GE-3A engine. (Lockheed)

General Electric J79GE-11A engine. (Jarosław Dobrzyński)

Left: *General Electric J79GE-11A engine. (Przemysław Skulski)*

Air starter of the General Electric J79GE-11A engine. (Jarosław Dobrzyński)

Two photo of the left AC generator of the General Electric J79GE-11A engine. (Jarosław Dobrzyński)

Stator vane variable geometry control mechanism of the General Electric J79GE-11A engine. (Jarosław Dobrzyński)

160

Two photos of the exhaust nozzle of the General Electric J79GE-11A engine.
(Jarosław Dobrzyński)

Tail section of an F-104F with closed engine exhaust nozzle.
(Przemysław Skulski)

161

Right: Tail section of a Norwegian CF-104 (F-104G) with open engine exhaust nozzle. Note ALR-43 Radar Warning Receiver antennae with red protective covers. (George Papadimitriou)

Below right: Tail section of a Danish CF-104 (F-104G) with open engine exhaust nozzle. (Przemysław Skulski)

Bottom: J79 Turbojet engine with afterbuner.
1. Air intake
2. Front gear case
3. No. 1 bearing house
4. Variable vane actuator
5. 17 stage compressor section
6. No. 2 bearing housing
7. Three stage turbine wheel
8. No. 3 bearing housing
9. Afterburner fuel manifolds
10. Exhaust nozzle flaps actuator
11. Tail pipe
12. Primary exhaust nozzle flaps
13. Secondary exhaust nozzle flaps
14. Tail pipe liner
15. Flame holder
16. Exhaust cone
17. Afterburner spray bars
18. Tail pipe temperature thermocouple
19. Three stage turbine section
20. Combustion chamber
21. Cross fire duct
22. Fuel nozzle
23. Horizontal accessory drive shaft
24. Transfer gear case
25. Variable inlet guide vans
26. Verical accessory guide vanes

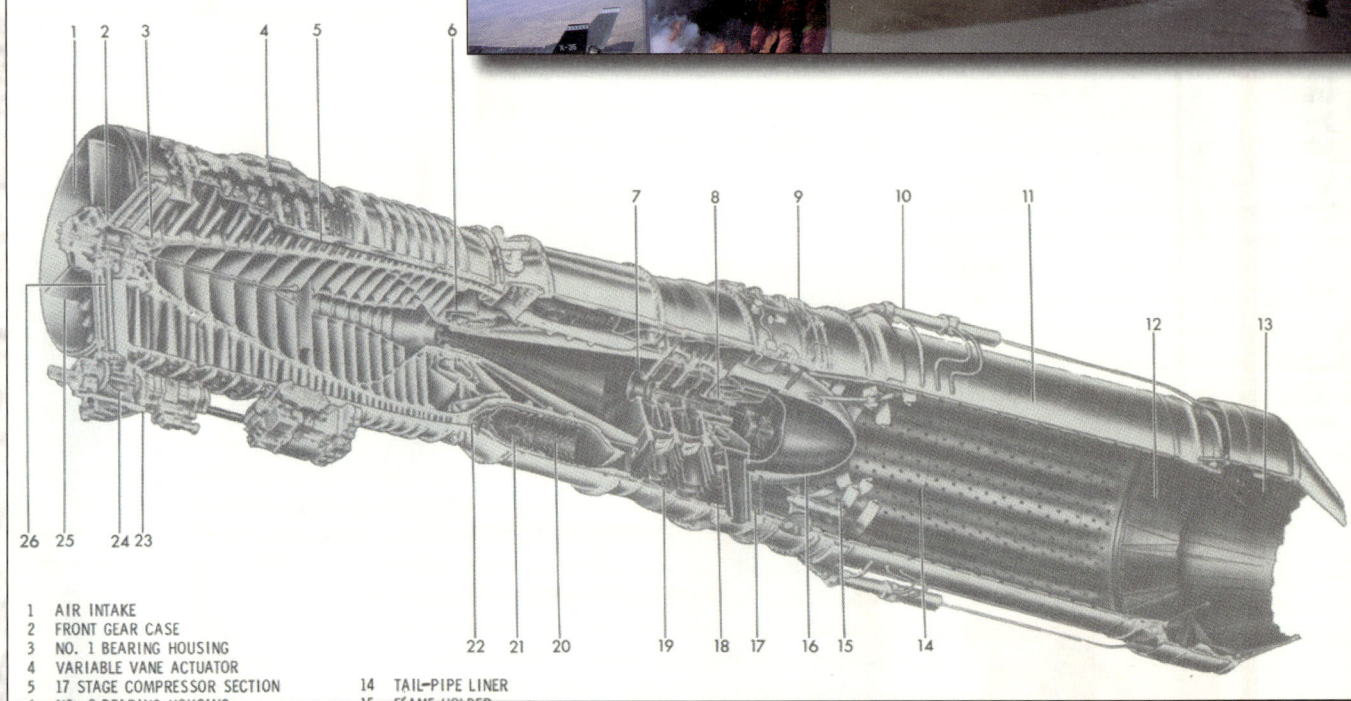

162

Fuselage details

GPS antenna under the third canopy section of an F-104S ASA-M. (Jarosław Dobrzyński)

Searchlight under the third canopy section of a Danish CF-104 (F-104G). (Jarosław Dobrzyński)

Gun gas vents in the F-104S ASA-M, although this aircraft was not fitted with the gun. (Jarosław Dobrzyński)

The interior of the Ram Air Turbine bay. (Jarosław Dobrzyński)

Temperature sensor for the Air Data Computer. (Jarosław Dobrzyński)

Heat exchanger air vents. (Jarosław Dobrzyński)

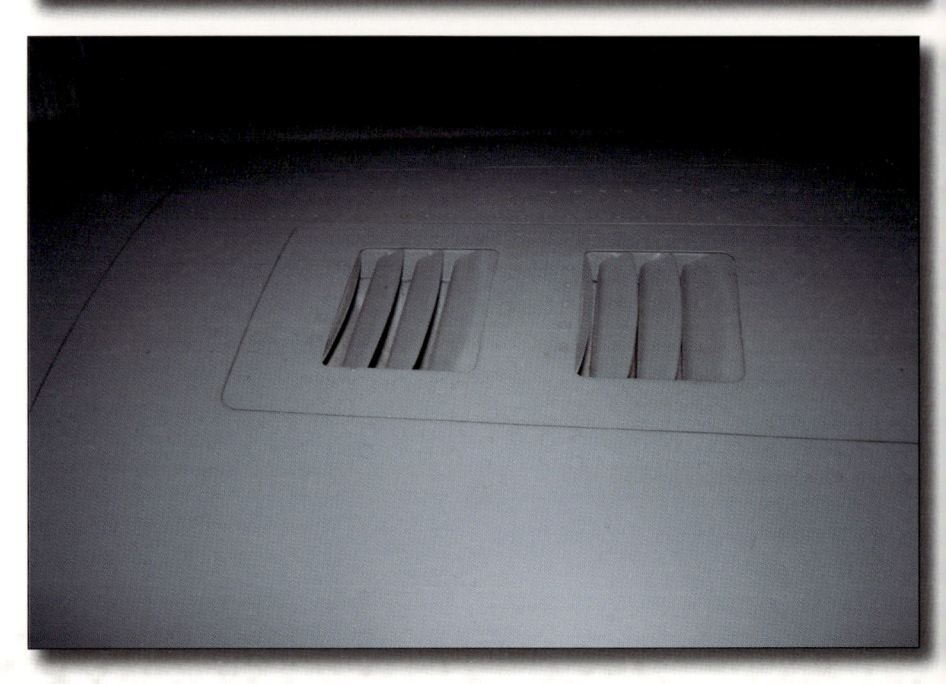

Left intake access door of the TF-104G. (George Papadimitriou)

Open intake access door of the F-104G. (George Papadimitriou)

Left engine auxiliary inlet door (EAID) of the F-104S ASA-M. Note different shape and larger area than in the F-104G. (Jarosław Dobrzyński)

Rear navigation lights in Danish CF-104 (F-104G). (Jarosław Dobrzyński)

Upper formation light. (Jarosław Dobrzyński)

Below, right: Upper red anti-collision light. (Jarosław Dobrzyński)

Below, left: Fuel tank selector switches. (Jarosław Dobrzyński)

Undercarriage

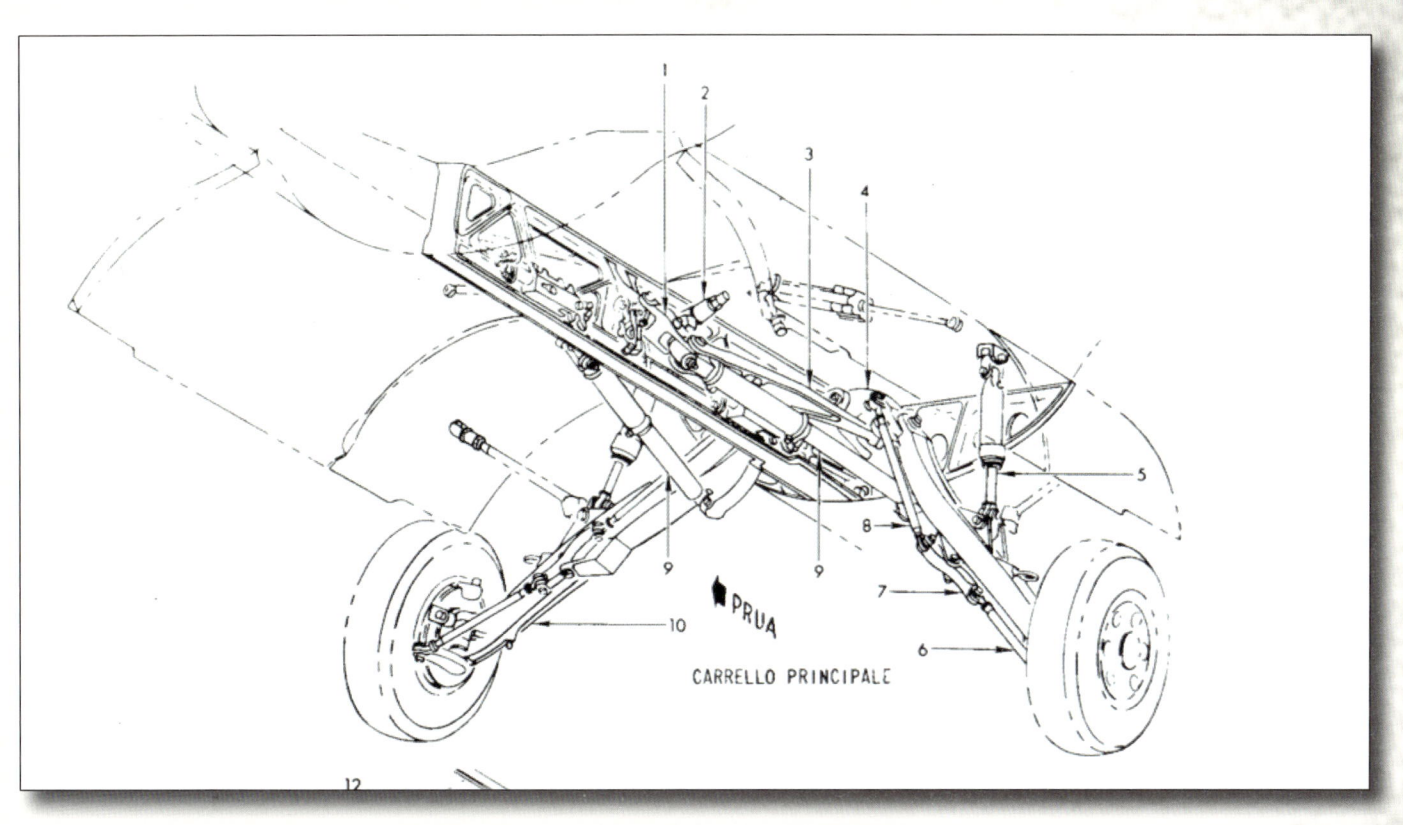

CARRELLO PRINCIPALE

Left main landing gear of a Danish CF-104 (F-104G). (Przemysław Skulski)

Left main landing gear liquid spring shock strut. (Przemysław Skulski)

Details of the left main landing gear of a Danish CF-104 (F-104G). (Przemysław Skulski)

Details of the right main landing gear of a Danish CF-104 (F-104G). (Przemysław Skulski)

Left main landing gear wheel of a Danish CF-104 (F-104G). (Przemysław Skulski)

The interior of the left landing gear bay of the F-104 ASA-M. (Jarosław Dobrzyński)

Left main landing gear of the F-104 ASA-M. (Jarosław Dobrzyński)

169

Right main landing gear of the F-104 ASA-M. (Jarosław Dobrzyński)

Details of the right landing gear bay. (George Papadimitriou)

Above: Details of the right landing gear bay.
(George Papadimitriou)

Right: Spring-loaded cover of the compressed air socket for engine startup in the right landing gear bay.
(Jarosław Dobrzyński)

Compressed air socket for engine startup.
(Jarosław Dobrzyński)

Left main landing gear liquid spring shock strut and landing light of the F-104 ASA-M. (Jarosław Dobrzyński)

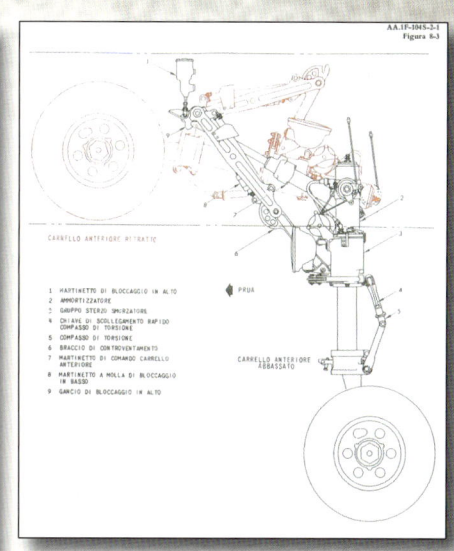

Nosewheel of a Danish CF-104 (F-104G). (Przemysław Skulski)

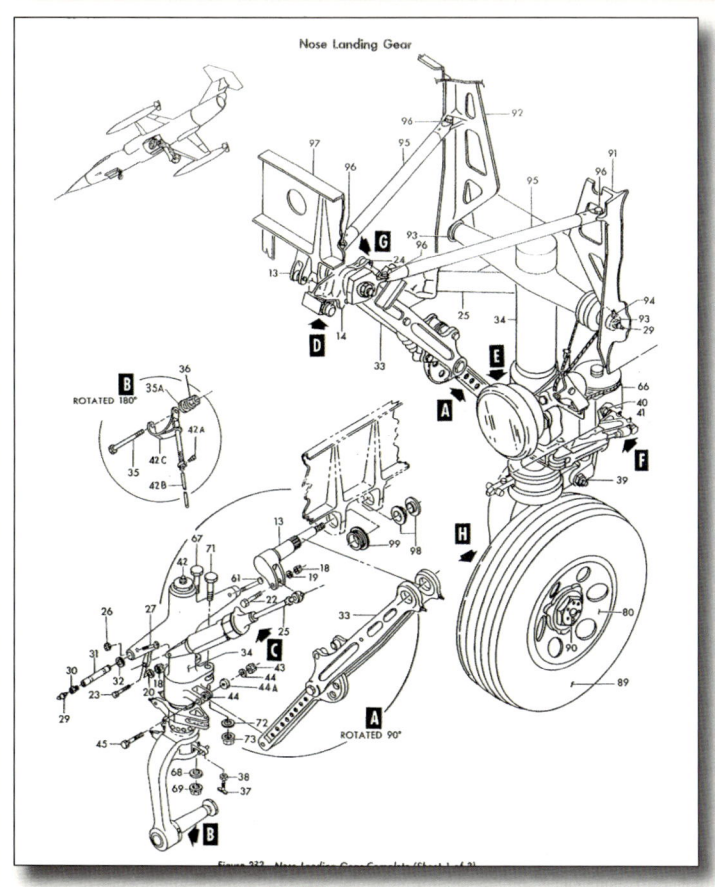

173

Nosewheel of a Danish CF-104 (F-104G).
(Przemysław Skulski)

Front view of F-104S Starfighter showing the undercarriage arrangement. (Ludovic Mac Leod)

Bibliography:

Books:
Bowman Martin W. , Matthias Vogelsang Lockheed F-104 Starfighter, Crowood Press 2000
Drendel Lou, F-104 Starfighter in Action, Squadron Signal Publications 1976
Friddel Philip, F-104 Starfighter in Action, Squadron Signal Publications 1993
Kinzey Bert, F-104 Starfighter, In Detail & scale, Detail & Scale INC. 1991
Lang Gerhard, Flugzeuge der Bundeswehr Lockheed F-104 Stazrfighter teil 1, AirDOC 2006
Rall Günther, My Logbook. Reminiscences 1938-2006.
Upton Jim, Lockheed F-104 Starfighter Warbird Tech Vol. 38, Specialty Press 2003

F-104B Flight Manual
F-104C Flight Manual
F-104D Flight Manual
F-104G Flight Manual
F-104S Flight Manual
F-104S Alenia Flight Manual
F-104S/ASAM-1 Flight Manual
F-104(T)GM-1 Flight Manual

Websites:
www.916-starfighter.de
http://www.aeroflight.co.uk/aircraft/types/lockheed-f-104-starfighter.htm

One of the proposed F-104G weapon load variants (never used) from a 1961 Lockheed catalogue. (Lockheed)